Communication and Development

The Freirean Connection

THE HAMPTON PRESS COMMUNICATION SERIES
Communication Alternatives
Brenda Dervin, supervisory editor

The Reach of Dialogue: Confirmation, Voice and Community
Rob Anderson, Kenneth N. Cissna, and Ronald C. Arnett (eds.)

Liberating Alternatives: The Founding Convention of the Cultural
Environment Movement
Kate Duncan (ed.)

Desert Storm and the Mass Media
Bradley S. Greenberg and Walter Gantz (eds.)

Hearing Many Voices
M. J. Hardman and Anita Taylor (eds.)

Theorizing Fandom: Fans, Subcultures, and Identity
Cheryl Harris and Alison Alexander (eds.)

Responsible Communication: Ethical Issues in Business, Industry,
and the Professions
James A. Jaksa and Michael S. Pritchard (eds.)

Value and Communication: Critical Humanistic Perspectives
Kevin F. Kersten, SJ, and William E. Biernatzki, SJ (eds.)

Communication and Trade: Essays in Honor of
Meheroo Jussawalla
Donald Lamberton (ed.)

Public Intimacies: Talk Show Participants and Tell-All TV
Patricia Joyner Priest

Communication and Development: The Freirean Connection
Michael Richards, Pradip N. Thomas and Zaharom Nain (eds.)

Fissures in the Mediascape: An International Study of Citizens' Media
Clemencia Rodriguez

Nature Stories: Depictions of the Environment and Their Effects
James Shanahan and Katherine McComas

forthcoming

The Arsenal of Democarcy
Claude-Jean Beltrand (ed.)

U.S. Glasnost: Missing Political Themes in U.S. Media Discourse
Johan Galtung and Richard Vincent

On Matters of Liberation (II): Introducing a New Understanding
of Diversity
Amardo Rodriguez

Communication and Development

The Freirean Connection

edited by

Michael Richards
Southampton Institute
University of Central England

Pradip N. Thomas
World Association for Christian Communication

Zaharom Nain
Universiti Sains Malaysia

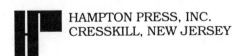
HAMPTON PRESS, INC.
CRESSKILL, NEW JERSEY

Printed in the United States of America

Library of Congress Catalog-in-Publication Data

Communication and development : the Freirean connection / edited by Michael Richards, Pradip N. Thomas, Zaharom Nain
　　　p. cm. -- (The Hampton Press communication series)
　　Includes bibliographic references and index.
　　ISBN 1-57273-243-1 -- ISBN 1-57273-244-X
　　1. Popular education. 2. Communication in education.
　3. Freire, Paulo, 1921- I. Richards, Michael, 1945- III. Thomas, Pradip. III. Nain, Zaharom. IV. Series.

LC196.C66 2001
371.102'2--dc21   00-050604

Hampton Press, Inc.
23 Broadway
Cresskill, NJ 07626

Contents

Preface   vii
Contributors   xv

PART I: COMMUNICATION AND DEVELOPMENT   1

1. The Freirean Legacy, Development, Communication, and Pedagogy
   Michael Richards   3

2. Participatory Communication Research for Democracy and Social Change
   Jan Servaes   13

3. The Communications Paradox: Inequality at the National and International Levels and the Communications Media
   Peter Golding   33

4. The Decentering of Cultural Imperialism: Televisa-ion and Globo-ization in the Latin World
   John Sinclair   45

5. Strategies for the Globalization of Culture in the 21st Century
   Aggrey Brown   65

6. Toward a People's Pedagogy: The Freirean Legacy and the Progressive Cultural Movement in the Philippines
   Maria Jovita Zarate   81

7. Action Research for Development Communications:
    Theory from Practice
        Edna F. Einsiedel   97

PART II: FREIRE AND PEDAGOGY   **107**

8. Freirean Pedagogy and Higher Education:
    The Challenge of Postmodernism and the Politics of Race
        Peter McLaren   109

9. Discourses of Discipline in South Africa:
    Rethinking Critical Pedagogies in Postmodernity
        Roger Deacon   131

10. Cultural Action and the Limits to Solidarity
    and Participation
        Costas Criticos   151

11. Questioning the Concept of Globalization:
    Some Pedagogic Challenges
        Michael Richards   171

12. Breaking Step: South African Oppositional Film and
    Media Education in Transition
        Jeanne Prinsloo   185

13. From Pedagogy to Praxis: Freire, Media Education,
    and Participatory Communication
        Zaharom Nain   209

14. Latin American Political, Cultural, and Educational
    Changes at the End of the Millennium
        Adriana Puiggros   225

15. Freirean Futures: Toward a Further Understanding
    of Participatory Communications
        Pradip N. Thomas   241

Postscript
Some Words from Freire: An Unfinished Journey   255

Author Index   257
Subject Index   261

Preface

The Political-Pedagogical Praxis of Paulo Freire (1921-97): Dreaming of a World of Equality and Justice*

Moacir Gadotti

We can say with certainty that Paulo Freire's thinking is both an existential and historical product. He forged his thinking in struggle and praxis, the latter understood as "action plus reflection," a definition he himself gave it. Brazilian and Latin American society of the 1960s can be viewed as a huge laboratory in which what became known as the "Paulo Freire method" was distilled. The intense political mobilization of that period profoundly affected Paulo Freire's thinking, whose roots lie in the 1950s. The historical period that Paulo Freire lived through in Chile is fundamental to explaining the consolidation of his work, begun in Brazil. In Chile, he found a political, social, and educational environment that was very dynamic, rich, and challenging, allowing him to rethink his methods in a different context, to evaluate it in practice, and to systematize it theoretically.

What attracted the attention of educators and politicians of the period was the fact that Paulo Freire's methods "accelerated" the

*This chapter was translated from Portuguese by Philip Lee. An earlier version of this article was published in *Media Development*, Vol. 3, 1997. Reprinted with permission of the World Association for Christian Communication.

process of adult literacy. He did not apply the methods applied to children to adults learning to read and write. It is true that others were already thinking along the same lines, but he was the first to systematize and to experiment with a method created entirely for adults.

Present-day constructivist theories are also based on the significance of lived experience, on the pupil's knowledge, but it is vital to know and to systematize it. However, Freirean constructivism goes beyond research and thematization. It shows not only that everyone can learn but that everyone knows something and that the subject is responsible for the building up of knowledge and for the resignification of what he or she learns. Children, young persons, or adults only learn when they have a life plan in which knowledge is meaningful for them. But it is the subject that learns through his or her own transforming action on the world. It is the subject who constructs his or her own categories of thought, organizes his or her life, and transforms the world.

Paulo Freire's work is interdisciplinary and can be seen from the perspective of researcher/scientist or educator. However, these two dimensions are caught up in yet another: Paulo Freire does not separate them from the political. Paulo Freire must also be seen as a politician. This is the most important dimension of his work. He does not think about reality as a sociologist, who only tries to understand it. He seeks, in the sciences, elements with which, understanding reality more scientifically, to be able to intervene more effectively in it. For this reason, he thinks of education as simultaneously a political act, as an act of knowledge, and as a creative act. His whole thinking has a direct relationship with reality. That is his benchmark. He did not commit himself to bureaucratic schemes, either schemes for political or academic power. He committed himself, most of all, to a reality to be transformed.

Paulo Freire proposed a new conception of the teaching relationship. It is not a question of conceiving education as the transmission of contents only on the part of the educator. On the contrary, it is a question of establishing dialogue. This means that the person educating is also learning. Traditional pedagogy also asserts this, but with Paulo Freire the educator also learns from the person being educated in the same way that the latter learns from the educator. No one can be considered definitively educated or trained. Each one, in his or her own way, together with others, can learn and discover new dimensions and possibilities about realities in life. Education becomes a shared and ongoing process of training.

However, Paulo Freire can still be read for his affinity to freedom. This would be a libertarian reading. As many of his interpreters assert, the central thesis of his work is that of freedom-liberation. From his first work on, freedom is the central focus of his conception of education. Liberation is the goal of education. The aim of education is to liberate oneself from oppressive reality and from injustice. Education aims at liberation, at the radical transformation of reality, to improve it, to make it more human, to allow men and women to be reconciled as subjects of their own history and not as objects.

Liberation, as the aim of education, is situated on the horizon of a utopian vision of society and of the role of education. Education and training must permit a critical reading of the world. The world around us is unfinished, which implies exposing the reality that oppresses, the reality that is unjust (unfinished) and, consequently, we need criticism that transforms, the proclamation of an alternative reality. Proclamation is necessary as the first step to a new reality to be created. Tomorrow's new reality is the utopia of today's educator.

CONSISTENCY BETWEEN THEORY AND PRACTICE

There are many examples of Paulo Freire's thought that could be cited, revealing most importantly the consistency between theory and practice. We only give one, the most recent, from his work as public administrator (1989–91) in the City Education Office of São Paulo.

For those who knew Paulo Freire well, his administrative abilities did not come as a surprise. His secret was knowing how to run things in a democratic way. In his almost two and a half years as Secretary for Education, he managed to create a team of five or six assistants who could work with great autonomy and who could substitute for him in any emergency. There was just one weekly meeting in which they talked about the general policy of the Education Office. If it was necessary, new bearings were taken. Paulo Freire fiercely defended his opinions, but he knew how to work as part of a team, far from the waywardness of which he has been accused. He had authority, but he used it democratically. He faced situations of conflict with enormous patience. He used to say that working for change in education demanded patience of a historical nature because education is a long-term process.

What were the most important structural changes introduced by Paulo Freire in the city's network of schools?

He himself gives the answer in his book on his experiences as Secretary (Freire, 1991): "The most important structural changes introduced into the schools affected their autonomy" (pp. 79-80). School councils and student clubs were restructured. However, Paulo Freire goes on: "The greatest step forward at the level of school autonomy was to allow the schools themselves to come up with their own teaching projects which with the administration's support could speed up change within the school" (pp. 79-80).

To illustrate this process, I give three examples: the program of ongoing training for teachers, the literacy program for young people and adults, and the practice of interdisciplinarity.

Ongoing Training for Teachers

From the beginning of his administration, Paulo Freire insisted that he was deeply committed to the question of the ongoing training of educators. His training program for the teaching profession was governed by the following principles (Freire, 1991):

- The educator is the subject of his or her practice, it being necessary to create it and recreate it through reflection about his or her daily work
- The training of educators must be ongoing and systematic because practice is done and redone
- Teaching practice requires understanding of the very genesis of knowledge, that is, of how the process of knowing takes place
- The training program of educators is a condition for the process of restructuring the school curriculum.

With this program, Paulo Freire wanted to train teachers to take a new stance on teaching, considering the authoritarian tradition in Brazil. No one could expect this to be overcome in a few years. For this reason, Paulo Freire put his well-known teaching patience to the test, in political decision making, technical competency, affection, and in the exercise of democracy. He ended up being successful. Teacher training goes far beyond, transcends, theoretical courses of explanation about democracy. Training takes place through practice, through genuine participation. Democracy in practice is worth a lot more than democracy in theory.

Literacy Programs for Young People and Adults

As well as the intense program of training the educator, Paulo Freire was the impetus behind a literacy movement in partnership with popular movements and alongside the expansion of evening classes and supplementary teaching.

This project, effectively initiated in January 1990, had great repercussions both in the city of São Paulo and in other Brazilian States because its aim was to strengthen popular movements. It was one of the rare examples of partnership between civil society and the state. It is obvious that in these circumstances such a relationship is not always harmonious but shot through with tensions. However, it is a necessary condition for the state and the popular movements to work in parity.

The MOVA-SP did not impose just one way of working or, as they used to call it, the "Paulo Freire method." It tried to maintain pluralism, without accepting nonscientific and nonphilosophical authoritarian and racist teaching methods. Even without imposing any methodology, the political-pedagogical principles of Paulo

Freire's theory of education were maintained, synthesized in a libertarian concept of education, underlining the role of education in constructing a new historical project, the theory of knowledge that sets out from concrete practice in the building of knowledge, the student as subject of knowledge, and an understanding of literacy not just as a logical, intellectual process but also as being deeply affective and social.

Practicing Interdisciplinarity

The vastness of Paulo Freire's work and his many journeys through different areas of knowledge and practice bring us to another central theme of his theory practice: interdisciplinarity. This is not just a teaching method or an attitude of the teacher. It is demanded by the very nature of the act of teaching.

The activity of teaching using interdisciplinarity or transdisciplinarity implies the establishment of a participatory and ultimate school in the training of the social subject. The educator, the subject of his or her teaching activity, is capable of drawing up teaching-apprenticeship programs and methods that can be introduced into his or her school in the community. The fundamental aim of interdisciplinarity is to experience a global reality that is written into the daily lives of the pupil, teacher, and people and that, in traditional schooling, is fragmented and compartmentalized. Articulating wisdom, knowledge, experience, school, community, environment, and so on is the aim of an interdisciplinarity that is translated into practice through working collectively and in solidarity in the organization of work in the school. However, there is no interdisciplinarity unless there is decentralization of power—unless the school has effective autonomy. Paulo Freire's last book, published in Brazil on April 10, 1997 less than a month before his death, is called the *Pedagogy of Autonomy.*

Paulo Freire left the City Education Office on May 27, 1991. After nearly two and a half years, he returned to his library and to his academic activities "in the manner of one who knowing, does" as he wrote in the epilogue to his book *A educação na cidade* (1991, p. 143). In fact, Paulo Freire remained actively present in the Office, translating his wide experience into the praxis of the projects carried out by the Office. At his farewell, he said, "Even though I am no longer Secretary for Education, I shall remain with you in another way. . . . You can continue to count on me in the formulation of an education policy, of a school with another 'face,' which is more joyful, companionable and democratic" (p. 144).

A TRANSPARENT PERSONALITY

How did Paulo Freire react to criticism of himself and his work? Attacks on him were extremely rare because his ideas might generate controversy, but not his person. His personality was transparent. He had no aversion to hypocrisy. He never responded to personal criticism, neither did he argue with critics of his work. Paulo Freire believed that humor is a teaching weapon that favors progress, but not controversy. Humor is constructive and controversy, frequently, destructive. For this reason, he never argued with any of his critics. This does not mean that he ignored them or made no reply.

He looked on criticism positively and tried to learn from it. When he responded indirectly in his books—and he did so systematically—he tried, most of all, to place his work in context, revealing him to be a child of his time. In this sense, we can say that there is an evolution in his thinking in which he overcomes a certain "ingenuousness"—as he himself says in *Pedagogia da esperanza* (1994, p. 67).

There are also critiques that come from very different and even contradictory readings of Paulo Freire's work—legitimate and serious readings. However, in this case, he had the right to disagree, and he did disagree with those readings: In many of them he did not recognize himself.

Certain conservative critics claim that he does not have a theory of knowledge because he does not study the relationships between the subject of knowledge and the object. He is only interested in the end product. This is not true: His thinking is based on an explicit anthropological theory of knowledge. Others accuse him of authoritarianism, saying that his method assumes the transformation of reality, and not everyone wishes to transform it. Therefore, his method is not scientific (because it is not universally applicable). His method would certainly be authoritarian if it obliged everyone to participate in the transformation. It is obvious that this criticism ignores the fact that Paulo Freire does not accept the idea of pure theory—for him an illusion—but critical theory rooted in a social and political philosophy. He rejects the idea of scientific neutrality—as he rejects academicism—and argues that the conservatives, on the pretext of the political neutrality of pure theory, are concealing their conservative ideology.

WHAT DOES AN EDUCATOR LEAVE AS A LEGACY?

In the first place he leaves a life, a biography. Paulo enchanted us with his gentleness, his mildness, his charisma, his consistency, his commitment, his seriousness. His words and actions were words and actions of struggle for a "less ugly, less wicked, less inhuman" world, as he used to say. Along with love and hope, he also leaves us a legacy of indignation in the face of injustice. In the face of it he would say that we cannot "sweeten" our words.

As well as the testimony of a life of commitment to the cause of the oppressed, he leaves us an immense bibliography in countless editions of books, articles, and videos scattered around the world. I was asked a number of times why his pedagogy was so successful. I replied that it was because a "pedagogy of dialogue" did not humiliate the student or anyone else. Conservative pedagogy humiliates the student, and Paulo Freire's pedagogy gave dignity to the student, placing the teacher at his or her side—with the task of orienting and guiding the educational process—as someone who is also seeking, like the student. He or she is also an apprentice. That is the legacy of Paulo Freire.

He did not see education as just a technique based on a theory of knowledge, but as a social, political, and anthropological matter. Because he based his theory and practice on an anthropology, he devised a profoundly ethical way of teaching. It is necessary to retain a conscience, but without violating the conscience of the other person.

In the development of his education theory, Paulo Freire managed, on the one hand, to demystify the dreams of the pedagogism of the 1960s, which claimed, at least in Latin America, that the school could do everything. On the other hand, he managed to overcome the pessimism of the 1970s, when it was said that the school was purely reproductive. Doing this, overcoming ingenuous pedagogism and negativist pessimism, he managed to remain faithful to utopia, dreaming positive dreams.

Several generations of educators, anthropologists, social and political scientists, professionals in the areas of exact, natural, and biological sciences were influenced by him and helped to construct a pedagogy founded on freedom. What he wrote is part of the lives of a whole generation who learned to dream of a world of equality and justice, who struggled and are still struggling for it. Many will have to continue his work even though he left no "disciples." There is nothing less Freirean than the idea of a disciple, a follower of ideas. He always challenged us to "reinvent" the world, to pursue truth and not to copy ideas. Paulo Freire left us roots, wings, and dreams.

REFERENCES

Freire, P. (1991). *A educacao na cidade* [Pedagogy of the city]. Sao Paulo: Cortez.

Freire, P. (1994). *Pedagogy of hope.* New York: Continuum.

Freire, P. (1997). *Pedagogy of autonomy.* New York: Continuum.

Contributors

Aggrey Brown, Professor, Carimac, The University of the West Indies, Jamaica.

Costas Criticos, Media Resource Centre, University of Natal, South Africa.

Roger Deacon, Media Resource Centre, University of Natal, South Africa.

Edna Einsiedel, Professor, Graduate Communications Programme, University of Calgary, Canada.

Moacir Gadotti, Director General, Paulo Freire Institute, Sao Paulo, Brazil.

Peter Golding, Head—Department of Social Sciences and co-director of Communication Research Centre, Loughborough University, UK.

Peter McLaren, Associate Professor, Graduate School of Education and Information Studies, University of California, Los Angeles, USA.

Zaharom Nain, Lecturer, Department of Communications, Universiti Sains Malaysia, Penang, Malaysia.

Jeanne Prinsloo, Lecturer, Department of Education, University of Natal, South Africa.

Adriana Puiggros, Member of Parliament and on the faculty of educational sciences, The National University of Entre Rios, Argentina.

Michael Richards, Professor of Media Studies, Southampton Institute, UK, and Professor, Department of Media and Communication, University of Central England, UK.

Jan Servaes, Professor, Department of Communications, Catholic University of Brussels, Belgium.

John Sinclair, Professor, International Communications, Victoria University of Technology, Melbourne, Australia.

Pradip Thomas, Director, Studies and Publications, WAAC, London, UK.

Maria Zarate, Media Visions, Quezon City, Philippines.

Part ▪ I

Communication and Development

INTRODUCTION

The objective of this section is to foreground the many ways in which Freire contributed to our understanding of what ought to be the relationship between communication and development. The chapters in this section attempt to highlight Freire's influence on both the theory and practice of communications for development.

If one were to conduct an audit of Freire's influence on the theory and praxis of communications and development, it would appear that key Freirean ideas—dialogue, participation, awareness, praxis, and so on—have become central aspects of the armoury of grassroots movements throughout the world. These intensely practical concepts become the bread and butter of communications-based strategies to name the world in order to change it. Quite fundamentally, the Freirean stance led to an integrated understanding of process—as an acting out of the abiding and mutually sustainable links between reflection and action. It led to many marginalized communities creating and using knowledge for their own empowerment. This nondualistic approach affirmed and enriched a variety of discourses of empowerment and led to a host of participatory communications projects—that ranged from the use of popular theater in the context of grassroots struggles against dictatorial regimes in Chile and Argentina, to film and video work in apartheid South Africa, to group media efforts in the Philippines and India, to awareness-raising workshops on a variety of issues of concern, both in the South and in the North.

1

What is less obvious is Freire's contribution to ongoing developments in the theory of communications and development, from the early preoccupation with modernization and reflected versions of development, to dependency and media imperialism, to participatory development, to globalization and theorizing the links between the local and the global. Although Freire was forthright in his condemnation of the cultures of domination, he was aware of the limits to the absolutization of liberation and of the need therefore to contextualize oppression and the strategies of change. Freire welcomed the many particular struggles and learned from the many cultures of struggle that were the unexpected, although wholly welcome byproducts of a dominant global order. This willingness to consistently critique the captivities of theory, to cross borders, and to engage in a politics of possibility has had a lasting influence on critical scholarship in communications and development.

Both the theory and the praxis of communications and development have been enriched by Freirean ideals. This section offers a glimpse of the many paths from and to Freire in communications and development.

Chapter ▪ 1

The Freirean Legacy, Development, Communication, and Pedagogy

Michael Richards

The work of Paulo Freire has made a major contribution to the theory and practice of "alternative" communications, although this has not always been recognized. In particular, the participatory framework of communications owes much to Freire's pioneering scholarship and praxis, especially in terms of his support for grassroots participation, access, local control, and cultural action for freedom. Of late, serious questions have been raised about the limits of participation, particularly in the context of identity-based struggles in an increasingly globalized media world. The following chapters in this book provide a critical introduction to Freirean ideas and their legacy in this new context, particularly as they relate to the theory and practice of communication and development and their pedagogies. This book celebrates the continuing relevance of Freire's philosophy through a reevaluation of some of his central concepts and examinations of the new environments that alternative cultural politics and participatory communication must negotiate.

Paulo Freire was one of the most influential philosophers of his era. His was a philosophy informed by experience and practice. In the 1950s he lived and worked in the slums of Recife in Brazil and began to recognize the significance of adult literacy to freedom and participation. He regarded illiteracy as an expression of an unjust social reality, a fundamental structural obstacle to self-realization;

therefore, he developed a new approach to literacy that linked what he called learning to read the word with learning to read the world. In 1962, he became coordinator of a large literacy program in Recife and soon after was appointed head of Brazil's National Literacy Programme, but following a military coup in 1964, the program was terminated and Freire was imprisoned and charged with subversion. These events and his subsequent exile to Bolivia and Chile convinced him of one of his central tenets, namely, that no education is neutral.

These experiences undoubtedly provided some impetus for his seminal work *Pedagogy of the Oppressed* (Freire, 1972). Through his radical pedagogy he believed that adults could learn to recognize social, political, and economic contradictions and would be able to take action against oppressive elements in life. Freire labeled this process "conscientization," a concept that was to become central to his pedagogy.

Freire condemned traditional educational processes that he identified as banking systems, in which students, at all levels, were positioned as passive recipients of deposits of knowledge from an all-knowing teacher. In contrast to this he advocated an education based on dialogue that would lead to an ongoing process of reflection, followed by action. He encouraged learners to assert themselves as creative subjects when learning to read and write. He discouraged the memorizing and repetition of syllables, words, and phrases "given" by the teacher and advocated critical reflection by the learner on the processes of reading and writing and a recognition of the profound importance of language as a source of power and enablement in everyday life. In this his ideas go beyond education and adult literacy projects and begin to suggest a framework for the role of mass communication in developing countries and a model of audience relationships to mass media throughout the world. The link between his concerns for adult literacy and development and emancipation in this much broader sense is that Freire's writing is centrally concerned with forms of cultural action. He claims that economic and cultural dominance is practiced by a metropolitan society:

> If we consider society as a being it is obvious that only a society which is "being for itself" can develop. Societies which are dual, "reflex" invaded and dependant on the metropolitan society cannot develop because they are alienated; their political, economic and cultural decision making power is located outside themselves in the invaded society. In the last analyses the latter determines the destiny of the former. (Freire, 1972, p. 130)

Freire's concept of the oppositional relationship between metropolitan and dependent societies accurately foreshadows the contemporary world of instant communication and global networks in which there is a profound interconnection between political, economic, and social action both within and between nation states. The decisions of those "metropolitan" nations who can choose may well have important implications for those who cannot. Freire (1972) argues that it is always though "action in depth that the culture of domination is culturally confronted" (p. 31). It is in this process that he saw education as either liberating or oppressive but never neutral, a process that can enable people to act upon and therefore transform their world or simply adjust to it.

Masterman (1985) has suggested that a transformation of social relations can be encouraged by a media education underpinned by a Freirean philosophy. For example, when interrogating media texts it is necessary to problematize objective knowledge, to ask how and why information has been selected, by whom and in whose interests and against whom and whose interests this knowledge is directed. This approach links directly to Freire's praxis. From the beginning he employed popular media to advance his pedagogy, for instead of working with text books he used photographs and images of local community life and social conditions as a focal point for discussion. As well as providing the building blocks for literacy work this method was to increase motivation by enabling learners to tackle issues that were important to them. So solid social resistance and conscientization had to be developed from the bottom up. Freire's conscientization method was designed to bring about new conditions by breaking through a culture of acceptance and silence and encourage active participation as a subject (Servaes & Arnst, 1993).

The right to participation and emancipation has been increasingly debated in the field of communication, as well as in education. Over the past 20 years communication studies have increasingly explored participatory approaches and attendant planning models that aim to theorize and implement development. Freire's premise that researchers should privilege and learn from the experience of ordinary people has been crucial to this area of research. In working to models of social change Freire's idea of "naming the world" has been particularly important for it is in the naming of the world that communication through dialogue plays an important role in participatory development. This line of thinking has been taken up by a number of development theorists. For example, Servaes's (1989) paradigm of multiplicity in one world looks to some of the major premises in Freire's critical pedagogy concerning popular participation in naming the world. It builds on Freire's work by emphasizing that cultures are varied and variable and operate with multiple interpretations and meanings. The role of communication, therefore, becomes crucial in exploring, cataloguing, and mediating the multiplicity of meanings within a single culture. Of course, communication itself makes multiple meanings, and for participatory development communication to be effective participants must know how to comprehend, construct, and negotiate these diverse meanings in everyday life. Being aware of this necessity is an essential first step in promoting participatory communication, but a second is that participants as social actors are empowered not only to name their world but also to theorize its relationships (Huesca, 1996).

These and other issues emanating from Freire's work are developed by the contributors to his volume. Perhaps one of the most enduring features of his scholarship will prove to be its accessibility and transferability to a range of contexts. Gadotti referred earlier to the universal dimensions of Freire's thinking and its influence on contemporary pedagogy. He refers to Freire's thinking in three distinct ways: first, as an existential product; second, as a humanist-internationalist educational philosophy; and finally, as a basis for praxis exemplified in Freire's own experience as a public administrator, particularly in relation to the permanent teacher training program, the adult literacy program, and the practice of interdisciplinarity. Gadotti shows how these aspects of Freire's work, in particular, have provided a basis for a universal extension of Freire's thought like no other in the history of pedagogical ideas.

He also points out that Freire is not without his critics. Ideas must move on if they are to be applicable to a changing world and wider spheres of social activity, and those thinkers are the key to the continued relevance of Freire throughout the world. This theme of change and continuing relevance runs through the first part of this book in chapters focusing on debates and issues in communication and development. Although Freire's contribution to critical education has been immense, his influence in the field of communication has thus far been less frequently explored and documented.

Since the 1980s there has been some waning interest in development communications, partly perhaps a reaction to a sense that the agenda had stalled on a limited set of issues. In particular, the "dominant paradigm," media imperialism, and participatory communications had each been a focus of debate and analysis, polemics and pronouncements, but more recently the study of communications and development has begun to move from these issues, with a new emphasis being on "participation," "access," "empowerment," and a more interdisciplinary and integrated approach to development. However, despite these "progressive" developments, relatively few substantive explorations have been undertaken in the last few years. One exception to this is research from Latin America, but those outside the continent have had little exposure to the theoretical and practical innovations that have been developed from Freire's work.

It is evident that, despite these developments, the principles and practices associated with the dominant paradigm and its various adaptations still maintains a ruling logic that simultaneously circumscribes and delegitimizes alternative approaches. Developments in the international order, including the collapse of the Soviet bloc and the widespread acceptance of monetarist economic policies, as well as the dilution of UNESCO's commitment to NWICO, have contributed to this situation. However, an additional factor has been the institutionalization of cultural politics and the inability to deal with emerging contradictions, as well as new configurations of interests that are beginning to affect processes of development, particularly in multicultural plural societies.

Some of these issues of cultural identity, empowerment, and the role of participatory communications in democracy and social change are addressed by Servaes in Chapter 2. He points out that three distinct models have underpinned theory and practice in development communications: the top-down model, whose validity was rooted in theories of modernization, which was subsequently challenged by a model based on media imperialism with its origins in dependency theory, and a participatory model of communications and development, which was based largely on Freirean concepts. This model, unlike the two preceeding models, emphasized localized media versions of access and control based on the ethic of participation. Servaes traces the history of the field and affirms the value of participatory models of communication to development, including both the dialogic model of community communication as well as the UNESCO-based media model that endorses the values of self-management, access, and participation. The chapter includes a case study of a participatory model of communications from Ecuador.

But there is another, "new" dominant paradigm that, according to Golding in Chapter 3, is linked to the debates about globalization and the role of the market as the great leveller—a precept that has wide currency in popular understandings of the nature of economic growth. Despite the enormous changes that have taken place in the global economy, for example, in the global syndication of culture, the world has not become a better place to live in for everyone. As Golding points out, economic data show that inequalities have increased, that the gap between center and periphery continues to widen, both between and within nations. He argues that inequalities are particularly evident in the context of the distribution of communication hardware and software between consumers. Taking the case of the United Kingdom, Golding traces the skewed nature of media distribution and the consequences of the gap between the information rich and the information poor. He concludes that, in order to reverse this trend, there is a need to realize the liberating potential of communications in and through actions for freedom.

One way of understanding the traditional limitations to such action is through the concept of media imperialism. In Chapter 4, Sinclair offers a critical reevaluation of the term in light of changes in the global economy characterized by globalization processes and the rise of transnational corporate empires emanating both from within the center and the periphery. Citing the cases of Televisa in Mexico and TV Globo as examples of a new wave of regional media entrepreneurship, Sinclair presents a refreshing analysis of the role of culture and language of origin as factors of comparative advantage in the establishment of international markets for audiovisual products. However, despite the fact that the internationalization as well as the pluralization of cultural production are clearly established phenomena, "dependent development" cannot be wished away, and indeed that may be the primary reason for the pursuit of overseas markets by regional media corporations such as Televisa and TV Globo.

So globalization, despite national variations in its perceived local impacts, is very much part of the agenda about communication and development. Brown, in Chapter 5, argues that the culture of globalization as well as the globalization of culture are two distinct but interrelated phenomena that have direct bearings on the nature of the contemporary information environment. The information industry is, as Brown notes, increasingly dominated by a handful of U.S.-based oligopolies. Citing the case of the Caribbean, he analyzes the nature of the cultural invasion and its manifestations and consequences for local culture as well as the reality of an acquiescent public who have actively supported this invasion of popular culture from the United States. There are, however, signs for optimism, for numerous efforts have been made to counter this cultural invasion through the production of local, indigenous media fare and the establishment of local and regional media structures and networks. Such initiatives include radio phone-in programs in Jamaica, distance learning developments at the University of the West Indies, the establishment of Caribvision—the regional broadcasting body—and the Caribbean Satellite network.

In Chapter 6, the empirical focus moves to the Philippines, where cultural action has always been a vital component of the people's movement. Zarate argues that active protagonists of the people's movement firmly believe in the paramount role of popular education and alternative pedagogy in conscientizing a critical mass for their enlightened, inspired, and sustained participation in the task of bringing about fundamental changes in Filipino society. She examines the historical development of cultural action in general and education and training within Filipino cultural movements in particular. The chapter considers the lessons and contemporary trends, as well as deviations from the extensions of the Freirean legacy that Filipino cultural activists have taken in cognizance of the particular attributes of Filipino culture and the strategic thrusts and particular features of the people's movement in the Philippines. The growing literature around participatory action research arising from Freire's work stresses the importance of development theory, of linking theory to development communication practice and of examining such a linkage in the context of social transformation. In Chapter 7, Einsiedel suggests that a useful approach to theory development for participatory communications is to examine development practice using grounded theory and the action research tradition as a means of understanding the reflexive relationship between theory and practice in the context of producing social change. She reviews research within the action research tradition and examines case studies of field experience within development projects and from this proposes a framework for communications research and teaching, which emphasizes communication as dialogue, communication as social practice, and communication as a social right.

Part II of the book returns to the heart of Freire's critical pedagogy for although his work does not explicitly address current political debates surrounding the pedagogy and politics of postmodernism, what can be loosely described as a postmodern social theory has been influential in, among other things, offering criticisms of material and economic causality by placing an emphasis on reading social reality as a text and on language as a mode of representation that helps construct social reality, power as both a condition and effect of discourse.

In Chapter 8, McLaren examines some of the central issues in this debate and advances a distinction between "ludic" postmodernism and resistance postmodernism. He addresses the general retreat within academic postmodernism from a politics of the concrete and a philosophy of utopia and liberatory praxis, as advanced by Freire, to a politics of cynicism and despair. Among the questions the chapter raises are: If the subject has been aestheticized and reduced to simply a "desiring machine," how can we address the concepts of morality and ethics? In addition, is it possible to build global alliances in the postmodern era that do not produce the same forms of technocratic capitalism that are part of the problem? Furthermore, if master narratives are colonizing practices that repress differences and the recognition of multiple identities, how should we begin to rethink and practice liberation? Indeed, how can we address pragmatically the project of human freedom based on the new understandings of desire by postmodernists?

Deacon, in Chapter 9, offers an analysis of Freirean ideas in the changing context, for example, that of South Africa. He argues that during the 1970s and the 1980s, new critical discourses emerged in South Africa in opposition principally to the ideology of apartheid and particularly in relation to its authoritarian and utilitarian dimensions. He shows how alternative discourses developed in popular education fueled both by critical pedagogies in community video projects in rural development and in the analysis of the position of the intellectual. Deacon's chapter illustrates the value of the "heterodoxal Freirean." Using the work of Derrida, Foucault, Bourdieu and Passeron, Spivak, and Freire himself, he argues that although the objectification of modernist discourses allows recognition and questioning of their characteristic features, the solution to the problem of emancipation in education lies in exploring the tensions between modernist discourses to highlight social difference and contradictory relations of power.

To teach that communication through participation is unproblematic would of course be misleading. In Chapter 10, Criticos examines some of the limits to solidarity and participation in South Africa. He observes that the revolutionary climate, inspired by responses to apartheid, has created a popular interest in emancipatory education, and that Freire's work was pivotal in providing a theoretical framework to foster it. Freire's work, Criticos argues, was crucial because its anticapitalist social theory helped in the analysis of education in South African liberation movements, that the context in which Freire's pedagogy was formed was similar to that of South Africa, and because Freire linked education with conscientization, which appealed to reformers and radicals in South Africa, and reinforced an interest in democratic education and Freire's work itself. Using concepts derived from border terminologies, Criticos examines examples of documentary production in which emancipatory participation was practiced and concludes that, despite difficulties, Freire has given us the language to challenge borders and that collective learning and cultural civil society enable groups to challenge, to cross, and to transform borders.

Chapter 11 continues the theme of exploring the pedagogical legacies of Freire's work by applying his ideas to the analysis of a concept central to the issues addressed in this book, that of globalization. Here Richards argues that the influential concept of globalization that dominates much of the contemporary debate in mass communications can reinforce the claims of the dominant paradigm of development and restate, as though it were unproblematic, how Western media sustain ideological practices of domination in developing countries. He challenges simplified notions of globalization and relates the globalization debate to some of Freire's central ideas, including those of questioning the nature of society, power and knowledge, control, consciousness, and pedagogy. Richards then proposes a pedagogy of communications specifically related to globalization, drawing on these Freirean concepts. He argues that the Freirean conception of traditional education echoes that of globalization; both are concerned with domination, oppression, cultural hegemony, the denial of the possibility of social action, and the ability of actors to reconstitute forms of knowledge and information that are given to them. Richards concludes that there is something distinctive about a pedagogy for globalization that has lessons for other parts of the communications curriculum, in particular, acknowledging ways in which national media belong to an international media system yet retain their own national distinctiveness, and that the experience of studying global media can provide a basis for broader critical development and observation from dominant discourses and modes of analysis.

Prinsloo, in Chapter 12, takes up part of this challenge by examining the Freirean legacy as it provides an underpinning for oppositional film making in South Africa. From an examination of the impact of Freirean education and film making, Prinsloo advocates the deployment of postmodern understandings to influence production practices, and she appeals for a media education that will develop critical thinkers. She argues that attention should be paid to cultural representations, the power of discourses, and through "border pedagogy" to the creation of learners who are both able to cross borders and to construct their own narratives and histories while recognizing those narratives that locate them and that constitute their subjectivity.

Nain, in Chapter 13, locates the relevance of Freire's project of liberation in two areas of communications—media education and participatory communication for development—and asks to what extent these two areas can be linked, particularly in the context of the developing world. Like some of the other authors in this volume, Nain examines the nature of the dominant paradigm and suggests why its position remains scarce in the new world order. He argues for the relevance of Freire's vision to a pedagogy of communication that seeks to demystify and liberate people from the forces of the marketplace in modern communications. While recognizing that practical media activity does not in itself guarantee a critical awareness, he suggests that even critical pointed scrutiny achieves little if, as Freire pointed out, a liberating education only changes our understanding of reality without changing reality itself. Nain maintains that this is not an easy goal to achieve and warns against overstating the possibilities of alternatives to current media structures and practices. Yet, in the final analysis, he argues Freire's philosophy provides at least hope, and possibly a way forward, for those who aspire to a democratic media as a significant force in people's lives locally and globally.

Chapter 14 by Puiggros picks up some of these issues. She offers a critical analysis of the lack of development of the Latin American popular education system. Examining some of the multiple determinants of this situation, Puiggros argues that they have combined to produce ruptures in the Latin American cultural structure, which grew in an uneven and mixed fashion at the end of the 19th century. She reminds us of some of the central ideas in Freire's work and argues for a new beginning, emphasizing a theoretical framework for action, based on these and the work of Giroux and Laclau, among others.

The authors of chapters in the second part of the book share the view that the contribution of Paulo Freire, both to alternative pedagogy and to cultural praxis, has been immense. His emphasis on the need to evolve counterhegemonic cultural strategies, based on the primacy of participation, access, solidarity, awareness, and cultural action, has provided the theoretical and practical basis for a number of alternative communication and development programs in Latin America, Africa, and parts of Asia. Freire's nondogmatic, open, and culturally sensitive political stance and his continuing dialogue with changing aspects of cultural politics today are reflections of his deep commitment to the humanization of life. Although not discounting the Freirean legacy, it is nevertheless necessary to contextualize its conceptual and epistemological foundations within the emerging framework of global, national, and local articulations that are the result of changes in the logic of capitalism and the emergence of national, language, and gender-based struggles against domination in various parts of the world.

In the final chapter in the book, Thomas examines the possibilities for a Freirean future based on an assessment of Freire's legacy to participatory communications. Thomas considers the continuing relevance of Freire in light of a number of contemporary challenges stemming from, for example, new theories of liberation, the increasingly complex relationships between consciousness, power, and social change, and the calling into question of the practical efficacy of development and inclusive intersubjectivity in localized models of participatory development. Thomas's conclusions are nevertheless optimistic. Freirean concepts must be critically assessed, adapted, even exorcised in order to become a valid language of critical discourse in the context of a changing global environment. The importance of context is paramount. Participatory communication strategies must be located in recognition of varied and ever-changing contexts, but in the final analysis "dialogue across cultures will need to form the basis for the practice of participatory communication as a 'pedagogy of hope.'"

REFERENCES

Freire, P. (1972). *Pedagogy of the oppressed.* Harmondsworth, UK: Penguin.
Huesca, R. (1996). New directions for participatory communication and development. *Media Development, XL(2),* 26-30.
Masterman, L. (1985). *Teaching the media.* London: Comedia.
Servaes, J. (1989). *One world. Multiple cultures. A new paradigm on communication for development.* Leuven, Belgium: Acco.
Servaes, J., & Arnst, R. (1993). First things first: Participatory communication for change. *Media Development, XL(2),* 44-47.

Chapter ▪ 2

Participatory Communication Research for Democracy and Social Change

Jan Servaes

The struggle for democracy is the centerpiece for the struggle for liberation. Yet it is also clear that democracy has different meanings for different peoples throughout the world. For some, it is synonymous with capitalism, the propagation of acquisitiveness and greed, the barbaric practices of colonialism, and conceptually opposed to socialism. For others, it is a process of achieving equality of social justice for all peoples through popular sovereignty.
—Paulo Freire (1993, p. xi)

The hallmark of modern consciousness, as I have been insisting to the point of obsession, is its enormous multiplicity. For our time and forward, the image of general orientation, perspective, *Weltanschauung,* growing out of humanistic studies (or, for that matter, out of scientific ones) and shaping the direction of culture is a chimera. Not only is the class basis for such a unitary "humanism" completely absent, gone with a lot of other things like adequate bathtubs and comfortable taxis, but, even more important, the agreement on the foundations of scholarly authority, old books and old manners, has disappeared. If the sort of ethnography of thought work I

13

have here projected is in fact carried out, it will, I am sure, but strengthen this conclusion. It will deepen even further our sense of the radical variousness of the way we think now, because it will extend our perception of that variousness beyond the merely professional realms of subject matter, method, technique, scholarly tradition, and the like, to the larger framework of our moral existence. The conception of a "new humanism," of forging some general "the best that is being thought and said" ideology and working it into the curriculum, will then seem not merely implausible but utopian altogether. Possibly, indeed, a bit worrisome.
—Clifford Geertz (1983, p. 161)

After the Second World War, the founding of the United Nations stimulated relations among sovereign states, especially the North Atlantic Nations and the developing nations, including the new states emerging out of a colonial past. During the cold war period the superpowers—the United States and the former Soviet Union—tried to expand their own interests to the developing countries. In fact, the United States was defining development as the replica of its own political–economic system and opening the way for the transnational corporations. At the same time, the developing countries saw the "welfare state" of the North Atlantic Nations as the ultimate goal of development. These nations were attracted by the new technology transfer and the model of a centralized state with careful economic planning and centrally directed development bureaucracies for agriculture, education, and health as the most effective strategies to catch up with those industrialized countries.

This mainly economic-oriented view, characterized by endogenism and evolutionism, ultimately resulted in the modernization and growth theory. It sees development as an unilinear, evolutionary process and defines the state of underdevelopment in terms of observable quantitative differences between so-called poor and rich countries on the one hand, and traditional and modern societies on the other hand.

As a result of the general intellectual "revolution" that took place in the mid-1960s, this Euro- or ethnocentric perspective on development was challenged by Latin American social scientists, and a theory dealing with dependency and underdevelopment was born. This dependency approach formed part of a general structuralistic reorientation in social sciences. The dependistas were primarily concerned with the effects of dependency in peripheral countries, but implicit in their analysis was the idea that development and underdevelopment must be understood in the context of the world system.

This dependency paradigm played an important role in the movement for a New World Information and Communication Order from the late 1960s to the early 1980s. At that time, the new states in Africa, Asia, and the success of socialist and popular movements in Cuba, China, Chile, and other countries provided the goals for political, economic, and cultural self-determination within the international community of nations. These new nations shared the ideas of being independent from the superpowers and moved to form the Non-Aligned Nations. The Non-aligned Movement defined development as political struggle.

Because the demarcation of the First, Second, and Third Worlds is breaking down and the crossover center-periphery can be found in every region, there is a need for a new concept of development that emphasizes cultural identity and multidimensionality. The present-day world, in general as well as in its distinct regional and national entities, is confronted with multifaceted crises. Apart from the obvious economic and financial crisis, one could also refer to social, ideological, moral, political, ethnic, ecological, and security crises. In other words, the previously held dependency perspective has become more difficult to support because of the growing interdependency of regions, nations, and communities.

From the criticism of the two previously described paradigms, particularly that of the dependency approach, a new viewpoint on development is emerging. The common starting point here is the examination of the changes from the "bottom-up," from the self-development of the local community. The basic assumption is that there are no countries or communities that function completely autonomously and that are completely self-sufficient, nor are there any nations whose development is exclusively determined by external factors. Every society is dependent in one way or another, both in form and in degree. Thus, a framework was sought within which both the center and the periphery could be studied separately and in their mutual relationship.

More attention is also being paid to the content of development, which implies a more normative approach. Another development questions whether "developed" countries are in fact developed and whether this genre of progress is sustainable or desirable. It favors a multiplicity of approaches based on the context and the basic felt needs and the empowerment of the most oppressed sectors of various societies at divergent levels. A main thesis is that change must be structural and occur at multiple levels in order to achieve these ends (for more details, see Servaes, 1989, 1999).

This chapter first briefly presents two communication models: a "diffusion/mechanistic" versus a "participatory/organic" communication model. These models should be seen as extremes on a continuum. Second, it discusses a framework for participatory communication research, which borrows from Freire's theory. Third, the chapter illustrates the distinct methodologies and approaches that could be used in such a participatory communication research perspective by way of the case study of Radio Enriquillo in the Dominican Republic, which is a role model of the Latin American popular radio movement. By way of conclusion, we end with a word of caution about the barriers to participation.

A "DIFFUSION/MECHANISTIC" VERSUS A
"PARTICIPATORY/ORGANIC" COMMUNICATION MODEL

Communication theories such as the "diffusion of innovations," the "two-step-flow," or the "extension" approaches are quite congruent with modernization theory. According to Everett Rogers (1986), one of the leading proponents of diffusion theory, this perspective implies "the the role of communication was (1) to transfer technological innovations from development agencies to their clients, and (2) to create an appetite for change through raising a 'climate for modernization' among the members of the public" (p. 49).

The elitist, vertical, or top-down orientation of the diffusion model is obvious. However, the reality often proves much more complex than the theory. Therefore, many authors and development workers point out that decision making and planning cannot be done by bureaucrats and policy makers for the people but only by these "experts" together with all concerned institutions and together with the people. In other words, in accordance with discussions on international political and academic forums such as UNESCO, FAO, or IAMCR, these people refer to newer insights on the role and place of communication for development that favor two-way and participatory communication.

The Diffusion Model

The 1950s was the decade of the communication model. Interestingly, one of the earliest and most influential of these came not from the social sciences or humanities, but from information engineering. Shannon and Weaver's linear "source-transmitter-channel-receiver-destination" model eclipsed the earlier, more organic, psychological, and sociological approaches. Lasswell, Hovland, Newcomb, Schramm, Westley and Mclean, Berlo, and others each devised a model of communication as they conceived it. This profusion of communication models may be attributed to three reasons.

First, because they identified communication basically as the transfer of information (the stimulus), they were amenable to empirical methodology, thus establishing the basics for communication as a distinct and legitimate science.

Second, theorists focused on the efficiency, or effects, of communication (the response), thereby holding vast promise for manipulation or control of message "receivers" by vested interests, or the "sources."

Finally, the communication models fit neatly into the nature and mechanics of mass or mediated communication, an emergent and powerful force at that time.

Therefore, in these years the discipline of communication was largely, and most importantly, its effects. The "bullet" or "hypodermic needle" effects of media were to be a quick and efficient answer to myriad social ills. Robert White (1982) wrote, "This narrow emphasis on media and media effects has also led to a premise . . . that media information is an all-powerful panacea for problems of human and socio-economic development" (p. 30), not to mention dilemmas of marketing and propaganda. Falling short of exuberant claims, direct effects became limited effects, minimal effects, conditional effects, and the "two-step flow."

In sum, we could characterize this communication perspective as "sender-and media-centric." In conjunction with the obsession with the mass media, it led to a conceptualization of communication as something one does to another. White (1984) argues this pro-media, pro-effects, and anti-egalitarian bias of communication theory "has developed largely as an explanation of the power and effects of mass communication and does not provide adequate explanation of the factors of social change leading toward democratization" (p. 2).

The main characteristics of this diffusion model are:

1. Derived from a world view of dominance over one's environment, the Western conception of communication is overwhelmingly oriented to persuasion. Akin to the modernization paradigm in both theory and ideology, the communication approach is undirectional, from the informed "source" to the uninformed "receiver."

2. Congruent with the modernization philosophy, the diffusion and development support communication approaches tend to assign responsibility for the problem of underdevelopment to peoples residing in those societies.

3. Development as modernization and communication as one-way persuasion reached their zenith through the diffusion of innovations, the two-step flow, and other "social marketing" strategies of attitude and behavior change directed at "underdeveloped" peoples.

4. Mass media play the preeminent role in the campaign of development through communication, and early predictions were of great effects. Bidirectional models and strategies such as feedback were added to render the initial message more effective.

5. Mass audiences were "influenced" with predispositions to development and social institutions. Such media technology has been taken either as the sole solution, the driving force, or simply a value-free tool in the process of development.

6. Research of the diffusion approach, like the modernization theory, suffers from an overemphasis on quantitative criteria to the exclusion of social and cultural factors. As a result, the manner in which foreign media hardware and software interact within a cultural context is largely unexplored.

The Participatory Model

The participatory model incorporates the concepts in the emerging framework of multiplicity/another development. It stresses the importance of cultural identity of local communities and of democratization and participation at all levels—international, national, local, and individual. It points to a strategy, not merely inclusive of, but largely emanating from, the traditional "receivers." Paulo Freire (1983) refers to this as the right of all people to individually and collectively speak their word: "This is not the privilege of some few men, but the right of every man. Consequently, no one can say a true word alone—nor can he say it for another, in a prescriptive act which robs others of their words" (p. 76).

In order to share information, knowledge, trust, commitment, and a right attitude in development projects, participation is very important in any decision-making process for development. Therefore, the International Commission for the Study of Communication Problems argues that "this calls for a new attitude for overcoming stereotyped thinking and to promote more understanding of diversity and plurality, with full respect for the dignity and equality of peoples living in different conditions and acting in different ways" (MacBride, 1980, p. 254). This model stresses reciprocal collaboration throughout all levels of participation. Listening to what the others say, respecting the counterpart's attitude, and having mutual trust are needed. Participation supporters do not underestimate the ability of the masses to develop themselves and their environment:

> Development efforts should be anchored on faith in the people's capacity to discern what is best to be done as they seek their liberation, and how to participate actively in the task of transforming society. The people are intelligent and have centuries of experience. Draw out their strength. Listen to them. (Xavier Institute, 1980, p. 11)

According to many authors, authentic participation directly addresses power and its distribution in society. Participation involves the more equitable sharing of both political and economic power, which often decreases the advantage of certain groups. Structural change involves the redistribution of power. In mass communication areas, many communication experts agree that structural change should occur first in order to establish participatory communication policies. Mowlana and Wilson (1987), for instance, state:

> Communications policies are basically derivatives of the political, cultural and economic conditions and institutions under which they operate. They tend to legitimize the existing power

> relations in society, and therefore, they cannot be substan-
> tially changed unless there are fundamental structural
> changes in society that can alter these power relationships
> themselves. (p. 143)

Consequently, the perspective on communication has changed. It is
more concerned with process and context, that is, on the exchange
of "meanings" and on the importance of this process, namely, the
social relational patterns and social institutions that are the result of
and are determined by the process. Another communication "favors
multiplicity, smallness of scale, locality, de-institutionalization,
interchange of sender-receiver roles (and) horizontality of communication links at all levels of society" (McQuail, 1983, p. 97). As a
result, the focus moves from a "communicator-" to a more "receiver-
centric" orientation, with the resultant emphasis on meaning sought
and ascribed rather than information transmitted.

With this shift in focus, one is no longer attempting to create
a need for the information one is disseminating, but one is rather
disseminating information for which there is a need. Experts and
development workers rather respond than dictate; they choose what
is relevant to the context in which they are working. The emphasis is
on information exchange rather than on the persuasion in the diffusion model.

Because dialogue and face-to-face interaction is inherent in
participation, the development communicator will find him or herself
spending more time in the field. It will take some time to develop
rapport and trust. Continued contact, meeting commitments, keeping promises, and followup between visits is important. Development
of social trust precedes task trust. Both parties will need patience. It
is important to note that when we treat people the way we ourselves
would like to be treated, we learn to work as a team, which also
brings about rural commitment and motivation. Thus honesty, trust,
and commitment from the higher ups bring honesty, trust, and commitment for the grassroots as well. This brings about true participation. And true participation brings about appropriate policies and
planning for developing a country within its cultural and environmental framework.

The main characteristics of this participatory model are:

1. The participatory model sees people as the controlling
   actors or participants for development. People will have
   self-appreciation instead of self-depreciation.
   Development is meant to liberate and emancipate people.
   Local culture is respected.
2. The participatory model sees people as the nucleus of
   development. Development means lifting up the spirits of a
   local community to take pride in its own culture, intellect,
   and environment. Development aims to educate and stimulate people to be active in self- and communal improve-

ments while maintaining a balanced ecology. Authentic participation, although widely espoused in the literature, is not in everyone's interest. Such programs are not easily implemented, highly predictable, or readily controlled.

3. The participatory model emphasizes the local community rather than the nation state, monistic universalism rather than nationalism, spiritualism rather than secular humanism, dialogue rather than monologue, and emancipation rather than alienation.

4. Participation involves the redistribution of power. Participation aims at redistributing the elites' power so that a community can become a full-fledged democratic one. As such, it directly threatens those whose position and/or very existence depends on power and its exercise over others. Reactions to such threats are sometimes overt, but most often are manifested as less visible, yet steady and continuous resistance.

TOWARD A FRAMEWORK FOR PARTICIPATORY COMMUNICATION RESEARCH

Traditional positivist–functionalist approaches implicitly still start from the assumptions that all knowledge is based on an observable reality, and that social phenonema can be studied on the basis of methodologies and techniques adopted from the natural sciences. However, as Giddens (1979) eloquently points out, the social sciences differ from the natural sciences in at least four respects: (a) with regard to the study domain the social sciences are, contrary to the natural sciences, in a subject–subject relationship; (b) they deal with a preinterpreted world in which the meanings developed by the active subjects form part of the production of that world; (c) the construction of a theory of society therefore necessitates a double hermeneutics; and (d) the logical status of generalizations in the social sciences differs from natural scientific generalizations. Therefore, in our opinion, the social sciences are hermeunistic and nomological in nature and need to be approached from a critical perspective.

Furthermore, the classic materialist–idealist distinction between political economy and interpretative approaches has become outdated. Therefore, we advocate the relative autonomy of a cultural analysis. In general, one can distinguish between two basic types of cultural critique. The first is of a philosophical nature, posing as an epistemological critique of analytical reason, of the Enlightenment faith in pure reason and in the social progress that rationality is supposed to engender. This type of critique attempts to demystify power and ideology. The second approach uses more empirical and therefore more conventional social science techniques to analyze social institutions, cultural forms, and the modes of discourse in social life.

Research Perspective

What we have in mind is a text that takes as its subject not a concentrated group of people in a community affected in one way or another by politico-economic forces, but the "system" itself—the political and economic processes, encompassing different space and time constraints. This kind of analysis, which builds on the ideas of Giddens (1984) and Marcus and Fisher (1986), should also involve the relative power-linked articulation and conflict over ideologies, world views, moral codes, and the locally bounded conditions of knowledge and competence. Although all social research presumes a hermeneutic moment, often it remains latent because researchers and research inhabit a common cultural milieu. Moreover, it is the study of the unintended consequences of action and the creation of meaning that some of the most distinctive tasks of the social sciences in general and communication studies in particular are to be found. At least two types of unintended influences can be distinguished: first, the unconscious ones, and second, influences conditioned by the context in which the different forms of social action take place.

Without disqualifying and underestimating the significance of other research contributions we advocate a research design that starts from a more dialectic and multicentered perception of power factors in the context of communication for social change. In other words, we advocate a framework that also takes counterpower or empowerment from a bottom-up or grassroots perspective into account. In general, three general problem areas can be discerned: (a) the mutual dependency between the macro-level of the society or a given structure and the micro-level of the social actions involved, (b) the position and the autonomy of organized subjects, and (c) the relationship of domination, dependency, and subordination versus liberation, selective participation, and emancipation of power and interest contrapositions.

The main actors of this new perspective are social movements with a concern for the previously indicated multiple public issues. Therefore, instead of one central, objective, and mainly economic "conflict," several segmented, subjective, and "postmaterialistic" issues can be identified. Instead of one central collective actor (the proletariat or exploited class), several different, sometimes opposing collective actors can be identified (see also Anderson, 1983; Beck, 1986; Escobar & Alvarez, 1992; Eyermann & Jamison, 1991; Gunder & Fuentes, 1988).

This research project must center around two problem areas. First, it must determine what actors or interest groups and what factors or structural constraints exercise influence from above. These influences can transform, reinforce, or weaken each other. What is required is a much more precise analysis of influence patterns that function from top down by means of power in the broad sense. The second problem area is the grassroots reaction to this influence. Research must be focused on the rational objectives of target groups and social movements. The difference from traditional anthropological research should be that the choice of the symbolic order for the research is determined by key concepts such as reproduction and identity. It is no more or less chance differences in rational objectives that are interesting, but the systematic tendencies and the thereby generalizable differences. This implies that the choice of the place and the context of research cannot be random but must be based on macro-structural insights.

Participatory Strategies

This policy and research model, which builds on the multiplicity paradigm, starts from more dialectic mobilization and conscientization strategies. Social resistance and conscientization is developed from the bottom up via interpersonal communication or media channels. This theme immediately brings to mind the conscientization method developed by Paulo Freire in Brazil. Because Freire himself clearly states that the third world is also found in industrialized societies (what is involved here is not a geographical but a relational and structural categorization), the "exemplarisch lernen" [imitative learning] method of Oskar Negt (1971), which originated in Western workers situations, can be mentioned as an important addition.

Freire's conscientization method is oriented to bringing individuals to critical reflection about their own living conditions, in which they break through the critique-free adaptation—the "culture of silence"—and actively participate in a historical process. The right to participation and emancipation regarding the social, cultural, and historical reality is a fundamental right for everyone. The basis of the conscientization method forms the philosophical and sociocritical notion that individuals must be able to achieve their essential goal—being a subject—and that the social structures, social relationships, and interpersonal relationships that interfere with it must be changed. The absence of any form of a guideline for political organization of those who are conscienticized is partially resolved by Negt. In this method, he tries to bring the marginal people in the society to see their individual need as a collective need that can only be satisfied in the context of organized groups.

In the literature, this approach is often described as "participatory action" or "participatory research." An appropriate definition used by the Philippine Partnership for the Development of Human Resources in Rural Areas (1986) is as follows:

> Participatory research is an alternative social research approach in the context of development. It is alternative, because although business, government and the academic also undertake research with development in the end view, little thought and effort go as to how the research project can be used for the benefit of those researched. The central element of Participatory Research is participation. . . . It is an

active process whereby the expected beneficiaries of research are the main actors in the entire research process, with the researcher playing a facilitator's role. (p. 1)

Eurich (1980), the Farmers Assistance Board (1985), Gran (1983), Huizer (1983), Kassam and Mustafa (1982), Kronenburg (1986), Seguier (1976), and Tobias (1982), among others, have attempted to identify the major characteristics of participatory research. Kronenburg (1986) summarizes them as follows:

1. Participatory research rests on the assumption that human beings have an innate ability to create knowledge. It rejects the notion that knowledge production is a monopoly of "professionals."
2. Participatory research is seen as an educational process for the participants in the research program as well as for the researcher. It involves the identification of community needs, augmented awareness about obstacles to needs fulfillment, an analysis of the causes of the problems, and the formulation and implementation of relevant solutions.
3. The researcher is consciously committed to the cause of the community involved in the research. This challenges the traditional principle of scientific neutrality and rejects the position of the scientist as a social engineer.
4. Research is based on a dialectical process of dialogue between the researcher and the community. Dialogue provides for a framework that guards against manipulative scientific interference and serves as a means of control by the community over the direction of the research process.
5. Participatory research is a problem-solving approach. The objective is to uncover the causes of community problems and mobilize the creative human potential to solve social problems by transforming the conditions underlying the problems.
6. The major asset of participatory research is its potential for the creation of knowledge. Close cooperation between researcher and community forms a condition enabling all participants to analyze the social environment and formulate adequate plans of action.

In other words, participatory research calls for upward, transactive, open, and radical forms of planning that encompass both grassroots collective actions (i.e., planning in the small) and large-scale processes (i.e., planning in the large). This kind of planning and research is centrally conceived with human growth, learning processes through mobilization, and the basic aim is to involve the people under study cooperatively in the planning and research process, with the planner or researcher as a facilitator and participant.

Therefore, one could call the conventional strategies "diffusion/mechanistic" models, as the human being is considered as just a "thing," whereas participatory strategies are more "organic," spiritually oriented, and "human," they believe in the humanness, the importance of people. Both models should be regarded as opposite positions on a continuum.

CASE STUDY: RADIO ENRIQUILLO

The island of Hispaniola in the Caribbean region is divided into Haitian and Dominican parts. From 1930 until 1952, R.L. Trujillo was the president of the Dominican Republic. He led a terroristic and dictatorial regime. After 1952, his brother became the president, but the former dictator kept the power behind the scenes. In 1960, the Dominican people stood up against the repression, and Trujillo was murdered in 1961.

Since 1966, the Dominican Republic is a presidential republic by constitution. Legislative power belongs to the Congress (a parliament like that in the United States). The political situation in the Dominican Republic has been unstable for the last 25 years. Cooperation between the 20 political parties seems impossible, but despite the problems, the politicians are still striving to attain a more orderly and democratic situation.

The Dominican Republic is economically dependent on the United States, with the export to that country accounting for 90% of total export. Agriculture is the most important sector of the economy, absorbing 70% of the working population. The main export product is sugar cane. Other products are cacao, coffee, and tobacco. In the poor southwest region, where Radio Enriquillo is located, the farmers produce sugar cane. There is much landlordism, so no matter how hard the farmers work, they remain poor.

Origins of Radio Enriquillo

Radio Enriquillo is a role model of the Latin American radio movement. Other participatory radios passed through the phases like Radio Enriquillo. Examples include Radio ERPE in Riobamba, Ecuador; "La voz de la Selve" in Iquitos, Peru; and Radio San Gabriel in La Paz, Bolivia (for more information, see Beltran, 1993; Cabezas, Rosario, Llorente, Contreras, & Ros, 1982; Ciespal, 1983; Fox, 1988).

Radio Enqiquillo was founded in 1977 in the village of Tamayo, in the southwest region of the country. The "Surenos" (the inhabitants from the southern province) were until then "the forgotten people" because the area was quite isolated and underdeveloped. Radio Enriquillo (named after a 16th-century Indian rebel) was established by Humberto Vandenbuleke, a Belgian missionary who later also founded the ALER, the Latin American Association of Radio Education.

Radio Enriquillo consciously seeks to support grassroots organizations in their social and economic demands. Observers agree that Radio Enriquillo was instrumental in the tremendous growth in the number of peasant associations and women's groups in the decade after its founding. In 1972, there were only a dozen associations of organized campesinos in the region.

Ten years later there were some 110 associations. Its programming is produced in coordination with local organizations. This includes participation in planning the program by the periodic meetings of regional and local organizations, participation in production by the leaders and representative of the various organizations, as well as the ordinary participation of the "voices" of many people in the region. It often broadcasts "live" and therefore completely unedited interviews. These interviews are about everyday things, the reality, and the problems of the region. Mistakes, misunderstandings, everyday language, all go on air. Therefore, over the years, Radio Enriquillo has developed a highly participatory working style, involving youth, women, and peasant groups in the identification of themes and content of programs ranging from news, debates, folk music, poetry, and drama.

For instance, after the military coup against the democratically elected Haitian President Jean-Bertrand Aristide in 1991, Radio Enriquillo exploited a journalistic loophole in a ban by the Dominican Republic on newscasts in Creole, the patois spoken by most Haitians. Musical broadcasts were permitted, so Radio Enriquillo reporters began singing the news in Creole twice a day to the accompaniment of guitars, flutes, and drums. It aired musical propaganda in support of Aristide's reinstatement.

The expected spillover of Radio Enriquillo is that local or national grassroot organizations recognize their collective problems. Through listening to and working with the radio, people can learn they are not the only ones to experience specific problems. When they get to know people who go through the same difficulties, they can organize and find solutions for the collective problem. This cooperation does not necessarily find its way through radio interaction, but it is possible that the radio establishes the first contact or recognition.

Appropriately, the station calls itself "La Amiga del Sur," or Friend of the South. However, because of its clear identification with the poor, those in power have accused it of "agitating" and generating conflict.

Radio Enriquillo has passed through the three phases typical of the Latin American radio movement.

These phases are, in chronological order:

1. "Radio schools" *(escuelas radiofonicas):* Radio as a medium to support education of the population. Specially formed listening groups received written material to support the radio education. This material and the radio

programs are designed to educate the poorer segments
of the population.
2. "Democratisation movement" *(radio popular):* In this peri-
    od the radio was used as a propaganda medium against
    the military dictatorships. Laborers (like the miners in
    Bolivia), farmers, and other opposition groups organized
    and used the radio to air their concerns and wishes.
3. "Radio as a communication medium" *(sistema de com-
    munication):* Radio is part of the communication process
    as a whole; that is, radio is there for the people and
    made by the people. Although participation is one of the
    key concepts, it is recognized that radio is only one com-
    munication medium, with the population also having
    other means of sending and receiving information. Most
    important in this phase is that people can be sender and
    receiver equally through one medium.

Objectives of the Radio Enriquillo Project

Radio Enriquillo is an audience-centered, participatory project.
Radio Enriquillo recognizes that the "public" or "audience" is in fact
made up of tendencies, tastes, and class interests that are often
antagonistic to each other. The audience is not one of individuals
but of people who are already organized into associations that are
both communicative networks and political entities. What is different
about Radio Enriquillo is that it does not pretend to be neutral. It
takes the side of the people. It respects and helps to strengthen the
people's own political organizations, without making an explicit
option for one ideological or political party. The basic philosophical
position of Radio Enriquillo is not a theory of "underdevelopment" or
"dependency," but a diagnosis of the actual situation in the region.
The diagnosis is that the dominant bloc is made up of an alliance of
landlords, state functionaries, military men, and industrialists. The
dominated bloc consists of small farmers, laborers, unemployed people who seek day labor, illegal Haitian immigrants, small traders,
and employees. The most important political organization in the
dominated bloc is the campesinos' associations. Radio Enriduillo
allies itself with these associations in a process of social change.
        The emergent practice of genuine participatory peoples' radio
in Latin America centrally involves issues of class, power, and cultural hegemony. The radios are an important part, but still only a
part of grassroots struggles for fundamental social change in their
region and in their country. The radios are used for direct political
organization (to call a meeting, to organize a campaign), but using
the radio also gives people self-confidence. Most of all this involves
the reevaluation of their language and culture. This culture process
may be a "long revolution"—the slow process of building a counter-
hegemony to the dominant political culture. But it is also linked
directly to political demands for fundamental social change. These

demands often find expression in local struggles for access to land and services, for jobs and housing, for clean water and schools. These demands of people organized in grassroots organizations can be noticed throughout Latin America.

Radio Enriquillo is dedicated to "horizontal" communication between the radio and its listeners. This means that the radio and the listeners are on the same level. There is no hierarchical structure within a teacher–student relation; anybody can learn from anybody. Everyone's voice is heard, and everyone's ideas are seriously considered.

Participatory Communication Strategies Employed

Generally speaking, participation is the main concept of Radio Enriquillo. "Evaluation" is a very important concept for a radio of the people. To encourage participation, the audience should be known. It is also an obligation for the radio station to make itself known and to know how the programs rate with the audience in terms of its needs and aspirations.

At first these evaluations were initiated by the financiers of Radio Enriquillo, but later the radio wanted to evaluate its own work. For example, regular meetings are held to examine the station's relationships with local and regional citizen's organizations. In 1982, the station undertook an 18-month research project with the assistance of the Latin American Association of Radio Education (ALER), an Ecuador-based group that specializes in participatory research for community radio stations. The evaluation proved worthwhile in helping the station explore the source of its popularity and to define ways to better serve the information and educational needs of local people (see Mata, 1985).

Since that time, changes have occurred at the station with the departure of original staff members and the addition of new ones. In addition, national elections brought about important political changes that had implications for the station and community organizations. As a result, in December 1988, the station staff decided to undertake another comprehensive self-evaluation to examine its achievements, limitations, and problems. The evaluation began in August 1989 and concluded in March 1990. It showed some deficiencies in the work of Radio Enriquillo, and changes were put through to improve the situation (see Camilo, Mata, & Servaes, 1990). The next evaluation is planned for 1995.

Participation and other development communication methods employed include:

1. *A Participatory Approach to Evaluation*: Because Radio Enriquillo had always emphasized democratic participation in its operations, the station staff has always been inclined to a participatory approach to evaluation. Everyone agreed that if staff were directly involved in the

determination of evaluation results, they would also be more committed to carrying out the recommendations. Thus the staff was involved at various stages of the evaluation process—selection of objectives, development of the methodology, data collection, and analysis. However, the process attempted to balance their in-depth knowledge of the station's operations with the research experience and independent perspective of "outside" coordinators of the evaluation.

2. *A Participatory Approach to Research*: Data collection was carried out with the involvement of station staff and village correspondents. Five methods were used to collect data: (a) surveys, (b) community meetings, (c) analysis of radio programming, (d) document analysis, and (e) participatory observation.

3. *Quantitative and Qualitative Research Methods*: Research methods employed focused on a combination and interpretation of quantitative and qualitative data. For quantitative data, clear cut conventions exist as to what can be done with data and how data should be collected. In the 1989 evaluation, some of these conventions (e.g., intercoder reliability) could not be met, due to the specific situations in which the research was executed (for instance, the "inexperience" of the interviewers with the previously discussed conventions). However, most of these methodological problems in the quantitative part of the research could be corrected through the qualitative research findings. The collection of qualitative data assisted in formulating the specific content of the questionnaires by identifying the most important key variables under which more specific data can be explored. It also aided in controlling the quantitative data. And, even more significantly, qualitative data enliven and make more concrete the statistical pictures that come out of survey information.

   Some standards of data collection, such as a high degree of statistical reliability, could not be met. First, because most data were gathered by associates of Radio Enriquillo, rather than by independent observers and, second, because many of them were inexperienced in the protocols of data collection, although there was a provision of training. It was agreeable that problems with quantitative measurements could be corrected through more in-depth qualitative research and careful data analysis and interpretation. The researchers also believed that the qualitative data would broaden the findings suggested by the statistical data.

4. *A Community Based Approach*: Why does the community have such trust and support for Radio Enriquillo? "Because the people that work with it are valuable

resources"; "because they have the support and acceptance of the people"; "because they make continual
efforts toward improvement, as in this evaluation."
These were the three answers most frequently cited by
respondents during the evaluation. They are the three
basic elements by which an organization such as Radio
Enriquillo can transcend its limitations, redefine vision:
a team that values people, works to revise its practice,
and ensures that the listeners recognize this radio as
their own.

5. *Edu-tainment*: Educative programs are aired in order to
   help the poor population develop. But the programs also
   have to appeal to the popular taste in music, to avoid
   switching to the commercial radio stations.

6. *Community Participation*: The audience needs to express
   its needs and wishes. The organization of the radio is
   democratic. This means that the population can cooper-
   ate in the development of radio programs. Access for
   anyone to radio microphones is most important. People
   express their feedback and their own ideas. Access for
   farmers in remote villages is made easier through the
   "*unidad movil*" (the mobile recording unit).

   Until now Radio Enriquillo has reached the people
   who were the target audience, the farmers. They have
   since become more conscious of their own situation and
   that it could be changed. Radio Enriquillo has gained
   the trust of the farmers.

BY WAY OF CONCLUSION: WORDS OF CAUTION

It should be obvious by now that no all-embracing view on development is to be offered. No theory has achieved and maintained
explanatory dominance. Each of the three perspectives discussed
here still does find support among academics, policy makers, international organizations, and the general public. In general, adopted
and updated versions of the ideas upon which the modernization
theory is built—economic growth, centralized planning, and the
belief that underdevelopment is rooted in mainly internal causes that
can be solved by external (technological) "aid"—are still shared by
many development agencies and governments. A revitalized modernization perspective in which some of the errors of the past are
acknowledged and efforts are made to deal in new ways (as outlined
in the multiplicity view) remains the dominant perspective in practice but becomes increasingly more difficult to defend in theory. On
the contrary, although the multiplicity theory is gaining ground in
academic spheres, in practice it is still looked on as a sympathetic
although idealistic side show.

Rigid and general strategies for participation are neither possible nor desirable. It is not an innovative formula that "experts" diffuse to the masses. It is a process that unfolds in each unique situation, and to prescribe how that unfolding should occur is not only conterproductive, it is often the antithesis of authentic participation. Authentic participation, although widely espoused in the literature, is not in everyone's interest. Such programs are not easily implemented, highly predictable, or readily controlled, nor do they lend themselves to quick name-enhancing results.

Behavioral response to an exogenous stimulus of passive reception of messages from the elite is not participation. Neither is it a strategy to make target audiences "feel" more involved and therefore more acquiescent to manipulative agendas. It is not a means to an end, but legitimate in its own right.

Participation can involve the redistribution of power at local and national levels. As such, it directly threatens those whose position and/or very existence depends on power and its exercise over others. Reactions to such threats are sometimes overt, but most often are manifested as less visible, yet steady and continuous resistance.

The main objective of bureaucrats and bureaucracies is their own perpetuation and expansion on both an individual and collective level. This necessitates an anti-participatory, institutional focus and the consolidation as opposed to the distribution of authority. Participatory communication is impeded by this stance. As such authentic government promotion of popular participation is quite unlikely.

Such barriers are not limited to government–populace relationships, but are prevalent both among bureaucratic organizations and communities as well. In India, for instance, the existence of casteism and the history of patron–client relationships exacerbates the situation.

It is asserted that the interaction between development organization and rural people is indeed cross-cultural communication. Various groups structure, indeed live within, different realities. Language differences go beyond words to the way those words are used and the resultant logical structures employed. A major misassumption of development practitioners is to assume their own logic and world view is correct, universal, and applicable to all.

In relation, participation should not be construed as the inclusion of the poor in government programs and services, but rather as the inclusion of government programs and services as per the informed and autonomous choice of the poor. In other words, the notion that people need to be "educated" for participation usually entails "education" as indoctrination and "participation" as subservience.

The assertion of a knowledge gap, of a disparity in valid knowledge between "experts" and local people, is wrong. Unless the "experts," through cooperation and learning from local people, can apply their knowledge in the context and to the benefit of those locals, "expertise" remains nothing more than piety.

As a result of the previously discussed points, participation does not always entail co-operation or consensus. It can often mean conflict and usually poses a threat to extant structures. Because of this, the question can be raised of whether participation is appropriate in all contexts.

Attitude is paramount for the facilitator. He or she must truly believe the participants are not only capable, but are indeed the most qualified persons for the task at hand. Therefore, beyond class and organizational interests, perhaps the major obstacles to participation are large egos and self-righteousness. The most important expertise, technique, or methodology cannot be operationalized. What is needed is a change of attitude, the patient fostering of trust, and the ability to listen.

REFERENCES

Anderson, B. (1983). *Imagined communities. Reflections on the origin and spread of nationalism.* London: Verso.

Beck, U. (1986). *Risikogesellschaft. Auf dem Weg in eine andere Moderne* [The risk society. Towards another modernity]. Frankfurt: Suhrkamp.

Beltran, L.R. (1993). Communication for development in Latin America: A forty years appraisal. In D. Nostbakken & C. Morrow (Eds.), *Cultural expression in the global village.* Penang, Malaysia: Southbound.

Cabezas, A., Rosario, A., Llorente, P.G., Contreras, E., & Ros, J. (1982). *La emisora popular* [The popular sender]. Quito, Ecuador: Editora Andina.

Camilo, M., Mata, M.C., & Servaes, J. (1990). *Autoevaluacion de Radio Enriquillo* [Self-evaluation of Radio Enriquillo]. Oegstgeest, Netherlands: Cebemo.

Ciespal. (1983). *Communication popular educativa* [Popular education communication]. Quito, Ecuador: Ciespal.

Escobar, A., & Alvarez, S. (Eds.). (1992). *The making of social movements in Latin America: Identity, strategy and democracy.* San Francisco: Westview.

Eurich, C. (1980). *Kommunikative partizipation und partisipative komunikationsforschung* [Participatory communication and participatory research] (R. G. Fisher, Ed.). Frankfurt: Verlag.

Eyerman, R., & Jamison, A. (1991). *Social movements. A cognitive approach.* University Park, PA: Penn State Press.

Farmers Assistance Board. (Ed.). (1985). *Participatory research: Response to Asian people's struggle for social transformation.* Manila, Philippines: Framers Assistance Board.

Fox, E. (1988). *Media and politics in Latin America. The struggle for democracy.* London: Sage.

Freire, P. (1983). *Pedagogy of the oppressed.* New York: Seaburg Press.

Freire, P. (1993). Foreword. In P. McLaren & P. Leonard (Eds.), *Paulo Freire. A critical encounter.* London: Routledge.

Geertz, C. (1983). *Local knowledge: Further essays in interpretive anthropology.* New York: Basic Books.

Giddens, A. (1979). *Central problems in social theory*. London: MacMillan.

Giddens, A. (1984). *The constitution of society. Outline of the theory of structuration*. Berkeley: University of California Press.

Gran, G. (1983). *Development by people. Citizen construction of a just world*. New York: Praeger.

Gunder, F., & Fuentes, M. (1988). Nine theses on social movements. *IFDA Dossier, 63,* 27-44.

Huizer, G. (1983). *Guiding principles for people's participation projects*. Rome: Food and Agricultural Organization.

Kassam, Y., & Mustafa, K. (Eds.). (1982). *Participatory research. An emerging alternative methodology in social science research*. New Delhi: Society for Participatory Research in Asia.

Kronenburg, J. (1986). *Empowerment of the poor. A comparative analysis of two development endeavours in Kenya*. Nijmegen, Netherlands: Third World Center.

MacBride, S. (Ed.). (1980). *Many voices, one world. Communication and society. Today and tomorrow*. Paris: Unesco.

Marcus, G., & Fisher, M. (1986). *Anthropology as cultural critique*. Chicago: The University of Chicago Press.

Mata, M.C. (1985). *Radio Enriquillo en dialogo con el pueblo* [Radio Enriquillo in dialogue with the people]. Quito, Ecuador: Aler.

McQuail, D. (1983). *Mass communication theory*. London: Sage.

Mowlana, H., & Wilson, L. (1987). *Communication and development: A global assessment*. Paris: Unesco.

Negt, O. (1971). *Soziologische phantasie und exemplarisch lerner* [Sociological imagination and teaching by example]. Frankfurt: Suhrkamp.

Philippine Partnership for the Devlopment of Human Resources in Rural Areas. (1986). *Participatory research guidebook*. Laguna, Philippines: Philippine Partnership for the Development of Human Resources in Rural Areas.

Rogers, E.M. (1986). *Communication technology: The new media in society*. New York: The Free Press.

Seguier, M. (1976). *Critique institutionelle et creativite collective* [Institutional criticism and collective creativity]. Paris: L'Hatmattan.

Servaes, J. (1989). *One world. Multiple cultures. A new paradigm on communication for development*. Leuven, Belguim: Acco.

Servaes, J. (1999). *Communication for development. One world, multiple cultures*. Cresskill, NJ: Hampton Press.

Tobias, K.J. (1982). *Participatory research. An introduction*. New Delhi: Participatory Research Network.

White, R. (1982, September). *Contradictions in contemporary policies for democratic communication*. Paper presented at the IAMCR Conference, Paris.

White, R. (1984, May). *The need for new strategies of research on the democratization of communication*. Paper presented at the ICA conference, San Francisco.

Xavier Institute (1980). *Development from below*. Ranchi, India: Xavier Institute for Social Service.

Chapter ▪ 3

The Communications Paradox: Inequality at the National and International Levels and the Communications Media

Peter Golding

INTRODUCTION

As communication studies have grown, in various guises, inevitably the professional apparatus of a burgeoning field has grown with it. We have our own journals, university departments, conferences, and associations. All this is welcome recognition of the central importance of communications institutions and processes in our lives. But there is also a concomitant danger. The more we isolate the study of communications in this way, the more we detach it from a fundamental concern with those radical and central issues within the social and human sciences that should command our primary attention.

In this chapter I briefly illustrate this anxiety by reference to some issues in international communications. Although few in communications research have fallen wholly prey to the raptures of technological euphoria that first greeted the global spread of communications, nonetheless we are faced with an uncertainty about how to address the obvious international diffusion of these apparatuses. Certainly, "nation shall speak unto nation," but as yet there has been little sign of swords being beaten into ploughshares. The massive efflorescence of international traffic in communications has attracted many claims, among them the observation that we have entered a new information age, global in scope, egalitarian in structure, and empowering in its essence.

It is this claim I want to contest. In particular, I will outline the inequalities that remain, and that are, indeed, in many ways deepening as communications advance. This is true both between and within nations, at a time when we are, probably prematurely, being advised to observe the disappearance from the world stage of the nation state. Inevitably, in the confines of this chapter only a few observations on this large theme are possible.

INVOKING FREIRE: THREE POINTS OF CONTACT

This volume takes as its spur the provocative and influential work of Paulo Freire. For many of us new to the politics of education in the heady days of social and political turmoil, which stirred many western countries in the 1960s and early 1970s, the appearance of Freire's writings on education was startling and revelatory. Alongside the work of other writers such as Fanon, it placed the familiar and comfortable world in which we lived firmly at the heart of change and new thinking emerging from what we now learned to call the third world.

On reflection, the lessons for communications research were not that well learned. This is not the place for a disquisition on Freire, although it is interesting that increasingly opportunities are being found to critically revisit his work (McLaren & Leonard, 1993). But I briefly mention three themes from his writing that seem to me enduringly worthy of the attention of communications scholars. First is the insistence on humans as reflective, objectifying the world in order to live within it:

> Engagement and objective distance, understanding reality as object, understanding the significance of men's action upon objective reality, creative communication about the object by means of language, plurality of responses to a single challenge— these varied dimensions testify to the existence of critical reflection in men's relationship with the world. (Freire, 1972, p. 53)

The constant interchange between reality and the language we employ to engage with it, and more importantly the extent to which that language is itself the construct of media of communication, and of social processes that render it contingent on structures of power and inequity, are central to the questions posed by communications research.

Second, it is useful to recall Freire's extension of this idea to explore the role of domination in those very social processes. In particular, he is, of course, concerned with the domination of dependent societies by powerful, metropolitan societies, resulting in the relatively exaggerated legitimacy of the voice and myths of the dominant. The result is stark: "The dependent society is by definition a silent society" (Freire, 1972, p. 59). Freire goes on to argue what is too often forgotten in later debates: that the inequality between what he terms dominator and object societies is in turn reproduced within societies, although this is not his main concern. It is, however, part of my purpose in this chapter to signal the importance of retaining a model of this "double inarticulacy" which mutes the voices of the repressed and powerless.

The third cue we should retain from Freire's work is the emphasis on activity; none of the previously discussed points is deterministic. We lose sight of the political potential and relevance of our analyses at our peril. Analysis is itself action and has the potential energy of radical resistance and reform. Cultural action for freedom, in Freire's resonant phrase, lies at the heart of communications policy. The massive uncertainties now sweeping through those nation states uncertain whether to retain or abandon traditional models of public service media, for example, derive from an inability to embrace cultural action for freedom as a proper objective of social policy (see Golding, 1993). Cultural action for freedom to "conscientisation," in Freire's famous term, is, he rightly warned, utopian in essence. But in communications policy analysis we are required to investigate the institutional forms and structural means that might render such ideals realizable.

The first step on this path is to understand the present, and I briefly outline next the central features of current media development that might inhibit such progress.

GLOBALIZATION: MYTH AND REALITY

The gradual creation in the modern era of a drift to a single, unifying, global culture seems irresistible under the combined force of a whole series of developments. The sense that we live, wherever located, at the heart of a common experience, whether imposed by malign and self-interested forces or through the benign evolution of a common project for humanity, has become almost commonplace. For the international traveller, the wearying sameness of airport lounges, hotel lobbies, and tourist clichés can induce a swift illusion of global consolidation into an inescapable marketing regime remotely controlled by the uninventive and the slick. Impressions can be misleading.

The essence of a global culture has four aspects. First is the observation that with the decline of the nation, rendered ideologically less viable by the traumas of two world wars, supranational ideologies—capitalism, Marxism, third-worldism—will offer large and all-embracing cultural resources from which people can derive identities dislodged from the previous certainties of nationality. More profoundly visible and attractive than previous identities, the supranational becomes the cultural association of greatest tenacity.

Second and of course related to this is the end of the nation state. The political and economic boundaries of the 19th-century nation state are no longer viable, it is argued, in the interdependent society of multinational industries and service economies of late 20th-century globalization. However, surviving within this global construct are the self-evidently potent cultures at the local level that play such central roles in many of the more destructive and enduring of conflicts across the globe, whether in northern Ireland, Balkan Europe, or in Africa.

Third to be offered in evidence is what a leading advertiser once hungrily described as the "syndicalization of experience." The global distribution of branded goods and the dramatic evidence of dominant imagery, from the "McDonaldization" of everywhere to the ubiquity of CNN, are evidence of an internationalization of dominant imagery that is difficult to deny. Yet the availability and dissemination of these images tells us little of their articulation with local and resilient cultures. As Smith (1990) points out, "The meanings of even the most universal of imagery for a particular population derives as much from the historical experiences and social status of that group as from the intentions of purveyors" (p. 179).

Finally the emergence of regional language blocs suggests how powerfully the residues of colonialism have seeped into the structures of contemporary discourse across whole populations. The obvious hegemony of English (Washington, Hollywood, and New York editions), and of French or Spanish needs little comment. But the assumption of the total globalization of the cultures they carry takes us further forward in the argument than the evidence would justify.

None of this is to deny the dissemination of a culture that is standardized, routinized, streamlined, and global. Often wedded to pastiche and superficial variation, it deals in slick symbol and diffuse connotation. But before we too readily accept the diagnosis of a global culture we need to ask some sharp questions (see also Ferguson, 1992). How far does it chime with the real experiences of the majority of nonmobile inhabitants across the variety of national, stratified, and local cultures? To what extent does it mistake the surface appearance for the material reality of sharply differentiated experience and life chances?

Certainly the changes in the world economy of the last two decades are real and possibly qualitative. The internationalization of companies, and of production and distribution, and the deregulation of capital flows and the major impetus given to the transmission of capital by the explosion in financial information and data flows in the last few years has certainly transformed much of the world's economy, in its manner of conduct and international division of labor.

Some such changes are immediately relevant to our discussion here. On the one hand, the decline of the United States as a global force has been moderated by the disappearance of the only other mid-century superpower. The intrusion of the Japanese and others into familiar territory in the United States (Sony and Murdoch, for example, into Hollywood and television, Bertelsmann and Maxwell into book publishing) change a familiar landscape. But before we too readily accept a picture of cultural uniformity and totally disorganized capitalism, I return to a few key features of the global infrastructure within which culture and communications operate.

A WORLD OF INEQUALITIES

We continue to live in a world of dramatic and harsh inequalities. No escape into the dizzying vistas of global culture can disguise that awkward reality. Real GDP per person in the United States was nearly $20,000 in 1988, compared to under $1,000 in Bangladesh, India, and Ghana. Overall the gap between industrialized countries and the "least developed countries" was of the order of 54:1. Some 1.4 billion of the world's 5.3 billion live in poverty, of which 1.2 billion are in the least industrialized countries (Townsend, 1993).

The gap continues to widen. On average GNP per person grew by 2.4% in industrialized countries between 1965 and 1989, but remained more or less static in the least industrialized ones. Efforts to affect a transformation in the international economy have foundered on the dams of self-interest. Aid, itself firmly locked into policies molded by economic interest, has in any case declined, especially from the wealthiest nations (e.g., aid dropped as a percentage of GNP from 0.56 to 0.19 between 1960 and 1990 in the United States).

The trend has intensified since the 1980–83 recession, propelled by protectionism, massive debt growth, and a fall in direct investment. For the poorest countries debt burdens grossly distort their economies. In 1988, the total external debt of the most severely indebted low income countries was 111% of their combined GNP and 488% of their combined exports. Through the 1980s, developing countries have been making net debt-related transfers of nearly $40 billion per annum to developed countries. Trade shifts continue to disadvantage the third world. U.S. and related manipulation of GATT, and also NAFTA and APEC, responds to an assumption of third world incursion into trading not yet exhibited in reality. In 1990, the most recent year for which data are available, the third world share of markets for manufactured goods in the industrialized countries was just over 4% in North America, and just over 3% in the European Community. The "threat from the south" does not seem too colossal. After all, the share of world manufacturing output accruing to the developing countries only grew modestly from 11.7% in 1975 to 14.5% in 1990.

Yet in the west the uncomfortable realities of recession, unemployment, and disruption require explanation. Desperate attempts to further liberalize trade have indeed globalized markets, but much more for financial flows than for goods. In 1991, for example, the market for "financial derivatives" was $7 trillion, a maverick free flow of capital provoking inevitable national protection in the traumatized western powers.

Third world countries have also been hit by falls in commodity prices. Real, non-oil, commodity prices fell by 23% between 1984 and 1988. Oil prices in fact fell 65% in the same period. As a consequence:

> The average real price of non-oil commodities for the whole of the period 1980-1988 was 25 per cent below that of the previous two decades and the terms of trade of non-oil developing countries were 8 percent below those of the 1960s and 13 percent below those of the 1970s. (South Commission, 1990, p. 60)

In the poorest regions of the world such as Africa south of the Sahara, what the IMF politely refers to as "pressures of adjustment" have "led to a downward shift in the expenditure shares for general public services, defense, social security and welfare, and transport and communications" (Heller & Diamond, 1990, p. 11). In fact, military expenditure in the third world rose from $17 billion in 1974-78 to $23 billion in 1984-88. Armaments arsenals like those that were so successfully "wasted" in the Gulf are only the most spectacular evidence of this. It was social expenditure and infrastructural investment that declined. According to UNICEF, in the world's 37 poorest nations, spending per head on health care was cut by nearly 50% in the 1980s and on education by nearly 25% in the same period.

The point to be noted is that although GNP per capita growth was higher in the third world than in OECD countries between 1970 and 1990, it was doubly maldistributed. First, the proportion in state expenditure has reduced as the private sector, especially the international arms of private capital, took over. More particularly, this reduced investment on welfare expenditure and on such infrastructural necessities as communications. Second, the third world itself became a meaningless conglomerate, within which growth rates in GNP per capita included Africa at 0.9% but also the newly industrializing "little dragons" of Thailand, Hong Kong, Singapore, Taiwan, and Korea at 6.5%. In Latin America per capita incomes were lower in 1987 than in 1980 in all but 5 of the 25 countries in the region.

The advice from the north was stern. As an OECD (1990) report puts it, the problem is "fundamental institutional and human resource weaknesses." It wags its finger disapprovingly and offers firm guidance:

> It is clear that a critical factor in enabling developing countries to participate dynamically in world trade, and thus to

adjust to the fundamental longterm forces now in play, is a
flexible robust, business sector. The individual business unit
is the key institution for intermediating between national
capacities and the world economy. (p. 58)

The need is for "market and efficiency-oriented growth policies and
their effective implementation by strong and competent governments" (p. 58). It does not take much imagination to translate these
epithets. As the report goes on, "constructive labour relations are an
important aspect of private sector development," and there is a "need
to rationalise the parastatal sector" (pp. 80-81). The reward for the
obedient, of course, will be, in that wonderful euphemism, structural
adjustment loans.

What emerges then is a pattern that goes full circle. From
Bretton Woods in 1944, through the rise of the nonaligned movement at Bandung in 1955, or more completely in 1961, and the
arrival of the third world on the international agenda of economic
decision making at UNCTAD in 1964 brings us to the brave new
world of the 1990s with the western economies on the edge of recession, and the third world riddled with dual economies, massive
debts, and over a billion people living in stark and absolute poverty.
On the demand side we find a rising appetite for imports fueled by a
pattern of demand nurtured by cosmopolitan elites and consequently
a growing dependence on the north for research and development,
technology, and education.

THE COMMUNICATIONS GRADIENT

It is not surprising, in this context, that the terrain occupied by communications goods and facilities is a hilly one, marked by soaring
peaks of advantage and dismal valleys of privation. It is essential,
however familiar some of this material may be, to review once again
how startlingly disparate the distribution of communications
resources is across the globe (see Golding & Harris, 1997).

Book production continues to be dominated by European
and U.S. publishers. The dominance of the English-language multinational publishers, especially in educational publishing, continues
to sustain what has been the longest established feature of the international media. In 1991, developing countries, with 77% of the
world's population, produced 26% of the world's books (UNESCO,
1996). Asia and the Arab countries now have a significant share of
the world's newspaper production, although over half the world's
production remains in the industrialized west. Conversely, Africa has
just 2% of the world's newspaper circulation, the same proportion as
a decade earlier. As discussed later, these figures are put further
into perspective when looked at on a per-capita basis. The same is
true for film production, in which significant centers of production,

especially within Asia, certainly disturb an unduly simple picture of U.S. hegemony.

The growth of broadcasting as the dominant medium in most regions has been swift and dramatic. The proportion of radio and television sets in Europe and North America has decreased during the last decade as a fraction of the world's total. But again European and North American people remain the owners of nearly two thirds of the total in each case, although they account for just 14.9% (Europe) and 5.2% (North America) of the world's population. Notable for its very limited incursion into this picture is Africa, with 12.1% of the world's population, but whose share of world radio and television sets is just 6% and 3%, respectively.

The extent to which the "lost decade" has seen the gap between rich and poor opening wider is starkly illustrated. Although annual book production in developing countries advanced from 153,000 titles in 1980 to 228,000 titles in 1991, the gap between developing and developed countries has scarcely been closed in the same period. There are over eight times as many book titles produced per capita in developed countries compared to the developing countries. The gap in newspapers per capita is of a similar ratio.

The gap in ownership densities is equally severe when reconsidered on a per-capita basis. The developed world has nearly 10 times as many radios per capita as the least developed nations and nearly nine times as many television sets. The picture these figures superficially represent does not, of course, illustrate the disappointments of the 1980s. If we look at Africa again, with just 39 televisions per 1,000 inhabitants in 1993 and just 173 radios, we realize how far behind some regions have been left (these figures were 17 and 104 in 1980). Yet in Europe the equivalent figures for 1993 were 628 (radio) and 802 (television), reflecting an increase in the decade greater than the African total.

The same picture can be seen in telecommunications. The routing of telecommunications is a simple reflection of the global capital structure. Four of the five top international telecommunication routes have the United States as one partner, and the USA is partner to 51% of international telephone traffic in the top 50 routes. Japan and the United States dominate world telecommunication equipment exports, accounting for 48% of the value of exports by the top 10 nations. Even within the developing world the overwhelming volume of traffic is among and between the major trading elites, with the top 25 routes including those between Hong Kong, China, Singapore, and Malaysia. No African country features in the top international routes among developing nations until we get down to number 15 (Namibia and South Africa). Yet, paradoxically, the biggest users of international telephony are a small number of affluent Sub-Saharan subscribers, living in a continent in which there is not even one line per hundred people. Although half the world's population has never made a phone call, a fraction are online and in touch to great effect and benefit.

However we portray these figures we emerge with a picture of massive inequalities in communications resources. It is important we do not lose sight of the complexities and variations within this overall pattern. But whatever the significance of the variation within the third world, the trends of the last decade, and the evidence of growing communications inequity, certainly do not look like signs of a global information village.

INEQUALITIES WITHIN: COMMUNICATION AND CITIZENSHIP

The vast inequalities of wealth and income between nations that underpin the communication disparities described here are also reflected within nations. The distribution of wealth in even the wealthiest societies produces massive inequity in the ability of many to take a full part in their society, whatever their standard of living measured on a global scale. In the richest country on earth, the United States, the poorest 20% earn just 5.6% of aggregate disposable income. Of the 1.4 billion living in poverty across the world, as mentioned earlier, the overwhelming majority are in developing countries. But 200 million of them are in the industrial countries, including 30 million in the United States (Townsend, 1993). We should not easily ignore the telling evidence of the Human Development Index constructed by the UN Development Programme, which shows that, when calculated for black people in the United States, their index is the same as for the population of Trinidad and Tobago.

In the UK the long-accumulated residue of a declining industrial base, and a regime committed to the massive reduction of public expenditure and to regulation by the market of public services have seen a return to levels and an intensity of poverty long thought abolished forever. Official statistics published in 1996 show that, for the UK between 1979 and 1991, the richest 10% received a rise in their income after housing costs of 62%, whereas the poorest 10% saw their incomes fall by 14%.

The consequence of this trend in relation to consumer goods in general and communications goods in particular is entirely predictable. We can see this in relation to the UK in looking at the ownership of a range of communications facilities among three contrasted income groups in the UK. As you might expect, television is more or less universally available, although this disguises the difference between the well-heeled household with a slimline fast Nicam stereo soundmaster set, and portables in every room in the house, and the dodgy four-channel secondhand small screen in the parlor of a less affluent neighbor.

But if we look at other goods a gap begins to appear. For example, video ownership, although relatively widespread in the UK (much stimulated by the royal wedding in the early 1980s), is much more common among higher income groups. Home computers, although increasingly available, are very inequitably distributed throughout the population. Even telephones, widely assumed to be universally available, are in fact not found in roughly 1 in 6 households, overwhelmingly those in lower income groups. Indeed, if those figures are broken down further, we find that phone ownership is even lower among single pensioner households and lone parents; just those groups we might assume are most in need of such facilities.

It is sometimes argued that this gap will diminish over time, just as it did for new "white goods" in 1950s. But this is unlikely to be so for two reasons. First, it is intrinsic to the nature of these goods that their ownership imparts cumulative advantage to those able to sustain them. This is because these goods require more than a single expenditure. They must be fed. Computers require updating, software, and addons such as printers or modems. Video recorders require blank or prerecorded tapes. Second, in the 1950s and 1960s, when the previous generation of domestic electrical goods became commonplace, there were periods of boom and declining inequality. Such economic dynamics are not likely to be replicated in the period in which the new communication goods are being established.

What we have in such a society is, in a cliché that nonetheless carries an unavoidable truth, the growing gap between information poor and information rich. Where information is only available at a price, the transformation of citizens into consumers brings with it a steep gradient of unequal opportunities to share in the communications revolution, and that in turn creates a form of democratic participation severely distorted by the accidents and structures of power and inequality.

CONCLUSION: COMMUNICATIONS—PROBLEM OR SOLUTION?

Freire (1972) proclaimed that "I only have one desire: that my thinking may coincide historically with the unrest of all those who, whether they live in those cultures which are wholly silenced or in the silent sectors of cultures which prescribe their voice, are struggling to have a voice of their own" (p. 18). That struggle is a far cry from the mystifying and Panglossian euphoria that too readily mistakes the technological gloss for the social reality.

I have suggested in this chapter that the globalizing tendencies of communications media should not be allowed to disguise the very real inequalities that persist at both the inter- and intra-national levels. Cast into silence by the stark realities of the marketplace, many would-be citizens of the political communications system find themselves excluded from this role and given the bit part of minor consumers in an economic game they can never win. We need urgently to return to Freire's exhortations to cultural action if we are not only to understand, but to realize, the liberating potential rather than the dominating capacity of communications media and institutions.

REFERENCES

Ferguson, M. (1992). The mythology about globalisation. *European Journal of Communication, 7*(1), 69-93.

Freire, P. (1972). *Cultural action for freedom.* New York: Penguin.

Golding, P. (1993, April). *The twin dilemmas of media research and media policy in Europe.* Keynote address given to the XIth Congress of the Nordic Media Research Association, Trondheim, Norway.

Golding, P., & Harris, P. (Eds.). (1997). *Beyond cultural imperialism* London: Sage.

Heller, P., & Diamond, J. (1990). *International comparison of government expenditure revisited. The developing countries 1975-86* (IMF Occasional Paper 69). Washington, DC: The IMF.

McLaren, P., & Leonard, P. (1993). *Paulo Freire: A critical encounter.* New York: Routledge.

OECD. (1990). *Development cooperation in the 1990s.* Paris: OECD.

Smith, A.D. (1990). Towards a global culture? In M. Featherstone (Ed.), *Global culture: Nationalism, globalisation and modernity.* New York: Sage.

The South Commission Chaired by Julius Nyergri. (1990, August). *The challenge of the south.* Oxford: Oxford University Press.

Townsend, P. (1993). *The international analysis of poverty.* Hemel Hempstead, UK: Harvester Wheatsheaf.

UNESCO. (1996). *Statistical Yearbook 1995.* Paris: UNESCO.

Chapter ▪ 4

The Decentering of Cultural Imperialism: Televisa-ion and Globo-ization in the Latin World*

John Sinclair

INTRODUCTION

The pattern in which television industries developed around the world in the 1960s gave substance to the durable critical paradigm of "cultural imperialism," in which the United States as a nation was seen as the center from which the national cultures of most of the rest of the world has come to be penetrated by the U.S. television system and its programs. This chapter takes the cultural imperialism paradigm as a reference point against which to assess both the actual changes in how cultural influences are exerted in the world and how they should be theorized.

On the one hand, the center-periphery model of world power has been made obsolete by the fundamental shifts of the last decade and the rise of "globalization." This is characterized by the eclipse of the nation state as the basic economic, political, and sociocultural unit of world order and the ascendance of the private corporation, with its power base in globalized industrialization, trade, and com-

*A similar version of this chapter has been published under the same title in Elizabeth Jacka (Ed.), *Continental shift: Globalisation and culture* (pp. 99-116). Sydney: Local Consumption Publications.

munication. On the other hand, the cultural imperialism paradigm's view of mass media as mechanisms of cultural "homogenization" is now challenged by the recent "ethnographic" trend in empirical audience studies and an emergent theoretical view of culture as a form of resistance through "mediation."

Furthermore, one of the blindspots of the cultural imperialism paradigm was its neglect of how commercial television was actively embraced by indigenous entrepreneurs in certain countries of what was then called the Third World. This is found in the case of Televisa in Mexico and TV Globo in Brazil, which now not only dominate their respective national media markets and the program trade within the Latin American region, but also have made incursions into certain European markets. As well, Televisa has played a major role in the development of the Spanish-language television industry in the United States, and in the advent of the world's first private international satellite service, which links the Americas with Europe. Thus, relative to the character of domestic markets and to commercial and technological innovations, culture and language of origin now emerge as factors of comparative advantage in building up international markets in audiovisual products.

The strategic global positions attained by Televisa and TV Globo calls for an analysis that takes account of the internationalization and pluralization of cultural production centers, particularly when geolinguistic factors are involved, and of the variable relations between corporations and the nation states in which they are based.

THE CULTURAL IMPERIALISM DEBATE

Cultural imperialism has been a durable critical metaphor of the post-colonial era. The term was adopted by the nonaligned movement of the 1970s as a way of conceptualizing the subordination that their former colonial masters and the United States were making them feel in the realms of communication and culture, which was seen as the superstructural counterpart to the more fundamental economic and political leverage that the West had continued to exert since decolonization.

In the West, progressive academics such as Herb Schiller in the United States and Armand Mattelart in Europe propagated the notion within critical discourse with such success that it has flourished until quite recent times. However, whatever analytic or rhetorical value it once might have carried has been overtaken by changes within the actual balance of forces within the world and the prospect of more complex ways in which they must be thought. It might seem then that there is no advantage in the critique of what now should be an obsolete paradigm. However, it has become lodged in the reflexes of a generation of communication academics and policymakers throughout the world, and still has its active protagonists and some popular currency. The point of this chapter is not so much to do battle against these residual pockets as to take the cultural imperialism paradigm as a reference point against which we can gauge both the changes in how cultural influences are exerted in the world and how we are to conceive of them.

Although cultural imperialism was seen to include such forms of cultural influence as tourism and education, it was the particular variant of media imperialism that drew the most critical attention and led to the formulation of demands for a New World Information and Communication Order (NWICO) in international forums, especially UNESCO, during the 1970s.

These demands were based on a critique of Western, and particularly U.S., dominance of the world's communication industries and on empirical studies of the "flows" of news and entertainment along a "one-way street" from the West to what was then called the Third World. Furthermore, just as the international news agencies Reuters, AFP, AP, and UPI monopolized news flows, and Hollywood and the U.S. networks dominated world film and television markets, U.S. advertising agencies were seen to be engaged in the "homogenization" of national cultures everywhere, conforming them to the market requirements of U.S. transnational consumer goods manufacturers. In all this, the natural, unproblematic assumptions were that U.S. foreign policy and U.S.-based private corporations proceeded in intimate mutual support, and that their communication industries were there to create a favorable ideological orientation among quiescent audiences in the subordinate nations so that U.S. interests could be pursued without hindrance.

Perhaps there was a stage in the 1970s when it really was like that, but the wisdom of hindsight and subsequent world trends suggest that the workings of international cultural influence are more subtle, complex in mediation, and "dialectic" than the cultural imperialism paradigm could ever have allowed for.

To invoke "world trends" is to draw attention to a whole range of familiar current phenomena that could not have been predicted out of the conceptual framework of cultural imperialism or other critical orthodoxies of recent decades. There is the decline of the U.S. national economy relative to the Japanese and their interpenetration; the disintegration of Cold War boundaries and the appetite for "market economies" in the countries formerly comprising the Soviet bloc; and in what was once the Third World, the industrial growth of the "tiger" nations of Southeast Asia and even of the major debt-laden nations of Latin America.

These changes and others have set the stage for a new era of globalization, characterized by the disaggregation of the nation state as the basic economic, political, and sociocultural unit of world order, and the ascendance of the private corporation, with its power base in globalized industrialization, trade, and communication. Although it would be rash to announce the demise of its time on earth, it is clear that the nation state's incapacity to control the electronic movement of information across its borders now undermines its power as a sovereign territorial unit, and as a consequence, its claims as guardian of "national cultural identity," a crucial issue in the cultural imperialism debate. This era has not just now appeared, but our critical conceptual frameworks have not been well suited to charting and analyzing its emergence.

Even from within the postcolonial world itself, indigenous theoretical initiatives for a long time misrecognized the changes taking place. The dependency theory of underdevelopment which originated in Latin America in the 1970s and subsequently became familiar in the West through the work of A. G. Frank, underestimated the capacity of countries in structural relations of dependent subordination and mass impoverishment to be able nevertheless to sustain economic growth. The coexistence of such growth with inequality, exploitation, marginalization, and indebtedness is now commonplace in the developing countries. This contradiction has been taken account of in Cardoso's more sophisticated and useful concept of dependent development, but the orthodox critical view of development as a zero-sum game that the postcolonial countries would always lose has not proven adequate to explain the present-day condition of much of what once was the Third World.

The blindspots that the concepts of cultural imperialism, media imperialism, dependency, and the variant cultural dependency can now be understood to share in common are attributable at least in part to an implicit center-periphery model of how power worked, derived in turn from the master metaphor of imperialism. To the extent that the historical phenomenon of imperialism was indeed one in which the center subdued and drew tribute from the periphery, we could say that the critique reproduces the principle on which the object of the critique once thrived; that is, theories of cultural imperialism reinforce the belief that the United States is the center of world power. But at any time in history there have been, to borrow from Che Guevara, one, two, three, many imperialisms, with greater or lesser, rising or falling centers. That is, instead of a single center for any age, we have to acknowledge the paradox of multiple centers, which in turn implies the possibility of overlapping, and perhaps, conflicting, spheres of influence. In Australia, for example, we are quite accustomed to recognizing that Britain, the United States, and Japan are centers that exert their historically and structurally overdetermined influence on us, although there is little attempt to apprehend that in theoretical terms.

Yet just as Foucauldians have "discovered" the diffuseness with which power is distributed within societies, and just as feminists and other postmarxist thinkers have "discovered" multiple forms of domination based on gender or race as much as class, so too should the conceptual and theoretical analysis of global influence take account of the "discovery" of plural and shifting centers of power, perhaps even dare to think that it has no center. That is the view taken by the anthropologist Arjun Appadurai (1990) in an often-quoted essay:

> The new global cultural economy has to be understood as a
> complex, overlapping, disjunctive order, which cannot any
> longer be understood in terms of existing centre-periphery
> models (even those that might account for multiple centres
> and peripheries). . . . The complexity of the current global
> economy has to do with certain fundamental disjunctures
> between economy, culture and politics which we have barely
> begun to theorise. (p. 296)

In elaborating his own pluralized conception of global cultural
processes, which will be referred to shortly, it is worth noting that
Appadurai is careful to acknowledge a debt to Frederic Jameson's
(1984) influential article "Postmodernism, or the Cultural Logic of
Late Capitalism." This is an indicator of the degree to which the
advent of postmodernism as a problematic has in turn allowed the
notion of globalization to be thought of, not least because of the theoretical liberation achieved through postmodernism's rejection of
what is now sometimes called the "dominant ideology thesis," which
subtended the cultural imperialism perspective. On the other hand,
that is not to say that the concepts of postmodernism and globalization should be allowed to be conflated with each other. Their analytic
and heuristic potential resides in their remaining related but distinct
and formulated with appropriate rigor. As Roland Robertson (1990)
warns, we should be circumspect in embracing a new paradigm in
which "there is considerable danger that 'globalization' will become
an intellectual 'play zone'—a site for the expression of residual
social-theoretical interests, interpretive indulgence, or the display of
world-ideological preferences" (pp. 15-16).

The inherent limitations of the center-periphery model do not
exhaust the flaws that now appear in the cultural imperialism paradigm. In particular, there is also what might be called the homogenization thesis, that is, the implicit argument that the invasion of the
peripheral airwaves with news, entertainment, or advertisements
from the center has an irresistible and uniform effect on their recipients, and furthermore, that this effect is whatever interpretation the
analyst (not the audience) ascribes to the ideological meaning of the
material in question. This is a variant of the dominant ideology thesis once common in ostensibly critical and progressive analyses, at
its worst the notion that the masses are mere ideological dupes of
omnipotent media, a view that now at last has been put under sustained challenge.

AUDIENCE STUDIES AND RESISTANCE THROUGH MEDIATION

Two lines of work are relevant here: the recent "ethnographic" trend
in audience studies, and an emergent theorization of culture as a

form of resistance through "mediation." The audience research is a naturalistic empirical investigation of the theoretical argument that media messages will be interpreted by actual audiences in different ways, depending on such social differences as gender, race, and class. The little of this work that has been done on a cross-cultural comparative basis reveals interesting variations in audiences' interpretations or "decodings" of the U.S. soap epic *Dallas,* that "perfect hate symbol" of the cultural imperialism theorists (Mattelart, Delcourt, & Mattelart, 1984, p. 90). Philip Schlesinger (1991) is concerned that audience research of this kind implies a relativized subjectivism, a "new revisionism" in which "an obsession with popular consumption for pleasure has tended to eclipse a concern with forms of dominance and control" (p. 306). However, such an assessment conflates the new audience research with other, unrelated tendencies that have arisen in media and communication studies over the last decade as the "dominant ideology paradigm" has lost its purchase on the field (Collins, 1990). Indeed, one of the strengths of the new audience research is its orientation to the disaggregation of audiences in the era of globalization, or in the formulation of one of its principal protagonists: "Our analysis of the cultural impact of any form of domination must always be differentiated, concerned to establish which groups, in which places, are receptive (or not) to it" (Morley & Robins, 1989, p. 27). When confronted with such assertions of the need for studies to articulate the differential consumption of media products on the one hand with the international structures of their production and distribution on the other, even Schlesinger (1991) concedes that "such belated acknowledgement of the obvious should be welcomed" (p. 306).

The other current approach that queries the homogenization thesis concerns the hitherto underestimated resilience, or at least, mediation with which cultures meet and transform foreign influence. From a globalization perspective, the notion of international flows of cultural influence becomes expanded beyond the flows of news and entertainment with which the cultural imperialism theorists and the NWICO debate were concerned. To refer back to Appadurai (1990), he discerns international flows of people, technologies, and finance as well as the flows of media and ideologies familiar from the cultural imperialism paradigm, but observes that these flows are subject to indigenization:

> At least as rapidly as forces from various metropolises are brought into new societies they tend to become indigenized in one or other way: this is true of music and housing styles as much as it is true of science and terrorism, spectacles and constitutions. (p. 295)

This process generates heterogenization, a dialectic counterpoint to homogenization. The influential Latin American theorist Jesus

Martin-Barbero (1988) identifies a similar dialectic when he observes:

> Not everything to do with transnationalization is the pure negation of difference: there is also a refunctionalization of difference in order to deal with the cultural entropy that the homogenisation of markets helps bring about. (p. 460)

Martin-Barbero has in mind not just the cynical hegemonic interests that salvage difference by packaging indigenous rituals and crafts for tourists, but also cites examples in which "the popular classes" have utilized radio or tape recorders to protect and communicate the subcultural language and music of their regions. Indeed, these allusions to grassroots forms of communication are indicative of a broader trend in Latin American communication studies to an interest in popular resistance (McAnany, 1989), not the notion of subversive pleasure found in some of the more familiar work in English (Fiske, 1987), but "a new perception of the popular that emphasises the thick texture of hegemony/subalternity, the interlacing of resistance and submission, and opposition and complicity" (Martin-Barbero, 1988, p. 462).

However, to take one last view of the dialectic mediation of cultural influence: Australian observers Stephen Castles and colleagues (Castles, Cope, Kalantzis, & Morrissey, 1990), evidently unimpressed by the postmodernist repudiation of the notion of authenticity and of the distinction between surfaces and depths, emphasize the alienation and loss that they see in heterogenization and articulate a common sentiment when they say:

> The British eat spaghetti, the Africans white bread, the Asians wiener schnitzel; but it all derives from the plants of world agri-business. The point is that homogenisation actually makes differentiation both possible and meaningless: we can get everything everywhere, but it has ceased to have any real cultural significance. Whatever we do is a celebration of the cultural dominance of the great international industrial structure, but we can kid ourselves on the basis of appearances that our culture or sub-culture is different. As difference loses its meaning, our need for it as a focus of identity becomes ever greater, as do our acts of self-deception. The attempt to preserve static, preindustrial forms of ethnic culture is an obvious example of this. The increasing integration of the world results in a simultaneous homogenizing and fragmenting of culture. (pp. 140-141)

A more empirical approach to the question of local cultural response to global influence is put forward by Colin Hoskins and Rolf Mirus

(1988) who have sought to demonstrate how a cultural discount applies in the international television program trade. That is, national television markets tend to exhibit a preference first for indigenous material and then for material from culturally similar sources. The more alien the material on offer, the higher will be the cultural discount and the weaker the preference. Thus, Australia might be receptive to Japanese capital and consumer goods, but not television programs. Similarly, in the international advertising industry, certain national markets have proven resistant to incursions by U.S. advertising agencies, notably Japan and France, both of which have instead provided a strong domestic base from which certain indigenous agencies have themselves become internationalized (Sinclair, 1987).

Most of all, and in spite of the doubts that can be raised about the actual content of the national cultures believed to have been under threat from cultural imperialism (Schlesinger, 1987), it is clear that language occupies a special position with regard to the maintenance of cultural difference. In the particular context of international television program flows, Richard Collins (1989) has argued that language is a "semi-permeable membrane," which has contributed to the quite uneven acceptance of British satellite television in continental Europe, with the consequent absence of transnational advertisers on that medium. David Morley and Kevin Robins (1989) sum up the effects of language-based cultural discounts in the current European television market in these terms:

> Attempts to attract a European audience with English-language programming, not unlike the attempt to create European advertising markets, do seem to have largely foundered in the face of the linguistic and cultural divisions in play between the different sectors of the audience. . . . There is a growing realisation that the success of American-style commercial programming in Europe is context-dependent in a very specific sense. US imports only do well when domestic television is not producing comparable entertainment programming—and whenever viewers have the alternative of comparable entertainment programming in their own language, the American programmes tend to come off second best. (p. 28)

Some of the elements that have been identified thus far—indigenization, language difference, and domestic market strength—are at the heart of another phenomenon that can now be found in cultural imperialism's blindspot, and that is the rise of other, nonanglophone "centers" of international media production and trade based on what might be called "geolinguistic regions": Mumbai for the Hindi film industry, Hong Kong for Chinese genre movies, Cairo for Arabic film and television, and Mexico City for film and television production in Spanish, particularly in the "indigenized" *telenovela* genre, as well as for dubbing U.S. programs into Spanish for reexport. These centers are not at all "new," having already been in evidence when Jeremy Tunstall (1977) wrote *The Media Are American* and predicted that their "hybrid" genres—what we would now call "indigenized" versions of the U.S. musical, action movie, and soap opera—would grow to form their own stratum in international exchange.

Armand Mattelart and his collaborators (1984) give attention to the geolinguistic factor in their investigation of the difficulties faced by the cultural industries of certain European and Third World countries in the development of a Latin audiovisual space within contemporary international image markets. As Schlesinger (1987) reminds us, "the audiovisual is both a symbolic arena and an economic one" (p. 228). The Mattelart work is tendentious in its origins, given that it was commissioned by the French Minister of Culture after a meeting in 1982 with his counterparts from Mexico and Brazil as well as Spain, Portugal, and Italy, which agreed to promote "co-operation between countries with a language of Latin origin" (cited in Mattelart et al., 1984, p. ix). It should be said that the Mattelart group (1984) distance themselves from the inherent traps of this patronage and pursue their own diverse interests. They strive to move beyond the determinism and functionalism that has characterized the cultural imperialism standpoint with which much of their own former work is identified and to an "internationalist" or globalized perspective that reaffirms the more dialectic qualities of thought to be found in the tradition of cultural Marxism and combines a skeptical empirical understanding of the media industries. They also are able to avoid the reflexive sloganized dogmatism of what Garnham (1984) has called "Third Worldism" and "cultural anti-Americanism."

As Anthony Smith (1990) has observed, the spread of a lingua franca throughout such a "culture area" as the Latin audiovisual space provides the potential rather than the necessary conditions for the emergence of transterritorial communications. In this case, the potential lies in the linguistic and other cultural similarities that might be cultivated to create an intercontinental media market across all those countries that have Latin-based languages—Spanish, Portuguese, French, and Italian—that is, the geolinguistic region of Latin America and Southwest Europe, itself a fusion of the cultural legacies of former empires.

The cultural imperialism approach and the critical theoretical tradition in general has had no more than a negative interest in the classical economists' concept of "comparative advantage," and even Ricardo would never have thought to apply the notion to language. However, in the context of the flow patterns of international trade in audiovisual products, and particularly when taken in relation to size and structure of the domestic market, language of origin emerges if not as a determinant, then at least as a factor of potential advantage in the international market. Richard Collins (1990) has drawn attention to the English sector of the global economy, although also emphasizing its potential rather than necessary status:

The size and wealth of the anglophone market provides producers of English language information with a considerable
comparative advantage *vis-à-vis* producers in other languages. But it is important to recognise that this is a *potential*
advantage which may or may not be realisable. Not all anglophone producers will succeed, and producers in other languages are not necessarily doomed to fail. (p. 211; emphasis
in original)

Indeed, an examination of the geolinguistic dimension of global
media flows, made with due regard to particular "multinationals of
the Third World" that have transformed themselves into "international multimedia groups" (Mattelart et al., 1984), demonstrates that a
kind of Latin audiovisual space is in fact being created by these private corporate interests, in which the comparative advantage of language is a key factor. These private corporations are Televisa, which
all but monopolizes the audiovisual industries of Mexico, and TV
Globo, the dominant television network in Brazil.

TELEVISA AND TV GLOBO

In the case of Televisa, the domination it has long held over its home
market in the world's largest Spanish-speaking nation has become a
raft for its various international ventures. Spanish is the second
most widely spoken European language in the world after English,
but like the other languages that have generated their own regional
media industries, it has only ever been in the peripheral vision of the
cultural imperialism perspective. TV Globo is different insofar as it
has had to decode and dub its programs to enter its several export
markets, but it too first based its international push into Europe and
Africa on its comparative advantage as the world's largest
Portuguese-speaking country, Portuguese being the world's fourth
most widely spoken European language after Russian (*World
Almanac 1992*, 1991). Once again, the critique reproduces its object
to the extent that native English-speaking critics of cultural imperialism, or indeed theorists of globalization (Featherstone, 1990), take
for granted the preeminence of English as a global language, and
hence their own position as beneficiaries of centuries of anglophone
colonialism. It is thus difficult to appreciate that Televisa and TV
Globo, based on the languages of an older era of colonialism, have
become the biggest television networks in the world outside of the
United States. Even if their markets are not as lucrative as the
English-speaking ones, and there is a heavy cultural discount
applied to foreign language programs in the anglophone world, a different set of relativities applies when the world is viewed from Mexico
City or Rio. To take a notable example, the Hispanic population of

the United States, although less than 10% of the total population and relatively deprived as a group, is nonetheless the sixth largest Spanish-speaking population in the world, and also the most affluent: on the face of it, a natural constituency for Televisa (Strategy Research Corporation, 1987).

Because comparative advantage is potential rather than actual, there are other factors to be taken into account in the expansion of these networks, but even these factors have not been within the range of vision of the cultural imperialism perspective. Because that view emphasized the technological and political strengths of the West, and especially the United States, it was inclined to see the adoption of new forms of the mass media as a process in which the United States imposed its new media technologies, television in particular, on weaker, less developed nations. This was seen to achieve a new market for U.S. transmission and reception technologies, that is, both producer and consumer goods, as well as for U.S. programs, not to mention access to audiences for U.S.-based advertisers and general control of the medium's ideological ethos. Because of this assumption of Western commercio-technological domination, and its theoretical commitment to impersonal structural forces as the prime movers of historical change, what the cultural imperialism perspective did not take account of was the degree to which individual entrepreneurs in the subordinate countries might have sought to attract and give active encouragement to this process, and so secure for themselves a place in the consequent structure of "dependent development."

This was particularly true of Mexico, where the progenitor of Televisa, Emilio Azcarraga Vidaurreta (Senior), not only inveigled the president of the time, Miguel Alemán Valdes (Senior), into adopting the U.S. commercial model as the basis for Mexico's television system when it began in 1950, but had long sought to organize the other media entrepreneurs throughout the region to do the same. He was assisted in this by Goar Mestre, who was active in developing the commercial television industry that flourished in Cuba prior to the revolution of 1959, and that gave birth to the *telenovela*, the Latin American soap opera that has since become the staple production and export genre. It should be acknowledged that Azcarraga had attracted investment from both NBC and CBS in his radio entrepreneur days of the 1940s, and subsequently built up his television program export activities with assistance from ABC in the 1960s (Sinclair, 1990a). As for Mestre, after being ousted from Cuba with the revolution, he emerged in Argentina and Venezuela, backed by capital from CBS and Time-Life. It was also Time-Life that provided the investment and technical advice to launch TV Globo in Brazil in the 1960s, but it is not often noted by cultural imperialism theorists that these and most other investments in the region were withdrawn by the early 1970s (Fox, 1988; Straubhaar, 1982). More important than the investments was the fact that this unofficial version of the "alliance for progress" forged between Latin American entrepreneurs and U.S. networks established the commercial model of television broadcasting as the norm throughout the continent. The subordination of public interest to private advantage that Latin American countries experienced in that formative era has thus continued to be a hallmark of their television systems (McAnany, 1984).

The cultural imperialism perspective also underestimated the degree to which the media entrepreneurs in the subject countries would come to use and adapt new technologies for their own innovation. In the Mexican case, the advent of videotape was seized on to build up program export activities, while at a later stage, satellite technology was exploited to interconnect the various Spanish-language television stations that Televisa for many years controlled throughout the United States itself (as mentioned, the sixth largest Spanish-speaking nation in the world, and the richest), thus establishing a national network for Mexican-originated programs and creating a national audience of Hispanics.

The international expansion of Televisa and its corporate ancestors has always been production-driven, based on an economics similar to the export of domestic product on which the U.S. cultural industries have built themselves. As early as 1954, Azcarraga (Senior) had attempted to sell his programs to U.S. networks, and when they were rejected as only fit for "ghetto time," began establishing his own stations throughout the United States, and a network to distribute programs and sell advertising in them. In these enterprises, his *prestanombre*, or front-man, was Rene Anselmo, a U.S. citizen. By 1986, a national network of broadcast stations, low power repeater stations, and arrangements with cable stations, all interconnected by satellite, was reaching a claimed 82% of Hispanic households, or 15 million viewers (bigger than NBC, it was said), supplying them with programs largely beamed up from Mexico City (Sinclair, 1990a). We will see later that this use of satellite technology to form a single national audience out of the dispersed and diverse Spanish-speaking populations throughout the United States was to become the model on which Televisa would later create a global market of Spanish-speaking nations, using an international satellite service.

The circumstances that prompted this transition had to do with Televisa being forced out of the U.S. broadcast television market after the Federal Communications Commission (FCC) decided in 1986 that Televisa was in breach of U.S. ownership restrictions and that Anselmo was just "an agent of foreign control." However, Televisa was permitted to retain its U.S. cable service, Galavision, which was not subject to the same restrictions. This it built into an international 24-hour Spanish-language entertainment and news service, which incorporated popular program transmissions from Mexico with ECO, a kind of Spanish-language CNN that Televisa had just initiated. This Galavision service now reaches North and South America as well as across to Spain by means of PanAmSat, the world's first private international satellite operation. We will discuss later that although PanAmSat is based in the United States, it was Televisa that initiated the venture as a crucial part of its expansion outside of Mexico, and that exploited its political connections in the United States to secure the required permission (Sinclair, 1990b).

This is to raise the issue of the relationship that Televisa as a transnational enterprise bears to the Mexican state. Mexico is still basically a corporate state ruled since the 1930s by one party, the Partido Revolucionario Institucional (PRI), or Institutionalised Revolutionary Party, which every six years ensures that its presidential nominee is elected. Televisa is in declared public support of the PRI, ideologically allied to its more conservative faction, and prepared to risk its credibility at home and abroad by favoring the PRI in its management of news and current affairs. However, although close to the party, Televisa is in longstanding struggle with the state, a struggle in which it seems able to maintain the upper hand. From time to time, presidential administrations have sought to assert control over the private oligarchy that owns and runs commercial television in Mexico, only to be defeated, compromised, or outmaneuvered by them. It was noted earlier that the Aleman presidential administrations in 1950 was persuaded to allow television broadcasting to be established on a laissez-faire basis. However, belated attempts by subsequent administrations to regulate the content and operation of private television, and when rebuffed, to develop a state television system, have only had the effect of consolidating and legitimizing the alliance of private interests that have become Televisa (Sinclair, 1986). The failure of the state's own venture into television as well as its embrace of deregulationist policies were both evident in the sale this year of the government's former networks (Golden, 1993).

Televisa in Mexico is more than the television broadcasting monopoly whose demographically and regionally segmented channels capture 70% of all advertising expenditure, and more than the conglomerate that reaches into most other branches of the media communications industries, hardware, and software alike. It has also institutionalized itself over the last decade as "the fifth estate" in Mexican society, competing with the state for hegemony over the "hearts and minds" of the Mexican people. This includes the intelligentsia, whom it cultivates through various links with formal education and the arts, even communication research (Trejo Delarbre, 1987). At the same time, Televisa has become more internationalized in its activities and interests. A general observation from British media theorist Nicholas Garnham (1984) is apt here:

> To focus too centrally on the State is also to fail to grasp the ways in which the development of the international economy is itself undercutting the role of the nation state. This, in fact, can give rise to a situation in which multinational producers of culture can actually engage in a battle with the State for the allegiance of its citizens. (p. 5)

In the case of Televisa, however, the multinational culture producer is rooted in the national soil, but should not be thought of as Mexican any more than we can think of News Corporation as

Australian or Saatchi & Saatchi as British. The story of PanAmSat's genesis shows how the sovereignty of the nation state can be more threatened by a domestically based than by a foreign transnational corporation. In 1982, the Mexican government sought to head off initiatives that Televisa had made in domestic satellite development. The constitution was amended to define all satellite communications as a strategic matter under the exclusive prerogative of the state. However, through Rene Anselmo and the Televisa companies in the United States, Televisa's retaliation was to raise the stakes beyond the jurisdiction of the Mexican government. A new United States subsidiary was created, PanAmSat, which applied for authorization to launch a private, U.S.-based satellite that could cover not just the United States and Mexico, but all the Western hemisphere. Because such a service was outside the whole international system regulated by Intelsat, it required special presidential assent: Ronald Reagan would have to sign a determination that the proposal was "in the national interest" of the United States. This Reagan did, no doubt assisted by the intercession of his associate John Gavin, former U.S. ambassador to Mexico, who was soon after to become head of Televisa's international satellite division. In this way, Emilio Azcarraga Milmo, the son who came to head up Televisa after the father's death in 1972 (Junior), had been able to mobilize contacts up to the highest level in the most powerful nation of the region in order to steal a march once more on the Mexican state (Sinclair, 1990a, 1990b).

The most recent chapter in Televisa's expansion makes clear its determination to establish itself as a true international media corporation. Five hundred years of Spanish America were celebrated in 1992, a year that saw two major initiatives for Televisa: its reinstatement in the United States as a partner in Univision, its former national broadcast television network there; and an international stock market float that gave it the capital to acquire new overseas holdings. These include a 49% share in a television station in Chile and 76% of another in Peru. There is also a special programming arrangement with an Argentinean station and distribution deals with Venevision of Venezuela, who are also their partners in Univision in the United States (Sinclair, 1993). However, the most notable venture has been with PanAmSat, a matter to which we return. As one of the New York brokers observed as the time of the float, "[Televisa] Management considers its target audience to be the 350 million Spanish-speaking people around the world, not simply the 82 million at home" (Warburg, 1992, pp. 5-6).

It is no accident that this expansion has emanated from a debt-ridden nation in which austerity measures, inflation, and devaluation have depressed advertising expenditures in the domestic market and given incentive to intensify international activities. These activities have diversified beyond broadcasting and program sales: Televisa set up subsidiaries in Spain to sell advertising space and duplicate home videos, whereas a U.S.-based subsidiary was established to manufacture video hardware, although the plant is located in the *maquiladora* zone of Mexico. In that regard, Televisa had joined the many U.S., -European-, and Japanese-based transnational manufacturers that also have been attracted to this zone because of its tariff concessions and access to cheap labor. Televisa also makes telecommunications components in this zone (Sinclair, 1990b). Other U.S. subsidiaries are in record promotion and telemarketing, whereas last year Televisa acquired the American Publishing Group. Based in Miami, this is the world's largest publisher and distributor of Spanish-language magazines (Moffett & Roberts, 1992).

As for TV Globo, it has been taking advantage of the proliferation of television services in Europe, where unlike in the United States, audiences are accustomed to seeing subtitled material and also for other cultural reasons are more receptive to Brazilian programs. Indeed, at one stage, Brazilian *telenovelas* acquired so strong a following in Italy that Roberto Marinho, head of the family that owns the TV Globo network, or Azcarraga's Brazilian counterpart, decided to invest directly in a television network, Telemontecarlo. Italian television is dominated by the state-run RAI and Silvio Berlusconi's Fininvest networks, which leaves Telemontecarlo with only 4% of the audience. However, Globo has strong backing from Italian capital, and there are long-term plans to develop the network on a pan-European basis (McCarter, 1990). At the same time, using tactics similar to those with which the U.S. audiovisual industries in the past opened up new markets, Globo has been selling dubbed *telenovelas* to France at a loss, hopeful of gaining access to the French-speaking world as a whole (Marques de Melo, 1989). And just as Televisa took itself into the former heart of the Spanish empire with Galavision, TV Globo bought a 15% share when the first private television network was created in Portugal (Besas, 1992).

It is clear that these communications conglomerates of the former Third World must be taken account of in discerning the new patterns of flow of cultural products in a globalized world, but we should not infer that they could ever occupy the same position as the expanding U.S. networks had when the cultural imperialism debate was first initiated in the late 1960s. The U.S. audiovisual industries are not yet a spent force and are assuming new forms with which the Latin global networks must compete. The latest chapter in the PanAmSat story is instructive.

It was recounted earlier how Azcarraga (Junior) had been obliged to sell off certain of his U.S. television broadcast interests as a result of the FCC decision in 1986. Given that PanAmSat had outlived its political usefulness as leverage on the Mexican state and seemed at that time to have little economic potential, Azcarraga sold it all to Rene Anselmo, the former U.S. partner whose business interests by then had been separated from Azcarraga's by fiat of the FCC. Anselmo's company. Alpha Lyracom, went on to make the necessary coordination arrangements with clients in the major Latin American and European countries, and after months of protracted negotiations with a reluctant Intelsat and its U.S. signatory Comsat, the first PanAmSat satellite was launched in 1988. Within a year, not only was it delivering Televisa's Galavision service to Europe and bringing the Italian state network RAI's service into Latin America, but also it was carrying some of the major U.S. cable channels into Latin America ("Separate systems," 1989).

For indeed, among those first to see the possibilities of the new private intercontinental service had been those U.S. cable channels that were already packaging programs in Spanish for the U.S. Hispanic market. Thus, Ted Turner's CNN, which was producing a news program in Spanish for the U.S. Telemundo network, mounted a 24-hour news service in Spanish to Latin America via PanAmSat. CNN soon after also introduced a dubbed version of its TNT entertainment service, whereas the U.S. cable sports channel ESPN, which is owned by the U.S. Capital Cities/ABC network, was sending out 15 hours a day of sports broadcasts in Spanish (Sinclair, 1990b; "Turner to launch," 1989). Confirming this trend for the largest U.S. suppliers to cultivate Spanish-speaking markets in both of the Americas has been Time-Warner, who now offers its U.S. cable movie service Home Box Office via PanAmSat to Latin America. With both Spanish- and Portuguese-tracked versions, it is called HBO Ole ("HBO plans," 1991).

It remains to be seen whether HBO Ole represents a move back to the future, that is, one in which U.S. programs dominate the new satellite-to-cable services that are flourishing throughout Latin America, just as they dominated broadcast television there in the 1960s. Certainly, the formation of a Spanish-speaking market in the United States has created a stimulus and a point of entry to the rest of the Latin world market for U.S. producers of programs in Spanish, thus challenging the preeminence of Televisa (and Globo) on their home ground. Latest among U.S. producers to offer a Latin American service have been Spelling Entertainment Group, MTV Networks, and GEMS Television ("U.S. TV trio," 1993). Spelling and GEMS have also opened up a direct service to Spain via Intelsat ("Satellite spotlight," 1993).

For those of us who live in the Asia-Pacific region, Televisa's competition within Latin America is of less direct interest than a most significant development closer to home: the fact that during 1993, Televisa acquired a half share in PanAmSat, bringing the Azcarraga and Anselmo families back together, this time with the blessing of the FCC. It has since announced a program of expansion that will bring it global coverage. Thus, by 1995, Australia will be within the footprints of both the Pacific and the Europe/Asian satellites that PanAmSat will have in operation by then. This prospect has provoked some concern that a pirate satellite service could be beamed into Australia, for PanAmSat would be technically well suited for such use (Fell, 1993).

However, Australian homes are not about to encounter Mexican news and *telenovelas* delivered from above the Pacific. Although PanAmSat is owned by the same people who first brought a national Spanish-language television network to the United States, clearly the Spanish-speaking market in the Asia-Pacific region is too small for the profitable distribution of Televisa programs. Rather, the motivation is the relative lack of satellite capacity in Asia and the fact that U.S. program providers, the foremost of whom are the same as those active in Latin America (Turner, HBO, and ESPN), are showing great interest in gaining access to the vast potential market for satellite television in Asia. Given that the Asian satellite service just acquired by Rupert Murdoch's News Corporation, Star TV, has a virtual monopoly over existing transponders on Asiasat, the presence of the rival program providers should assure PanAmSat that there will be demand for capacity on its new satellites as the Asian market continues to expand (Brauchli & Witcher, 1993; Goll, 1993).

The unforeseen development of intercontinental media markets based on the comparative advantage of geolinguistic region, domestic market size, and technological adaptation does not repudiate the basic rationale of the cultural imperialism critique as it developed in the 1970s, insofar as it sought to comprehend the cultural dimension of unequal relations between nations. Of course, basic structural inequalities still remain. The suggestion sometimes made that Televisa's incursion into the U.S. market or TV Globo's exports to Portugal and Italy are forms of "reverse cultural imperialism" is a canard, based on cynicism at worst or ignorance at best (Rogers & Schement, 1984). Indeed, as it has been suggested in this chapter, the energetic pursuit of overseas markets by Televisa and TV Globo can be explained in terms of the constrictions that inflation, economic crisis, and the imposition of debt discipline have placed on their growth in their respective domestic markets, which are still in a condition of "dependent development."

What can and should be said against the cultural imperialism perspective is that it was limited by its undialectic center-periphery model of structural relations between nations, its assumption of credulous, homogenized consumers of cultural products and of a supine *comprador* bourgeoisie in the subordinate countries, and its disregard for the specificities and complexities to be found among the various regions and nations of the erstwhile Third World. The processes of national disaggregation and interpenetration between new international entities in the era of globalization calls for less abstract and dogmatic, more particular and empirical ways in which to apprehend the world.

REFERENCES

Appadurai, A. (1990). Disjuncture and difference in the global cultural economy. In M. Featherstone (Ed.), *Global culture: Nationalism, globalization and modernity* (pp. 295-310). London: Sage.

Besas, P. (1992, March 23). Globo grabs the TV jackpot in Brazil. *Variety*, p. 82.

Brauchi, M., & Witcher, K. (1993, July 27). News Corp. acquires control of Star TV. *Asian Wall Street Journal*, pp. 1, 3.

Castles, S., Cope, B., Kalantzis, M., & Morrissey, M. (1990). *Mistaken identity: Multiculturalism and the demise of nationalism in Australia* (2nd ed.). Sydney, Australia: Pluto Press.

Collins, R. (1989). The language of advantage: Satellite television in Western Europe. *Media, Culture and Society, 11*(3), 351-371.

Collins, R. (1990). *Television: Policy and culture.* London: Unwin Hyman.

Featherstone, M. (1990). Introduction. In M. Featherstone (Ed.), *Global culture: Nationalism, globalization and modernity* (pp. 1-14). London: Sage.

Fell, L. (1993, May). Will PanAmSat's "truth and technology" triumph? *Australian Communications*, pp. 61-66.

Fiske, J. (1987). *Television culture.* London: Methuen.

Fox, E. (1988). Media policies in Latin America: An overview. In E. Fox (Ed.), *Media and politics in Latin America* (pp. 6-35). London: Sage.

Garnham, N. (1984). Introduction. In A. Mattelart, X. Delcourt, & M. Mattelart (Eds.), *International image markets: In search of an alternative perspective* (pp. 1-6). London: Comedia.

Golden, T. (1993, July 19). Big Mexican retailer wins bidding for state-owned TV. *New York Times*, pp. C1, C6.

Goll, S. (1993, July 13). Tough rivals prepare to battle Star TV. *Asian Wall Street Journal*, pp. 1, 8.

HBO plans pay TV launch in Latin America. (1991, March). *Broadcasting Abroad*, p. 4.

Hoskins, C., & Mirus, R. (1988). Reasons for the U.S. dominance of the international trade in television programs. *Media, Culture and Society, 10*(4), 499-515.

Jameson, F. (1984). Postmodernism, or the cultural logic of late capitalism. *New Left Review, 146*, 53-92.

Marques de Melo, J. (1989). Las Telenovelas en el Brasil [Telenovelas in Brazil]. *Apuntes, 16*, 46-59.

Martin-Barbero, J. (1988). Communication from culture: The crisis of the national and the emergence of the popular. *Media, Culture and Society, 10*(4), 447-465.

Mattelart, A., Delcourt, X., & Mattelart, M. (1984). *International image markets: In search of an alternative perspective.* London: Comedia.

McAnany, E. (1984). The logic of the cultural industries in Latin America: The television industry in Brazil. In V. Mosco & J. Wasko (Eds.), *The critical communications review, Vol. II: Changing patterns of communications control* (pp. 185-208). Norwood, NJ: Ablex.

McAnany, E. (1989). Television and cultural discourses: Latin American and United States comparisons. *Studies in Latin American Popular Culture, 8*, 1-21.

McCarter, M. (1990, December 17). TV net grows in Italy. *Advertising Age*, p. 22.

Moffett, M., & Roberts, J. (1992, July 30). Mexican media empire, grupo televisa, fasts an eye on U.S. market. *Wall Street Journal,* pp. 1, A6.

Morley, D., & Robins, K. (1989). Spaces of identity: Communications technologies and the reconfiguration of Europe. *Screen, 30*(4), 10-34.

Robertson, R. (1990). Mapping the global condition. In M. Featherstone (Ed.), *Global culture: Nationalism, globalization, and modernity* (pp. 15-30). London: Sage.

Rogers, E., & Schement, J. (1984). Introduction. *Communication Research, 11*(2), 163-182.

Satellite spotlight: GEMS plans new programming for Spain. (1993, June 14). *Satellite News,* p. 3.

Schlesinger, P. (1987). On national identity: Some conceptions and misconceptions criticized. *Social Science Information, 26*(2), 219-264.

Schlesinger, P. (1991). Media, the political order and national identity. *Media, Culture and Society, 13*(3), 297-308.

Separate systems—New era for global communications. (1989, September). *Broadcasting Abroad,* p. 6.

Sinclair, J. (1986). Dependent development and broadcasting: "The Mexican Formula." *Media, Culture and Society, 8*(1), 81-101.

Sinclair, J. (1987). *Images incorporated: Advertising as industry and ideology.* London and New York: Croom Helm.

Sinclair, J. (1990a). Spanish-language television in the United States: Televisa Currendersits Dom. *Studies in Latin American Popular Culture, 9,* 39-63.

Sinclair, J. (1990b). Neither West nor Third World: The Mexican television industry within the NWICO debate. *Media, Culture and Society, 12*(3), 343-360.

Sinclair, J. (1993). Unpublished research in progress.

Smith, A. (1990). Towards a global culture? In M. Featherstone (Ed.), *Global culture: Nationalism, globalization, and modernity* (pp. 171-191).

Strategy Research Corporation. (1987). *1987 US Hispanic Market Study.* Miami: Strategy Research Corporation.

Straubhaar, J. (1982). The development of the telenovela as the pre-eminent form of popular culture in Brazil. *Studies in Latin American Popular Culture, 1,* 138-150.

Trejo Delarbre, R. (Ed.). (1987). *Televisa: El Quinto Poder* (2nd ed.). Mexico: Claves Latinoamericanas.

Tunstall, J. (1977). *The media are American.* London: Constable.

Turner to launch Latin American film service. (1989, July). *Broadcasting Abroad,* p. 3.

U.S. TV trio gets the Latin beat. (1993, February 1). *Variety,* p. 47.

Warburg, S. C. (1992). *Grupo Televisa SA de CV: Company report.* Investext, Thompson Financial Networks.

World Almanac 1992. (1991). New York: Pharos Books.

Chapter ■ 5

Strategies for the Globalization of Culture in the 21st Century

Aggrey Brown

THE CONCEPT OF GLOBALIZATION

Globalization is a phenomenon of the information/communication (infocom) age. The concept could not have emerged meaningfully earlier because the infocom technologies that give it meaning did not exist. Computers had first to be mass produced and popularly consumed; satellites had to be proven commercially viable as information and data delivery technologies, and digital telephony had to become widespread if not commonplace. It is the convergence of these technologies and the traditional mass media that have made globalization possible.

Although the term *globalization* has multiple meanings, it is best understood as an evolutionary syncretic process, the outcome of which is a composite greater than the sum of its parts. Such a meaning of the concept is implicit when it is used with reference to culture as in the phrase "the globalization of culture." What is suggested by this precise usage however, is the emergence or evolution of an entirely new human phenomenon: that of a nonparticularistic expression of human culture; a plurally inclusive, holistic, and universal concept.

Such a universal concept is an ideal that is yet to be achieved for a variety of reasons, some of which will become evident as we examine the structure of the international infocom industry.

THE STRUCTURE OF THE GLOBAL INFOCOM INDUSTRY

The convergence of computer, electronic mass media, and telecommunications technologies has led to the emergence of an enormous global infocom industry comprising both hardware and software dimensions.

Estimates are that by the turn of the century, the entertainment hardware segment alone of the industry will be worth $US 3 million ("Survey," 1989). In the United States, the entertainment industry generated some five and a half thousand million dollars in 1988 and was second only to the aerospace industry in that country's foreign earnings.

Given huge returns on economies of scale as well as equally vast requirements for software (programmed material) generated by consumer electronic hardware sales, hardware/software technological convergence is a characteristic of the global corporate conglomerates that compete for market share in the industry. As the Deputy President of the Sony Corporation is quoted as having said: "[the] hardware and software parts of the entertainment industry can no longer be talked about separately" ("Survey," 1989).

Of course, technological convergence comes at a price in the competitive, market-driven global environment especially with respect to the setting of technical standards. Specifically with reference to the battle over digital television standards, one report asserts that:

> With the convergence of the communications industry—from broadcasters to phone companies to media concerns to consumer-electronics giants—the digital age is exposing powerful conflicting business interests and visions. For example, it's little wonder that computer makers are clashing with consumer-electronics companies: at stake is some $150 billion in sets for receiving digital TV. ("Digital divide," 1997, p. 68)

Another characteristic of the major players in the infocom arena is that they are vertically as well as horizontally integrated behemoths. John Chesterman and Andy Lipman (1988) estimate that within the foreseeable future, no more than three or four of these conglomerates will control the world's entertainment industry.[1]

Among the megaconglomerates that comprise a veritable global infocom/ entertainment oligopoly are the following:

---

[1]This includes lesser known entities involved in defense systems, electronic security, computers, semi-conductors, and other aspects of telecommunications.

1. Time-Warner ($13 billion merger in 1989 and subsequently—1996—including CNN as well), Thorn EMI, Gulf and Western, and MCA, which subsume such well-known names as HBO, Cinemax, Paramount, and Universal Studios as well as the publications *Time Magazine, Sports Illustrated,* and publishers Simon and Schuster.
2. RCA, General Electric, Coca-Cola Citicorp, subsuming NBC TV, Random House, and entities in cable TV, electronic hardware, defense and security systems, home appliances, and consumer electronics.
3. The Sony Corporation, Columbia (now Sony) Pictures, CBS (now Sony) Records—the world's largest record manufacturer—Loews, and the News Corporation (Rupert Murdoch), including Twentieth Century Fox, Fox TV, BSkyB channel, Star TV, a Hong Kong-based pan-Asian satellite broadcast service, and lesser entities involved in telecommunications, consumer electronics including the Walkman, the Watchman, digital audio-tape (DAT), CD players, Betamax VCRs, and newspaper publishing.
4. Fujisankei Communications, which includes television and radio stations, newspapers, records (including Virgin Records, which acquired Island Records, which had previously acquired rights to late Jamaican reggae superstar Bob Marley's music) and video and film production companies.
5. Matsushita, which owns Panasonic, one of the best-known names in consumer electronics as well as Universal Studios, one of the biggest Hollywood studios.
6. Bell Atlantic Corporation and Tele-Communications Incorporated (TCI)—a 30 thousand million dollar merger linking cable, telephone, and entertainment businesses, which have 42% of the U.S. population as customers.

In addition, there are a number of independent transnational entities that participate in the global infocom industry in either the hardware and software sectors and that are big enough to influence developments in their sector. A well-known independent player in the hardware sector is the Japan victor Company (JVC), whose Video Home Service (VHS) video recording system is the international standard in consumer video recording and playback systems. In the software sector, MTV is a veritable household name in television throughout the globe.

Most noticeably, the major players in the global infocom industry are either Japanese, European, North American, or partnerships of these.

At the macro level, therefore, the global infocom sector is not only vertically and horizontally integrated and dominated by a handful of megaconglomerates, but also it is divided into discrete but interrelated subsectors comprising information, entertainment, news, hardware and software manufacturing, research and development, and distribution and marketing. (Brown, 1991).

STRUCTURED GLOBAL INEQUALITIES

Popularly understood and applied to the structural status quo of the contemporary infocom industry, the term *globalization* is merely descriptive of the ubiquity and global reach of infocom technologies as they purvey their fare. Because that fare emanates from an oligopoly and is predominantly North American and more specifically Hollywood in origin, the term *globalisation of culture*, thus used, essentially describes the global spread of (largely) Hollywood entertainment and entertainment products by contemporary infocom technologies.

Obviously, in such a context, culture has to be understood in its narrowest sense as creative expression rather than holistically as the symbolic, instrumental, and social responses of collectivities of people to their environment (Brown, 1991).

Demonstrably, the present oligopolistic structure of the world's infocom industry mitigates against the development of syncretistic expressions of an authentic global culture, and the very technologies qua technologies inherently contribute to the present state of affairs.

If we understand communication as the interactive transference of meaning between intelligencies (Brown, 1981), that is, as a social phenomenon, then it is clear that most of the mass consumption technologies around which the global infocom industry is built are not communication technologies; rather, they are very potent information transmitting technologies. As such, they can contribute to the process of communication as it is self-evident that in order to communicate, information must be transmitted. However, it is equally clear that the mere transmission of information does not constitute communication. Communication as social process and as a sociological phenomenon is a dialogic encounter between intelligences that results in understanding through shared meaning.[2]

At the level of general consumption, the most popular contemporary infocom technologies are noninteractive, image-processing technologies: television and video and their various permutations. Unlike the telephone that is, archetypically, a bona fide communication technology, these technologies are nothing of the sort. Crucially, however, the mass media are powerful point-to-multipoint information-transmitting technologies. And like all technologies, they mediate our relationship with our environment. In fact, it is the unique manner in which these potent information-transmitting technologies

---

[2]Failure to achieve understanding constitutes miscommunication or what Karl Mannheim (1936) calls "talking past each other."

mediate our relationship with our environment that sets them apart from all other technologies in that environment.

In the first instance, infocom technologies are consciousness-shaping technologies. That is, they are technologies that affect the user's perceptions as well as conceptions of external reality. (Not without good reason, some analysts refer to the infocom industry as the "knowledge" industry.) And second, in the process of shaping consciousness, they separate the activities of information production from those of information consumption and thereby the producers of information from the consumers of information. Indeed, particularly in its dominant entertainment aspect, the global infocom industry's very existence is based on this defining characteristic of the marketplace, the crucial separation between the producers of information (as entertainment) and the consumers of information (as entertainment).

At the extreme, some infocom hardware, such as Nintendo and Sega Genesis video game systems, are entertainment-dedicated, incapable of transmitting anything but programmed information in the form of entertainment. So third, and most importantly, the "interactivity" of these systems is illusory because the player (consumer) is limited to the preprogrammed parameters structured by the system creator(s).

The vast majority of contemporary infocom technologies are of this sort. They are noninteractive and nondialogical. They therefore are exclusive rather than inclusive with respect to their use for expressing creative imagination. More precisely, the program makers, the creators of software in its various forms—whether as television programs or video games—define the world for the consumers of both hardware and software. The program makers' creative expression and cultural conceptions are being *globalized*, not the expressions and conceptions of the consumers.

In the process, a culture of globalization is also being forged by these infocom technologies that mediate relationships in the environment, predictably, the world over. Super Mario Brothers, Double Dragon, Superman, and Ninja Turtles games are played mostly by children the same way, with the same variations, the same outcomes, and perhaps the same consequences the world over. Whether the children are Japanese, American, Malaysian, or Jamaican, their engagement with these games is as predictable—no more, no less as inhaling and exhaling.

To be sure, predictable behavior is not creative behavior. On the contrary, predictability is the antithesis of creativity. In the sphere of videography, the use of satellite and fiber optic technologies for delivering preprogrammed information globally, also contributes to the nurturing of a culture of globalization among the consumers of such information. However, the latent and overt values imbedded in the prepackaged information are the values of those who generate the information and not necessarily of those who consume it. Although in many instances their influence is not analyzed, those values do have an effect on the indigenous cultures of consumers.

In the Caribbean, given its geography, sociohistorical and cultural heritage and, in the case of the Anglophone Caribbean, a common language, contemporary infocom technologies have had varied effects.

In the first place, the region falls within the ambit of U.S. domestic satellite (domsat) signals. And second, as those signals become more powerful as a result of technological developments, it is possible to capture them with smaller and smaller TVROs.[3] Citizens of the region with the financial wherewithal can access multiple television channels from U.S. domsats by investing in TVROs, and many have been doing so since the late 1970s.

As of 1992, out of a population of 2.5 million comprising over 600,000 households, there were some 20,000 privately owned dishes in Jamaica. Given the cost of TVROs, the percentage represents almost all the consumption potential of this particular technology within the upper-middle and upper-income segments of the population. During the 1980s, these segments of the Jamaican population comprised an elite as far as the consumption of entertainment-dedicated infocom technologies was concerned. Currently, however, a much larger percentage of the Jamaican population has access to satellite-delivered material through cable distribution. Virtually every major middle and lower-middle income housing development in urban Jamaica, and some in rural Jamaica as well, now have access to cable-delivered television as a result of extralegal efforts by slick entrepreneurs with an eye for satisfying the demand for cable service. And only recently and after the fact has the government of Jamaica attempted to regulate the mushrooming of these privately owned, community-based cable television systems within the country.[4]

The latest addition to this cornucopia is DBS—Direct Broadcast Satellites—introduced in late 1996 and now available throughout the English-speaking Caribbean and Latin America. These services are capable of providing consumers with over 150 digital video and audio channels.

Notwithstanding, in spite of the widespread consumption of multiple video channels within Jamaican society, many Jamaicans still do not have access to multiple channels and must remain content with programming provided by two local television stations that themselves transmit more than 70% imported content on their services. In this vein, the Jamaican case is not unique in the Anglophone Caribbean (Brown, 1987).

Although other factors account for many of the observable changes that have occurred within Caribbean societies in the recent past, including ease of travel between the region and the United States, tourism, and so on, the media have played a significant role in nurturing the culture of globalization.

---

[3]Television receive-only dish antennae.

[4]In September 1993, the Broadcasting Commission made recommendations to the GOJ for regularizing and rationalizing cable TV services. As of mid-1997, CTV was still operating extralegally in Jamaica.

Basketball has become a popular sport in every Caribbean country within the past decade, and hairstyles, clothing fashions, and slang evolve simultaneously in Harlem, San Francisco, Kingston, and Port of Spain as a direct result of media influences.[5]

At an earlier time, these media effects were interpreted by many Caribbean observers and commentators as the result of cultural penetration or worse, cultural imperialism. But that interpretation ignored or left unexplained the very important fact that Caribbean citizens were and are willing consumers of infocom technologies with all their consequences: cumulatively, what I have characterized as the culture of *globalization*—the uncritical participation in the consumption of the cornucopia of commodities concocted by "communication" conglomerates to market their own and other commodities globally.[6] The culture of globalization is in fact a culture of conspicuous consumption, which in an earlier time was said to be the self-indulgent pasttime of the leisure class.

DIALOGUE AND THE GLOBALIZATION OF CULTURE

Writing the "Foreword" to the 1970 English-language edition of Paulo Freire's *Pedagogy of the Oppressed*, the U.S. scholar Richard Shaull (1970) said the following: "Our [the US's] advanced technological society is rapidly making objects of most of us and subtly programming us into conformity to the logic of its system. To the degree that this happens, we are also becoming submerged in a new 'culture of silence'" (p. 14).

Of course, for Freire, the notion of a "culture of silence" is the very antithesis of authentic freedom. Such freedom is based on the individual's capacity to "name the world" for self, and only free individuals can "name the world" for themselves. It is in and through "naming the world" that one consciously participates in making history and creating culture. Clearly then, the "naming of the world" for self is not a selfish act, but one that is undertaken and achieved through dialogue and in collaboration with others. That is to say, authentic human culture emanates from the actions of human beings who can and do speak for themselves in dialogue with other "free" human beings.

Cultural invasion—a technique of oppression—subverts the emergence and expression of authentic culture (a culture of freedom)

---

[5]The latest media gadgets are themselves part of the syndrome: Walkmans, Boom Boxes, CD players, camcorders, and so on, are fairly commonplace urban consumer durables, especially among young people.

[6]The culture of globalization also has its political/economic aspects as propounded by such "international" institutions as the World Bank and the IMF. Structural adjustment, liberalization, privatization and deregulation are in fact crucial characteristics of the culture of globalization.

by imposing the views of one set of persons on others. Those invaded become submerged in a "culture of silence" because avenues for participating in dialogue—for "naming the world"—are made inaccessible.

Freire's vision of a world of liberated citizens is yet to be realized fully on a global scale, although there have been significant political developments in Europe, South Africa, and elsewhere.

The "culture of silence" imposed on millions of people throughout the world, particularly in Eastern Europe by communism, has been broken by the demise of that dogma. The release of Nelson Mandela from prison by President F.W. DeKlerk and his subsequent elevation to the Presidency of that country established dialogue among protagonists in South Africa—dialogue that is incrementally but inexorably leading to freedom for both blacks and whites in South Africa—thereby clearly demonstrating the central role of dialogue in the process of human liberation.

No doubt the mass media and other infocom technologies played and continue to play a big part in informing the world's people about transforming events such as those in Europe and South Africa. But simultaneously, these same media are also used to anesthetize—to nurture—the "culture of silence."

To the extent then that contemporary infocom technologies do not intrinsically foster dialogue between people, to that extent they are not technologies of freedom. On the contrary, to the extent that they are inaccessible and/or inhibit, by design or otherwise, such dialogue they are technologies of domination. Recall that the mass media inexorably separate the producers of information from the consumers of information and by that very fact invest the producers of information with enormous potential power to prescribe for the consumer: what he or she sees, hears, reads, and thinks about, as well as even how.

It is this phenomenon that explains the fact that the anesthetizing influence of the media, that which Shaull observed in U.S. society at the dawn of the decade of the 70s, has since been globalized. The "culture of silence" is a direct result of strategies pursued by the oligopoly of conglomerates that comprise the global infocom industry. This is perhaps the most significant consequence of the culture of globalization.

The paradox, however, is that the potent information transmitting capabilities of contemporary infocom technologies also allow them to be utilized in the service of freedom.

When used in the service of freedom, contemporary infocom technologies can contribute to the globalization of culture, but when used as tools of invasion, they consolidate the culture of globalization.

Put somewhat differently, as long as the information transmitted by the globe-spanning infocom technologies originate from and reflect the collective values, beliefs, and perspective of only a single and homogenous source (albeit oligopolistic), the technologies will continue to be utilized in the service of invasion and its consequence, the culture of globalization.

Strategies for the globalization of culture, therefore, are those strategies that attempt to utilize contemporary infocom technologies to serve the purposes of dialogue between people globally. Such strategies run counter to the strategies of those who nurture the culture of globalization. The culture of globalization is invasive, nonparticipatory, and nondialogic, but the globalization of culture is liberating because, as process, it seeks to be participatory and dialogic as it taps the creative potential of all members of the human family. And as it does so, it expands human consciousness to the inherent creative possibilities of the species.

There are therefore at least two dimensions to strategies for the globalization of culture: a technological and a creative one. And the technological dimension itself has two aspects.

The first of these aspects can be conceptualized as the problematic of how to use the extraordinarily potent one-way or point-to-multipoint information transmitting technologies extant to achieve communication, which is, as we have seen, an interactive process.

The second aspect is less immediate if only because it is more difficult to realize, which is inventing or devising potent and accessible information transmitting technologies that are also communication technologies. The telephone—a bona fide communication technology—when linked to the broadcast media is indicative of the possibilities. Forms of computer conferencing made possible through the Internet, as well as video and audio teleconferencing, also represent the possibilities for genuine communication utilizing inventively and imaginatively existing infocom technologies. However, research and development efforts must seek to go beyond these present constructions to woo into existence new technologies that do not now exist.

Although the majority of existing consumer infocom technologies are used for entertainment, with some of them incapable of being used for anything else, the purposes for which some of them are and can be used are genuinely liberating. A few examples from the Caribbean may be illustrative.

SOME CARIBBEAN CASE STUDIES

Radio Call-in Programs in Jamaica

In the 1970s, the Michael Manley-led government of Jamaica espoused a Democratic Socialist ideology, which among other things, envisioned the pursuit of participatory politics as an end in itself. As a direct consequence in 1974, the government-owned broadcasting service—the Jamaica Broadcasting Corporation (JBC)—started the daily telephone call-in program "The Public Eye." For an hour and a half every weekday morning, citizens of the country with access to a telephone were able to call the moderator of the program and discuss any matter of interest to the caller circumscribed only by the legal parameters of libel, slander, and defamation governing broadcasting. At the time, there was only one other national radio station, the privately owned RJR. In competition for listeners, RJR was soon to start its own call-in program "Hotline," which was aired at the same time as "The Public Eye" but which lasted for only one hour. As of this writing, 23 years later, "The Public Eye" and "Hotline" are still being broadcast and have become institutionalized vehicles for public expression on matters of personal or public interest.

As a result of late 1980s liberalization policies, the Jamaican media environment expanded exponentially with the addition of five new radio stations—most of which have call-in programs of one sort or another. One of these stations, KLAS FM, increased popular access to the medium by pioneering toll-free telephone calls to its programmes. One consequence of toll-free calling is that any citizen with access to a phone (including call boxes), and not just those who own a phone, can call and express his or her views freely—and at no cost. As a result of this innovation, telephone calls to programs now originate from all over the country and are no longer limited primarily to the metropolis and capital city, Kingston. Predictably as well, the other stations soon followed the KLAS lead by introducing toll-free calling to their programs as well, thereby greatly increasing public access nationally to radio.

Going beyond KLAS, two Jamaican radio stations introduced live hookups with sister stations serving Jamaicans living in New York and Miami respectively, on a weekly basis. These links allow Jamaicans as well as others to air their views and share their concerns with listeners in these U.S. cities and Jamaica simultaneously. Such linkages are also made with radio stations elsewhere in the Caribbean.

In spite of the demise of Democratic Socialism, and as a result of the expansion of the number of radio stations and heightened competition between them, the telephone call-in phenomenon has become an institutionalized aspect of radio broadcasting in Jamaica and provides citizens and government alike a popular forum for communicating their concerns to each other. In the process, the national dialogue created through this particular medium contributes to the "naming of their world" by Jamaicans.

Distance Teaching at the University of the West Indies

The University of the West Indies (UWI) is a regional tertiary institution with three campuses serving some 14 Anglophone Caribbean countries stretching from Jamaica in the North to Guyana on the South American mainland and Belize in the West in Central America. Jamaica, where the main campus of the University is located, is well over 1,000 miles from Guyana. The University has two other campuses: one in Barbados (Cave Hill) and one in Trinidad (St. Augustine). However, there are University Centers in all the English-speaking territories of the Caribbean.

The UWI began investigating in 1978 the use of telecommunications as a means of better serving its scattered constituents with a two month USAID-funded experiment called "Project Satellite," which linked Jamaica and Barbados by satellite (video out from Jamaica and two-way audio).

Following the success of "Project Satellite," a three-year feasibility study was undertaken to determine whether and how interactive distance teaching and teleconferencing could contribute to education and public service in the Caribbean. The University of the West Indies Distance Teaching Experiment (now Enterprise)—UWIDTE—was the outcome of these two projects.

The experiment started in 1982 with five interactively audio-linked Centers, one in each of the campus countries and one each in University Centers in Dominica and St. Lucia, respectively. Today there are some 19 Centers on the network located in all the territories served by the university.

The range of programs offered on the network is wide and includes University-certified courses and programmes in education, the social sciences, continuing medical education and other short professional courses in such areas as public health, labor administration, day care, nutrition, and so on. Additionally, the facility is used to conduct certain administrative chores of the University, thereby obviating the need for frequent travel for such purposes between campuses. From time to time and with increasing frequency, the facility is also used to link the UWI to other Universities, inside and outside of the Caribbean, undertaking collaborative programs. Regional NGOs also utilize the network on an adhoc basis.

Currently, teleconferencing is a fully institutionalized part of the UWI's outreach capacity, and regional governments have given the UWI responsibility for increasing the region's skills bank to face the 21st century. A direct consequence of that mandate is the UWI's decision to become a "mixed mode" institution having parallel intramural and extramural programs, with the latter being based entirely on distance-teaching infocom technologies. With the rising cost of University level "education" in the Caribbean, the use of these technologies significantly increases access of the economically disadvantaged and remote users to the services of the University of the West Indies. Infocom technologies that now comprise the UWI's distance-teaching system include: audioconferencing, computer conferencing, e-mail, local area networks on each campus and in the foreseeable future, video conferencing, as well as a regional computer network linking campus as well as noncampus sites. All these technologies are interactive and hence facilitate dialogue between and among users. The Mona campus of the university also uses its campus radio station—Radio Mona—for nonformal distance teaching.

The Caribbean Broadcasting Union—the CBU

Research undertaken for UNESCO (Brown, 1987) showed that on average over 80% of programming carried by English-speaking

Caribbean television services originated from outside the region and primarily from North America. Moreover, the research also showed that the proliferation of television services in the Caribbean, including cable TV, only increased the volume of such material. Indeed, the study merely confirmed what most professional media practitioners in the Caribbean had already been aware of and what some had labeled cultural imperialism, namely, that the region was being inundated with externally generated images and lifestyles from the United States. In fact, given its geography and therefore exposure to U.S. domsat transmissions, the Caribbean was effectively the first region of the world to be exposed to the effects of DBS as well as the culture of globalization.[7]

The Caribbean Broadcasting Union (CBU), established in 1970 as a broadly representative umbrella organization of regional broadcast systems—including some from the non-English-speaking Caribbean systems—committed among other things to redressing the imbalance of regionally produced material on regional television screens. With financial and technical assistance from the Friedrich Ebert Stiftung (FES) of Germany, "Caribvision" was the initial response that was created to attempt to break a regional "culture of silence" utilizing the very technologies that helped to impose it in the first place.

"Caribvision" is a nightly television news programme produced by the CBU based on local items supplied by its regional television member systems. The program is coordinated and distributed from the headquarters of the CBU in Barbados and is available to all CBU member systems who are free as well to contribute items to it. It is also available to broadcasters outside the region. "Caribvision" is the CBU's flagship program and, as would be expected, is very popular with television viewers throughout the region.

The regional success of "Caribvision" resulted in the CBU producing and distributing regionally and extraregionally a number of additional programs including: "Caribscope," a weekly half-hour cultural magazine; "Caribbean Sports Digest," a weekly half-hour review; "Caribbean Business," a weekly half-hour magazine and "Caribbean News Review," a weekly half-hour news program.

Reaching beyond the Caribbean, the CBU also distributes these programs to the Atlanta-based Tropical Television Network (TTN), which reaches over 7 million cable TV viewers in New York, New Jersey, Florida, and Georgia. It also includes in its distribution to TTN a number of other regional independent productions including travelogues, soap operas, documentaries, and cultural magazines. In short, the CBU has moved from being a mere loose association of regional broadcasters to becoming both a source of regional television programming and a distributor of such programming extraregionally. As the Caribbean affiliate of World Educational Television (WETV), a Canadian-based global access alternative televi-

---

[7]Although this was not how the problem was conceptualized at the time.

sion service, the CBU also distributes two hours worth of regional material globally via WETV on a weekly basis. In the foreseeable future, the Union projects having its own dedicated satellite network linking all television member systems of the region in real time.

Although it is still constrained by technological and marketplace imperatives, the potential exists within the CBU's eclectic programming to create forms of cultural expression that can transcend the particular. The emergence of such syncretic material would be an augury of the potential that resides within the human family and that can be given expression when the "culture of silence" is broken and citizens of the world begin to "name their world" in dialogue with each other.

The Caribbean News Agency—CANA

The nonprofit Caribbean News Agency was established under the aegis of UNESCO in 1976 in direct response to the call for a New World Information Order. Its mandate was to redress the imbalance of news flows within the Caribbean and between the Caribbean and the rest of the world. Up until that time, news flows within the region were dominated by the British-based Reuter News Agency. Although spawned by regional governments, from its inception CANA's independence has been assured by both its structure of ownership and management. Regional governments are minority shareholders with majority ownership and control resting with 12 privately owned media houses.

Starting with a basic print news service, CANA generated and delivered some 3,000 words per day to regional subscribers via teletype. As of this writing it generates some 20,000 words per day and delivers them to subscribers regionally and extraregionally via satellite. Among its clients are the BBC, *The Financial Times* and the *Miami Herald*.

In a region in which both poverty and illiteracy are fairly widespread and in which, therefore, many would be excluded from accessing its information, CANA started a radio news service, CANA Radio, in 1984. As expected, its original daily 15-minute radio news program, the "Caribbean Today," became an overnight success with regional radio listeners. Currently, over 30 regional and extraregional radio stations carry CANA Radio's programs that include a thrice daily, five-minute news program, as well as a variety of other developmental programming on such issues as gender, the environment, tourism, and export. CANA Radio also carries live commentary of the regional and international cricket competitions, the latter involving the West Indies cricket team.

With links to the World Radio Network, a global nonprofit radio service that rebroadcasts international public radio, CANA Radio also supplies a daily 15-minute Caribbean news program for global dissemination. The program has an audience of 41 million listeners.

Utilizing satellite technology, CANA Radio has also put in place the infrastructure to begin continuous region-wide broadcasting. Starting with a 12-hour broadcast day, it proposes to become a global 24-hour-a-day news disseminator by the end of 1997 (CANA Business, 1997).

BY WAY OF CONCLUSION

With few exceptions, contemporary infocom technologies are not intrinsically communication technologies, but they are extremely potent information transmitting technologies. As such, a defining characteristic of these technologies is that they separate the producers of information from the consumers of information—a separation that leads to the commodifying of information. Although this chapter has not focused attention on the differential access that people have to information as a commodity, it is decisively one of the consequences of the culture of globalization. In fact, some contemporary societies are already being stratified on the basis of access to information, with distinctions being drawn between the "information rich" and the "information poor."

This commodifying of information in its various manifestations, whether as databases, text, entertainment and so on, is a deliberate strategy of the megaconglomerates that comprise a structural oligopoly within the international infocom sector. That is why an analytical distinction must be made between the two distinct phenomena: the culture of globalization and the globalization of culture. Aided and abetted by such international institutions as the IMF and World Bank, the culture of globalization largely results from the deliberate strategy of the major actors in the international infocom industry, whose businesses revolve around the mass consumption of new infocom hardware and software that are, for the most part, entertainment dedicated. Satellite and fiber-optic distribution technologies have created a single global market for the products of the infocom industry. These distribution technologies have also contributed to the globalization of the culture of globalization, one effect of which is what Paulo Freire calls "the culture of silence."

Ultimately, therefore, strategies for the globalization of culture must be strategies that seek to break this imposed "culture of silence," thereby allowing the majority of the world's people to participate in the kind of dialogue with each other that will lead to the evolution of a genuine world culture, eclectic in composition, humanistic in content, and syncretistic in manifestation. For such a nonparticularistic and universally valid manifestation of culture to emerge, innovative ways have to be devised of utilizing one-way transmitting-media technologies to serve the ends of dialogue between those entrapped in "the culture of silence," providing them opportunities for naming their world. And, simultaneously, every support must be given to efforts that seek to create genuinely new communication technologies that will be accessible to the majority of the world's people for purposes of dialogue.

As the examples from the Caribbean indicate, the passive and conspicuous consumption of many contemporary infocom technologies fostered by the culture of globalization is being countered by efforts to appropriate some of those very technologies in the service of freedom—the original and still to be consummated task of a pedagogy of the oppressed. That some of the regional efforts are still constrained by the limits of the technologies extant, namely, the one-way flow of information from a single source to many "silent receivers," and the fact that the voices that are "naming the world" are indigenous and are seeking to do so from a Caribbean perspective, is a step in the right direction. Without such small steps, the globalization of culture would remain an ideal beyond the making of the majority of the world's people and captive of those who would stymie its realization by perpetuating the culture of globalization.

REFERENCES

Brown, A. (1981). Dialectics of mass communication in national transformation. *Caribbean Quarterly, 27*(2 & 3), 42.

Brown, A. (1987). *TV programming trends in the Anglophone Caribbean, Kingston.* Paris: UNESCO.

Brown, A. (1991). Caribbean cultures and mass communication technology in the 21st century. *Caribbean Affairs, 3*(4), 48.

CANA Business. (1997, January/February). p. 22.

Chesterman, J., & Lipman, A. (1988). *The electronic pirates.* London: Routledge.

Digital divides. (1997, April 21). *Newsweek*, p. 60.

Mannheim, K. (1936). *Ideology and utopia.*

Shaull, R. (1970). Foreword. In P. Freire, *Pedagogy of the oppressed.* New York: Herder & Herder.

Survey, the entertainment industry. (1989, December 23). *The Economist.*

Chapter ▪ 6

Toward a People's Pedagogy: The Freirean Legacy and the Progressive Cultural Movement in the Philippines

Maria Jovita Zarate

In evaluating and critically assessing the legacy of Paulo Freire, we must initially consider our similarities and differences as peoples of the world and as catalysts of social change. Honestly, I feel more challenged to single out varying differences among ourselves and use these as reference points in the colossal task of evaluation and appraisal of the Freirean legacy in the different parts of the globe. Discerning and putting more emphasis on our differences may eventually lead us to discovering more of the Freirean methodology in our pedagogical work—the "universality" of its relevance to different societies and how variances in its actual application may be breeding grounds from which to develop new alternatives.

The gap that gnaws between our societies is both immense and disturbing. Relative economic affluence and political stability govern most of the countries present in this gathering. Most have wrested themselves free of colonial control and are treading the path toward economic self-reliance and progress. However, neocolonialism persists in its many guises, ravaging the lands and its peoples of the South. Class tensions mark social relations, aggravated by racial strife and patriarchal rule.

In the Philippines, the people's movement prevails as the most viable response to the structural arrangements that have spawned poverty and oppression. We may ask: What exactly is the people's movement? In the context of the Filipino people's struggle for liberation and national democracy, the people's movement is the organized and consolidated expression of the people's resistance to the prevailing social structures. Much of its strength is derived from the decisive participation of the basic masses—the workers, peasants, fisherfolk and the urban poor—and the able support of other patriotic forces—the students, professionals, intellectuals, and the national bourgeoisie.

The existence and continued vitality of the people's movement in the Philippines may be the most important element that stands in the chasm that separates our society from the countries of the North. A recognition of this element is invariably important to be able to historicize and contextualize the breadth and depth of Freirean influence in our pedagogical enterprise. The people's movement is the rich soil from which the seeds of our pedagogical work blossomed and bore fruit for our people. And the present state of our people's movement—its gains and losses, the challenges it confronts and the imperatives for the future—shall provide both the theoretical and practical rigor in the critical appraisal of Paulo Freire's legacy.

Pedagogy of the Oppressed reached Philippine shores in the late 1970s, a time of gradual but sustained development of the people's movement amidst the reality of martial rule. At an instant, it encountered kindred spirits in the people's movement. Recognizing similarities between the struggle of the Filipino and Brazilian peoples, cadres and cultural activists immediately utilized it in the more comprehensive area of political education work. Freire's clarification on the nature of banking education only heightened their renunciation of the educational system as institutionalized by the U.S. colonizers. Pioneering attempts led to new discoveries and gave birth to more specific spheres of concern such as human rights education, literacy and numeracy work, development education, and art and literary education and training.

How far has it developed in the hands of the Filipino people? What in Freirean thought persists in our pedagogical work in the people's movement? What are the extensions and deviations from the original premises of Paulo Freire? What alternatives can we create to reinforce the theory and praxis of pedagogy and make it the cultural activist's principal weapon in combating centuries of ignorance, illiteracy, exploitation, and oppression.

The general parameters of this chapter are the people's movement, the historical bases, and a distinct set of principles. Particular emphasis is given the progressive art and literary movement as an inextricable component of a cultural revolution and as one of the main proponents and practitioners of what is now being referred to as people's pedagogy.

HISTORICAL BACKGROUND

The people's movement in the Philippines take its roots from the Propaganda Movement and the subsequent Philippine Revolution of 1896. Although the Propaganda Movement was initiated by Filipino expatriates in Spain, notably Jose Rizal, the Philippine Revolution was led by Kataastaasang Kagalanggalang Katipunan ng mga Anak ng Bayan (Most Noble and Respected Sons and Daughters of the People) which was founded by Andres Bonifacio, a member of the working class. As the Propaganda Movement agitated for reforms from mother Spain, the Philippine Revolution had national sovereignty and independence as its foremost battlecry. The anticolonial struggle confronted issues of national magnitude: military depredations of the guardian civil, forced labor, heavy taxation, the feudal system of agricultural production and the accompanying forms of exploitation it generated, and abuses perpetrated by the Spanish friars. The Katipunan was able to mobilize men and women to rise up in arms; however, they failed to attain victory because of the duplicity of the United States and the class betrayal of the ilustrados, notably General Emilio Aguinaldo.

The conquest of the Filipino people by the United States continued the status of the Philippines as a colony. But the anticolonial struggle persisted in the U.S. Occupation and in the Commonwealth regime of the 1930s. Agrarian unrest, which initially simmered during the Spanish colonial period, culminated in a series of bloody peasant revolts, most notable of which are the colorum revolts of 1924 and the Sakdalista uprising of 1935, which ended in a massacre of peasants by the military on orders of the colonial government.

Although the peasantry remained the majority class in the entire society, a class of urban factory workers grew in number due to the increase in agricultural production in the countryside. Minor manufacturing companies were erected to process raw materials from the countryside and then directly siphoned out of the country. As early as 1901, the first Filipino labor union was formed by Isabelo de los Reyes. Unremitting colonial and class oppression agitated a broad base of workers and peasants.

In November 7, 1930, the first Communist Party of the Philippines was formed by Crisanto Evangelista. The party strove to integrate the theories of Marx and Lenin, as well as the experiences of the October Revolution of 1917, to the concrete conditions of Philippine society.

Spontaneous mass actions, peasant demonstrations, and industrial strikes intensified as the U.S. colonial government employed ferocious methods to quell popular protest. It was during this time that ferment in art and literature emerged alongside the political upheaval. The theory of art for art's sake, as advocated by the idealist and romanticists, clashed with the emerging ideology of proletarian art, as articulated by university professor S.P. Lopez. The proponents of art for art's sake argued for the autonomy of art against social and political considerations, whereas the ideologues contested this premise and asserted that art should be an instrument for social change and should principally serve the toiling masses, as well as reflect their conditions and aspirations. Soon his ideology would gain many followers, most of whom are now enshrined in the history of nationalist art and literature.

One of the most gifted poets of Philippine literature, Amado V. Hernandez, amplified the tenets of proletarian literature by concretely applying this to the practice of his poetry. His voluminous works, which continue to serve as inspirational and educational materials to the struggle, delineated the conditions, dreams, and world outlook of the enlightened members of the peasantry and working class.

With the end of World War II and the Japanese Occupation of the Philippines in 1945, the ideals of nationalism came to the fore. A few writers and intellectuals assailed the continuing subservience of the Philippine government to the United States. It holds for a fact that the nationalist sentiment would ebb with each passing epoch, suffering severe blows during the Cold War period, and most of the time thwarted by the systematic and colonial miseducation of the Filipino. but time and again it would be resurrected in the collective consciousness of the nation, each time renewed and revitalized by the attempts of the Filipino people to organize and galvanize their unity toward more decisive political action.

THE CONTEMPORARY PEOPLE'S MOVEMENT

The decade of the 1960s was marked by the intensification of political mass actions spearheaded by students and intellectuals against, among others, the conscription of Filipinos to the Vietnam war. Militant student organizations were formed such as the Kabataang Makabayan (Nationalist Youth) and the Samahang Demokratikong Kabataan (Association of Democratic Youth). Soon the students managed to go beyond the confines of their campuses to live and learn with the basic masses of peasants, workers, and urban poor. Their sustained and highly motivated organizing work paid off as thousands of workers and peasants were proselytized into the basic tenets of the national democratic struggle.

Teach-ins, discussion groups, symposia, and fora characterized forms of teaching and proselytization. There was a marked tendency toward simplification of concepts. Student activists of this generation recollect how they managed to teach class analysis of Philippine society. A triangle is always the starting point, with the tip representing the ruling class and the broad base representing the basic masses of workers, peasants from whose labor the very few rich continue to enrich themselves. The "three magic weapons" of the national liberation struggle was illustrated by a man with a shield in his right hand and with a gun in his left: the head symbolized the Communist Party, which provides the ideological foundation; the shield symbolized the united front which, drawing strength from their numbers, no dictatorship can frighten; and the rifle represented the people's army, which wages armed struggle. Art and literary works bloomed and mushroomed in the soil of the people's popular movement. Skits, songs, poetry, and fiction revitalized the call for proletarian art during the Commonwealth era, as cultural troupes and literary organizations founded by the students experimented with various form of protest art. In the visual arts, politicized artists valued the production and dissemination of art works with optimum visual impact such as murals and political graffiti. Inspired by Mao Tse Tung's treatises on art and literature as articulated in Talks at the *Yenan Forum*, student activists went for the more didactic and direct forms of presentation, as well as the use of satire.

It is worth noting that at this time there did not exist a distinct theoretical framework for the teaching of art and literature. Cultural workers learned from the actual exercise of the craft. For instance, the theater artists learned a variety of theater forms and devices from their interaction with the director, with the text as material itself, with the audience and, of course, among themselves. Writers armed themselves with the tools of literary mass criticism, as well as erudite appreciation of formalist and traditional literary forms.

It can be said for a fact that it was during these years that cultural work assumed the character of a mass movement. As a mass movement it set forth its definite tasks and imperatives vis-à-vis the overall people's movement, while defining its relations with other lines of work. It attracted and flourished a great number of constituents who all strove to improve their artistic craft because this was the principal tool by which they engaged in the struggle, while sharpening their analytical skills and refining the conduct of their political work with the masses.

In December 1968, a few young men, having repudiated the capitulationist strategies and tactics of the existing Communist Party, gathered to form a new organization. The new Communist Party of the Philippines renewed the call for armed resistance through a protracted people's war. It is a fact that this underground organization commanded a significant number of cadres, who, in turn, influenced and directed the course of the popular resistance.

The declaration of martial law in 1972 simmered the cauldron of protest. Yet undaunted by military crackdown and incarceration, the activists persisted. Most went to the countryside to engage in mass work and directly participate in the armed struggle, whereas those who opted to stay in the city centers were assigned to the urban revolutionary work, specifically organizing factory workers, urban poor, and professionals.

Although the repressive years wore on the activists and the cadres, this was also a period of daring experimentation in the use of forms in artistic and literary production, as well as in methods in reaching out to a captive audience.

In the countryside, the image of the cultural worker cum people's army was one who went to the barrios in the hinterlands and regaled the peasants with their songs, poems, and skits. With a rifle hung on one shoulder and a guitar on the other, they spent days traversing one site to another, bringing delightful entertainment and political education to thousands of peasant folks. Because the majority of the cadres in the countryside came from the universities with some steeped in artistic and literary tradition, they sought ways and means by which to teach forms of creative writing, music, and drama to the peasant folks. Thus, this was also a time of a marked rise in productivity in various fields such as the performing arts, visual arts, literature, and music. A number of literary anthologies produced by the underground press could attest to the bountiful harvest of painstaking cultural work among the basic masses. Although most of the writers who filled up the pages of these anthologies were the students and the professionals, still a number of them came from the peasantry.

In the meantime, the urban city centers were governed by a dominantly popular and legal form of struggle. Labor unrest was stirring, and unions were being formed even in the big multinational corporations. Facing threat of eviction and demolition, the urban poor faced organized community associations. Student councils were revived and rallied against tuition fee increases and undemocratic forces in the campuses. Martial law may have silenced many, but still there were souls who "raged against the dying of the light." It was in this context that cultural work took an exciting turn. Professional organizations of dramatists, filmmakers, writers, visual artists, and others had been formed on a national and/or regional basis. These entities incorporated in the articulation of their mission and program of action a commitment to the broad movement for social change.

The result was that committed art and literature saw in these years a phenomenal development as new forms were devised to elude the direct and biting commentaries on the social order. Circumvention of artistic forms came be the most convenient way to address social issues. Thus, allegory, farce, and historical drama dominated the theater scene. In the literary arts, discourses on committed art, mostly extensions from the Marxist analyses, lent credibility to the forays in fiction and poetry by a group of poets and writers whose battlecry was to bring back literature to the bosom of the people.

It was in 1973 that the Philippine Educational Theatre Association (PETA), a theater company formed in 1968 and committed to the pursuit of Filipino theater, ventured into giving theater workshops in the grassroots communities. Its basic integrated theater arts workshops later on came to be popularly known as BITAW, its acronym. Its basic content was composed of five main subjects woven throughout the entire duration of the workshop: creative drama, body movement, creative sounds and music, creative writing, and visual arts. Inasmuch as the course content seemed multifaceted to include the primary disciplines of art, theater was its cornerstone. All the other art disciplines were utilized to serve the ends of theater; thus, exercises in creative writing were geared to script writing, creative sounds and music to composition for the theater, and the visual arts served the ends of production design for a theater performance.

Its philosophy for the theater was anchored on the reality that creative powers reside in each individual, even those who have been bereft of formal schooling. Viola Spolin, dramatist and exponent of improvisational theater, provided for them a framework for a theater training course. According to Spolin, to be creative one has to open the mind to new vistas. It means digging inside the furrows of one's self. In the process of discovering one's inner resources, one's personhood, he or she becomes sensitive to others. Such sensitivity is the building block of a fruitful working relationship with others, a much needed requirement for successful theater work.

In her book, *Improvisation for the Theatre*, Spolin expounds on it:

> We learn through experience and experiencing and no one teaches anyone anything. This is as true for the infant moving from kicking to crawling as it is the scientist for his equations.

> If the environment permits it, anyone can learn whatever he chooses to learn; and if the individual permits it, the environment will teach him everything it has to teach. "Talent" or "lack of talent" has little to do with it.

> We must reconsider what is meant by "talent." It is highly possible that what is called talented behaviour is simply greater individual capacity for experiencing. From this point of view, it is in the increasing of the individual capacity for experiencing that the untold potentiality of a personality can be evoked.

> Experiencing is penetration into the environment, total organic involvement with it. This means involvement on three levels: intellectual, physical and intuitive. Of the three, the intuitive, most vital to the learning situation, is neglected.

And so it was witnessed: The peasants took up courses in the theater with the field as their classroom; the workers applied the rigidity of assemblyline work to the more tedious but challenging demands of mounting a play; the urban poor youth shied away from the temptations of prohibited drugs as they were initiated into the community theater groups that they formed after the workshops transpired.

In the meantime, there were stirrings in other art disciplines. *Galian sa Arte at Tula* (Workshop for Literature and Poetry/GAT) was

formed in 1973. Its roster of members drew mainly from the intelligentsia class, mostly students and young university professors. As the
martial law years wore on the people, committed cultural groups lived
and died. In the latter years the participation of the basic sectors in art
and literary work became more pronounced, largely due to the efforts
of the enlightened middle-class artists and writers who committed
themselves to the vision of democratizing the tools of artistic and literary production. It must also be noted that the commitments of these
middle-class artists and writers went beyond their artistic and literary
calling for they were indeed protagonists of a broader social movement
who were struggling against the dictatorship and for a national democracy. KAISAHAN (Unity), an organization of visual artists, dedicated
themselves to the propagation of committed art. Social realism pervad-
ed over abstractionism and impressionism. In their canvasses were the
stark realities of urban blight, feudal exploitation and peasant unrest,
forlorn children bitten by the pangs of poverty, and government
neglect. Beyond these painful realities, the visual artists also touched
on the people's struggle, using the metaphors of history to articulate
contemporary struggles.

The tools of the artists and writers in educating the people
became a major element in their bid to promote the creation, production, and dissemination of committed art and literary works. After
all, the crux of artistic and literary endeavor lies in the artists' abilities to create art. The process of creating (or "producing" art) is, of
course, governed by inner laws and more importantly a fundamental
knowledge of the language and the medium of art and literature.

But being artists and writers goes beyond producing works of
art and literature. Most of them embarked on a modest endeavor to
teach their art to others. Their university schooling in art became the
vantage point from which they developed, and improved on, their
training methodologies. Poetry and fiction was taught in an "experiential" manner, with the budding writers conducting a reading of
their works, and then subjected to criticism, with the "established"
or "older" writers singling out the redeeming literary qualities of the
creative work, both in form and in content, but never glossing over
its weak points, ranging from defective poetic syntax to certain
inconsistencies in the handling of the literary material. The political
perspective was the absolute framework for all reading and all interpretation of the literary text.

The visual artists of KAISAHAN, steeped from the fine arts
education in the universities, also ventured into actual teaching of
the craft. However, they limited themselves to transmitting skills in
the use of popular forms in the visual arts, for example, comics,
political graffiti, and installation art from available environmental
materials.

Paradoxically enough, it was in the darkest years of martial
rule that alternative methods for disseminating and sharing social
knowledge were pioneered through the efforts of the progressive
cluster of the Roman Catholic Church. They launched a program
called Building Basic Christian communities. Nuns and layworkers

conducted literacy classes in the hinterlands; soon they were able to tap the support of other professionals.

Inspired by the force of the liberation theology, members of the Catholic clergy combined literacy classes with political education work. Even the literacy and numeracy classes had a predilection to incorporate in the teaching of reading, writing, and counting the economic, political, and social realities of the illiterates. The program and its advocates maintained that illiteracy is only a function of underdevelopment and poverty, and that power to understand the world is the only way to change the world.

Soon they conducted parateacher training courses for the initial graduates of the literacy and numeracy classes. It was through institutional support that came from the progressive Catholics that Education Forum, an institution committed to literacy for the grassroots and realizing an alternative agenda for Philippine education, came into being.

The "lifting" of martial law in 1981 was made to coincide ostensibly with the papal visit as a display of the regime's commitment to "democratic principles." It was immediately followed by presidential elections that further "legitimized" the rule of Marcos. These cosmetic moves hardly made any significant changes in the social and political life of the nation and its people. The state structures remained firm and intact—a corrupt bureaucracy, an abusive and repressive military, a conservative Catholic clergy, a muzzled media, and a silenced citizenry. The people's movement continued to struggle to prove its viability as an organized force with a comprehensive paradigm for social transformation and a clearly spelt-out program for attaining its goals. Amidst the reality of state repression (the martial law years count as much as 10,500 political detainees and 2,400 victims of involuntary disappearances or "desaperacidos"), the people's movement in the Philippines grew stronger. In the words of one Filipino intellectual, it is the only social movement in Asia that endures as a force to reckon with, an organized and widespread enterprise that is capable of marching into the corridors of power.

FREIREAN LEGACY WEAVES WITH THE ART AND LITERARY MOVEMENT

The need to disseminate art and literature as a principal tool for the national democratic project necessitated the development of a pedagogy that will ensure the democratization and, thus, demystification of the tools of artistic and literary production.

The totalizing tasks of a cultural revolution emanated both from Mao Tse Tung and Paulo Freire. Demolishing oppressive and exploitative social structures and the corollary task of erecting a new social order more than a conscienticized citizenry, it required a populace tempered—and beaten—by the gleaming lessons of political praxis.

When Freire's seminal work *Pedagogy of the Oppressed* reached the Philippines in the late 1970s, it immediately provided theoretical backbone to the emergent practice of education work within the people's movement. Although the framework provided by Viola Spolin opened new vistas for the artist-trainer, it was bereft of any class bias and thus was not hinged to the glaring economic and political realities of the poor masses. Spolin's assertions were revolutionary in itself, as she liberated theater from the dictates of the readymade text. Spolin believed that the human mind, body, and spirit conquering time and space are the animating elements of the theater. In Spolin's theater, the unschooled and the illiterate had a comfortable niche.

A highly organic combination was destined for the merging of Spolin's theater and Freirean thought. As the human body discovered—through movement, dance, sound and rhythm, and words—its capacity for creating art, Freirean method historicized and contextualized pedagogy, not only tapping the creative reservoir of the students, but situating the entire educational process so that it makes use of the actual realities—economic, political, and cultural—confronting the participants. Freire, unlike Spolin, did not pose neutrality, believing that education is either designed to preserve the status quo or change people's consciousness and thus liberate society.

Although credit must be given to PETA for pioneering training modules that combined the basic tenets of Spolin for improvisational theater with the keystones of Freirean thought, the cumulative efforts of the regional cultural groups based in the countryside, and thus more immersed with the realities confronting the peasants, broadened and deepened the training design and extended its theoretical and practical possibilities for use in the basic sectors. It was through these endeavors that theater became highly charged with profound meaning as it assumed two dimensions—one as a process, and the other as a finished product. For the politically conscious cultural workers, the process and the product assumed equal importance. As a finished product, its dramatic material drew much from the generative themes, or "hot issues," of which the audience have strong feelings. Thus there is a close link with entertainment and the motivation to act on these issues. As a process, it made the actors aware of the creative forces inside them and made them realize what they can accomplish as a group. Community presentations are events that allows them to write, rewrite, and revise the play, not only from the standpoint of the actors or creators, but more importantly of the audience for which the final product is dedicated. The process and the product are two separate but related components; when combined, they become more inextricably related to the process of community conscientization, organization, and political action.

Community theaters in the provinces referred to PETA's initial training design as the vantage point for their own pedagogical efforts. As early as 1975, a priest and some layworkers from Negros Oriental, a province famed for its big sugar estates owned by a few privileged families and the abject poverty of the sugarworkers, attended PETA's theater workshop. The priest became critical of the absence of an organizing perspective in the training design. When they went back to the communities of their diocese, they used the PETA training design as a reference for innovating a community theater training design, one that will cogently combine artistic training with cultural administration and management. In Mindanao, the largest island in the Philippines, a community theater program was launched in Magsaysay, Lanao del Norte as early as 1976, from the impetus provided by the Mindanao-Sulu Pastoral Conference Secretariat-Creative Dramatics team in 1977, an institution supported by the progressive bloc of the Catholic church in Mindanao. It may be accurate to say that the early efforts of the progressive Church in the field of cultural work are the seeds from which the fruits of cultural work in the provinces can be traced.

Thus, being a committed artist also meant being a partisan trainer, and being a partisan trainer meant conducting painstaking mass work with the basic sectors of society—urban industrial workers, out-of-school youth, peasants in the hinterlands, agricultural workers, illiterate women of upland communities, barefoot children who will never step into a schoolhouse. Much demystification happens, therefore, to the valorized role of the teacher. Facilitator, animator, trainer, cultural cadre—these terms became imbued with more meaning as the artist realized the primacy of living with the masses if only to render the training and learning cycle as meaningful and effective. The philosophy recognized the participants as thinking, creative people with the capacity for artistic and/or literary creation. The artist-trainer's role was to help them identify the aspect of their lives that they want changed, and then they proceeded by using these aspects as breeding grounds for generative themes.

As a way of generalizing the different approaches to the pedagogy of theater combining contributions of both Spolin and Freire, the following items form an essential part of a training design:

1. Priming and Unfreezing: The participants are introduced to a series of exercises that allow them to discover their bodies. Games and other group dynamics exercises serve as warmups and introduction to complex group work.
2. Introducing the Elements of Theater: A series of exercises, structured learning experiences, and lecturettes are designed to introduce them to the elements of art and drama and allow them unlimited space to discover the potentials of their bodies and minds. Exercises graduate from simple to complex, with all demanding collective action.
3. Tapping Generative Themes as Sources of Dramatic Material: This component covers social investigation, dialogue among themselves and with the immediate community, exposure to the immediate and surrounding community, critical analyses through group discussions,

and a summative structural analysis of the social, political, economic, and cultural elements in the community.

4. Mounting and Rehearsals: It takes more than one person to mount a theater performance. Thus, group work is emphasized in this aspect. The process of coming up with a play, from germinal ideas and generative theme to finished product, is essentially discursive and dialogical. The group sits down to discuss their ideas, initially zeroing in on the content; ideas are exchanged, and debates conducted to come up with a coherent working outline.

5. Community Presentation: These are special and valued community events. The sponsoring people's organization sends notices to the community members of a performance by the cultural troupe. While the presentation is going on, the actors will learn a lot from the audience reactions including their silences, laughter, applause, or even walk-outs. Dialogue with the community members are held after the presentation. Thus, these community events are also validation processes that allow community members to "authenticate" the presentation, give insights, and volunteer their suggestions for the improvement of the play.

6. Summative Evaluation and Organizational Planning: The evaluation and assessment of the entire training cycle are ensured by the trainers and organizers. The summative evaluation provides opportunity to crystallize lessons as well as formulate recommendations for the future. Most of the time the recommendations are stepping stones for the organizational planning component; future activities are also drawn up. In general, this is the part of the process that assures in the short and longterm the continuity of the learning process.

In the Freirean approach, issues of principal importance were presented to the participants. These generative themes, or hot issues, were transformed as basic sources of art and literary materials. In the countryside, themes of flesh and blood dimensions became the generative themes, and because they were close to their lives as a people, they tapped—and zapped—into the energies of the people. These themes revolved around landlord–peasant relationships, militarization and human rights violations, cooperative formation and socioeconomic work, and even issues of national import such as debt servicing and graft and corruption in the government bureaucracy.

Boal came into the picture in the early 1980s as a response to the growing need to develop and practice a pedagogy with a strong foundation in the theater and the arts. Boal's contributions to the enrichment of the pedagogy of Freire is revolutionary and groundbreaking in itself.

In Boal's approach, theater became a participatory act. Extending Bertolt Brecht's treatises on breaking the fourth wall, Boal allowed the audience to smash that imaginary wall that divides them from the performers and then direct the course of dramatic action. Thus, the process went beyond the dialogue; it spurred action, collective decision making, and response. More aptly, Boal called it a "rehearsal for the revolution." The bigger the stage of life, the more exciting dramatic action happens when the masses rise up and shape history.

This method of Boal is being integrated into the basic workshops for popular and political theater in the different grassroots communities in the country. The method is laborious and requires mental facility from the trainers to make it truly authentic and effective. When used to its maximum effectiveness, it becomes a truly liberating exercise.

In 1986, we tried utilizing the method in a basic theater workshop for workers initiated by the union. In September 1993, the factory union emerged victorious in a certification election that pitted them against the management-supported union. Spirits were still high, and morale had just received a boost, but apprehension loomed over their heads. A strike seemed forthcoming. Company management had been violating provisions in the collective bargaining agreement: The 15-peso across-the-board wage, and the regularization of contractual women workers.

After a series of priming and unfreezing exercises on the theater, the workshop participants sculpted images of a workers' union planning for a strike. In one frame they were able to capture diverse images—intense discussion and debate, fear and apprehension, resoluteness, and militancy. The exercise allowed them to create extensions to the single frame that they had initially created.

It is interesting to note that the series of theater exercises became fitting and effective rehearsals for a strike that they successfully waged, much to the consternation of the management. But it was through the series of theater exercises that they were able to formulate step-by-step actions that logically led to the strike—the first move was a work slowdown, then a general walkout, and then a strike, if the company refused to heed their demands.

The conduct of an art and literary training group is always a nodal point in the organizational life of a cultural group. More often than not, it is the very process of artistic training effectively combined with political education that these groups get started, or, if the group had been formed a long time ago, establish their bearing or sometimes get started. Both in the trade union and peasant movement, once the leaders of the people's organizations witness the lively, dynamic, and dialogical processes of art and literary trainings, they immediately take interest in adapting such methods in the political education programs of their respective organizations.

The formation of regional cultural networks and a national cultural network, immediately after the people power uprising that brought Corazon Aquino to power, heightened the imperative and concern for a more totalizing pedagogy. The political situation was drastically changed with the dissolution, albeit informal, of the broad antidictatorship front. Some political quarters suddenly hinged their hopes for social change with the popular president and her much vaunted democratic space.

But for some, the lessons of history remain crystal clear: Emancipation lies with the people, not with a government that continues to support and be supported by its colonial masters.

TOWARD A PEOPLE'S PEDAGOGY: CONTEMPORARY CHALLENGES AND IMPERATIVES

Freire—and subsequently Boal—provided a theoretical framework for the political education and training work that is congruent with the guiding principles of the people's movement in the Philippines. Freire historicized and contextualized pedagogy in a society already rife with class contradictions and struggling for national sovereignty. Adapting Freirean philosophy to art and literary work, the teaching of art and literature and subsequently the democratization of the means of artistic and literary production became immensely realizable.

Literature and the other disciplines of art can glean much from the great strides achieved by the theater. Learning the rudiments of creative writing can seem to be more taxing than theater because the form requires a high degree of functional literacy. I had one experience of teaching traditional poetry to the peasants. Because the form relied on elaborate rhyming schemes and uniform meters, the peasants had to grapple with a literary form externally imposed.

Years of apprenticeship and study of contemporary trends in the literature of resistance gave birth to a generative theme that we now refer to as testimonial literature. This has been the basis of most creative writing training courses implemented with the basic masses. Testimonial literature, drawing from the human impulse to narrate his or her life story, veers away from the formalist school of thought that ascribes to formal elements of literature such as linear plot in the case of fiction or metric and rhyming schemes in the case of poetry; instead, it values capacity of the individual to "narrate" his or her views, insights, life events, and stories in his or her own terms. Testimonial literature is necessarily political literature as it captures the voices of suppressed groups and uncovers their perspectives of themselves, their community, and society.

The decade of the 1980s also gave rise to corollary concepts of pedagogy. Popular education and adult education have become buzzwords among nongovernment organizations and people's organizations in their bid to weave training and education as part of their centerpiece programs. However, these trends, in their attempt to become increasingly "popular," are always in danger of diluting the class partisanship of Freirean methodology and thus turn against the fundamental principles of the people's movement. Although employing participatory and dialogical learning methods, the educational content of these popular education modules has a way of obscuring the contradictions engendered by feudalism and capitalism. For instance, course content is heavily geared to creating a belief that people's organizations and communities can realize democratization and development by peaceful coexistence with the oppressive and exploitative structures of the state. Most of these programs are funded by foreign development agencies that initially requires that recipient agencies assume a nonconfrontative stance vis-à-vis the government.

The encounter of Freirean pedagogy and feminism has not been an easy one. From the onset, Freirean pedagogy has identified its emphasis on contradictions among social classes. Reading Freire with a gender lens, one can very well perceive the invisibility of women in his texts. Nonetheless, for some time now, cultural activists with a feminist consciousness have been addressing gender issues in their training modules. More exciting are forays in the development of women's art and literary groups who are able to trace the connections between gender and class contradictions, painstakingly strengthening the unity of the women's liberation movement with the national liberation movement. As I have said, it has not been easy. Some quarters in the feminist movement, following the line of popular educators, have blatantly declared their nonespousal of the basic principles of the people's movement. Sadly, such belief is reflected in their approaches to pedagogical work. Strong resistance to the reality of class oppression mars their attempts to develop training courses for women. Thus, gender issues such as domestic violence, prostitution, and reproductive rights are taken as isolated issues emanating only from patriarchy and in no way related to the totalizing perspective of undemocratic social structures.

Toward a people's pedagogy: This includes two key words—*people* and *pedagogy*. In time, these words have attained diverse, sometimes even eclectic meanings, always allowing some latitude of deviation. *People* mean the disenfranchized sectors of society, thus affirming the strong class and, of late, the gender partisanship; *pedagogy* means the transmission of social knowledge necessary to shape history and change society through decisive political action of the working class and peasantry, not through token reforms from the ruling class.

If we affirm and reaffirm both the profound and operational definitions of these concepts, we will not be lost in the arduous journey of conscienticizing, arousing and organizing our people as creative, dynamic subjects of history.

REFERENCES

Boal, A. (1979). *Theatre of the oppressed.* London: Pluto Press.
Spolin, V. (1973). *Handbook of acting and directing techniques.* London: Pitman.

Chapter ▪ 7

Action Research for Development Communications: Theory from Practice

Edna F. Einsiedel

Action research has had a long and distinguished tradition in the literature. As a research tradition, it offers a means of understanding the reflexive relationship between theory and practice and an opportunity for building theory from practice in the context of social change.

This chapter describes our experiences within a development project that provided an opportunity to conceptualize some theoretical dimensions of communication on the basis of development practive.

PROJECT BACKGROUND

My involvement in a development project in coastal communities in central Philippines provided the impetus for this study. The project, funded by the Canadian International Development Agency from 1988 to 1994, focused on food systems. The emphasis was on food as an entitlement, with three important dimensions: (a) as an inalienable right to a sustaining and nutritious diet; (b) as a right defined by social, economic, legal, and other structures; and (c) as a framework for empowerment and self-realization (Armstrong, 1991).

Of immediate concern to the project was the issue of unequal access to food and the antecedents and consequents of this problem. As Armstrong (1991) elaborated in one of the project's occasional papers:

> Our objective is to help move the patterns of entitlement towards an adequate and nutritious diet among the different groups in the *baranggays* [villages]. But the means and the ends are inextricable linked: to improve the access of at-risk groups (the end) can only really be achieved by involving them directly in a cooperative endeavor to do so (the means). The challenge is to encourage the empowerment of the disadvantaged, to ensure that different community voices are heard, to ensure that different community voices are heard, to insist that gender equality and environmental awareness are treated as central to the processed of change. (p. 4)

In practice, this philosophical framework involved a broad-changing program of community organizing and mobilization. In the first two years of the program, we tended to look at the community food system in fragmented fashion, examining specific livelihood systems and looking at health and nutrition as an end-product. Our project was similarly administratively structured, with community organizers and modules selected along livelihood areas. For example, we had agriculture and fisheries technicians and health and nutrition experts. An opportunity for reorganizing was accompanied by— indeed necessitated—a major reconceptualization of the project framework and implementation practices.

My direct role on this project was primarily in the areas of communication planning and monitoring and evaluation. In the course of thinking about the role of communications in the implementation of the project, we engaged in a reflexive process of action and reflection, of thinking and doing, and, in the process, of theorizing about communication in development that grew out of development practice.

THE CONTEXT

The Philippine Fisheries Sector

The natural resource base of the Philippines has included a wealth of marine resources that has been the basis of major economic activity throughout the country's history. The fishing industry consists of capture or culture, industrial and service activities featuring processes of catching, processing, manufacturing, and trading of fishery products.

Three categories define the country's fisheries sector: municipal fisheries, inland fisheries, and commercial fisheries. Municipal fisheries essentially involve subsistence fishing, sometimes carried out by small craft and/or fishing boats that operate primarily in coastal areas. Municipal fisherfolk are said to supply 55% of the country's food fish. Inland fisheries are comprised of activities in freshwater and brackish water areas, whereas commercial fisheries consist of fishing conducted in open seas in boats of more than three tons.

It is generally conceded that the evolution of the fisheries sector in the direction of export development has benefitted the big business element in this sector. Against the backdrop of this rich fisheries sector and the fact that the country lies in one of the richest fishing grounds in the world, the poverty of coastal communities of small fisherfolk remains a startling social paradox. Small-scale fishing families have been categorized by government reports as occupying the second lowest rung of the national poverty ladder, next only to the "poorest of the poor," or the landless workers. The average annual income of municipal fishing households averaged about P6810 in 1988, or less than half of the poverty threshold of P15, 260. This economic circumstance has necessitated small-scale fishing households to engage in income-generating activities such as rice farming, labor rental, retail selling, and cottage industries.

The Communities

The three *baranggays* or villages are all located on the northern coast of the province of Aklan in central Philippines. The province is one of the poorer provinces, with agriculture and fishing as its main industries. The three communities have a total population of over 9,000 individuals. Most households are engaged in some form of agriculture, but fishing also occupies as important place in these communities.

Some of the project activities generated included the following:

- Group income-generating activities including handicrafts and a communal fish pond
- Communal activities such as vegetable gardens, with school children in charge of preparation, planting, and maintenance, and the community benefitting from seeds and seedlings
- An herbal garden started by a group of women, which provided the sources for indigenous medicinal drugs, distributed through a communal *botika* or pharmacy
- A number of community day care facilities, built by the community members themselves and run by volunteers and managed by groups of women.

DEVELOPING A COMMUNICATION PLAN

Communications were central to these development activities. These included community mobilizing and group formation, with community organizers as facilitators; group discussions and dialogue; and information dissemination and educational activities. In thinking about communications, we considered the following issues:

- Where did knowledge reside?
- What context did we need to know in order to understand each other's communication practices?
- Who claims ownership to knowledge?
- What approaches to education/mobilization/information dissemination would be feasible and appropriate?
- Outside of ourselves (our project), which groups did we need to reach out to share our learning experiences?

In thinking about these questions, we were guided by the principles of participatory action research that saw development efforts as a method of social investigation that was participatory, a method that was educational for all concerned and oriented to social transformation (Fals-Borda & Rahman, 1991; Hall, 1979).

Where Did Knowledge Reside?

Early on there was recognition of knowledge being resident in all participants; as collaborators, we were all engaged in teaching as well as learning. For those of us from the West, there was recognition that part of our responsibility was to ensure that we did not contribute further to the imbalance of information flow from North to South. Not only could we learn from the considerable expertise within the South; we could also facilitate the flow within the South. One of the distortions in history has been the all-too-frequent occurrence of southern groups learning about themselves from northern colleagues; within the media, segments within a local population might learn about themselves or about their other southern neighbors purely from western voices. Recognizing the considerable expertise that fish stocks, we had to start with the theories already subscribed to by the fisherfolk.

Among the outcomes was a local plan for community education about fishing regulations and for community enforcement of zoning regulations. Many of the violators were commercial trawlers, fishing off shore at night, using illegal-size nets. A community watch program was put into effect, and community reports of violations encouraged the appropriate federal agency to enforce these regulations.

SOME THEORETICAL CONSIDERATIONS

In thinking about the process of "theorizing," we kept in mind some of the axioms discussed by Fals-Borda and Rahman (1991) which we recapitulate here.

First is the idea of collective research. They described it as "the use of information collected and systematized on a group basis, as a source of data and objective knowledge of facts resulting from meetings, socio-dramas, public assemblies, committees, fact-finding trips and so on" (p. 8)

Second is the critical recovery of history. This involves an effort to discover, by means of collective memory, those elements of the past that are helpful to the struggle for conscientization. There is thus extensive use of popular stories and oral tradition, a search for concrete information on periods of the past in family coffers, folk heroes, community archives, and so forth.

Third is the principle of valuing and applying folk culture and of being open to the users. Ownership is a step beyond accessibility; it means asking ourselves to whom the information ultimately belongs, and who has a say as to its repository and use? In this project, we emphasized the importance of bringing knowledge back to the community via meetings. As a rule, it also had to be in a form accessible to everyone. In this case, community members came up with their own ways of information dissemination that were easily comprehensible to everyone. For example, in a food system cooperative that was started, documentation of savings and loans was done by members via simple bar graphs and graphics that were posted for everyone to see.

Communication as Knowledge Reconstruction

In our initial discussions with fisherfolk, it appeared that information dissemination about more effective fishing techniques and technologies would be a primary need. However, in the course of further discussions and problem analysis, the groups recognized that fisherfolk's fishing practices and nutritional habits were very much enhanced or constrained by fishing regulations, the international market for seafood, or the lack of government action on pesticide runoff or enforcement of fishing regulations. Before we could start talking about innovations in fishing practices, we had to learn about the nature of these practices and the knowledge base behind these practices. Our marine scientist colleagues had to do an assessment of the nature and distribution of marine species in the bay, but had to be informed by the rich local knowledge already available. In understanding the problem of depletion "different subgroups are shunned, and, in subsistence economies, experimentation and mistakes are often regarded as conveying unacceptable risk" (Fals-Borda & Rahman, 1991, p. 202).

We kept this in mind as we learned to take into account differences in communication style amongst ourselves, between women and men, and between young and old.

In the process of understanding our communities; communication practices, we discovered certain oral traditions that were beginning to disappear. These included the production of spontaneous poems or oral recitations, particularly during festive or significant occasions (e.g., the opening of a new school), which had a number of functions: to salute an individual, to express celebratory thoughts, to describe an event, or to educate. A number of individuals within the community were known for their oratorical skills and were usually called on to render these recitations. One women was particularly adept at colorfully describing events and used these descriptions to help audiences remember details and to instruct. For example, in describing and celebrating a gathering of women learning to prepare herbal medicines, she developed her ideas in rich descriptive detail, allowing her words to remind the women participants about the occasion and about the medicinal significance of some of the herbal plants in their environment.

Whose Knowledge?

The essence of this question is at the heart of democratic communication. This embodies the notions of access and ownership of information. Access might be described in terms of the appropriate channels of communication (communicating in a medium that is "accessible," i.e., comprehensible and culture-resided within the region), and we made it a point to facilitate the flow of information and knowledge bases within the South.

To illustrate, in setting up a modest library dealing with issues of health and nutrition and community development, we exerted special efforts to locate local materials and resources, research sources that talked about health and nutrition within the local contexts. In addressing such issues as the lack of pharmaceutical drugs in the *baranggays,* we learned from the existing storehouse of knowledge from other communities that had catalogued the medicinal properties of local plants.

The Nature of and Context for Communication Practices

Freire (1970) maintained that "in order to communicate effectively, educator and politician must understand the structural conditions in which the thought and language of the people are dialectically framed" (pp. 85–86). As part of this process, there is a need for understanding each other's practices and the structural or cultural conditions that maintain or sustain such practices.

Although dialogue is a simple enough concept, and despite Habermas's (1970) attempt to describe an "ideal speech situation" as being dialogically based, dialogic practices remain culturally conditioned. Participation in the Western sense may entail different values and behaviors than that demonstrated in other cultural contexts.

Finally, there is the axiom of the production and diffusion of new knowledge. This technique is essential to the research process of participatory action research because it involves (a) a division of labor among and within groups, and (b) incorporates a variety of approaches for systematizing new information and knowledge according to levels of political understanding or consciousness of group members.

How do these issues relate to theorizing and action research? In this section we briefly review some of the seminal ideas on action research that have influenced our own thinking. Then we present some ideas about the process of theorizing from action research, particularly as they relate to communications.

Our Early Mentors

The focus on social practices and the ways that research and reflection leading to theoretical insight might inform the process of social change is called praxis, introduced by the Greeks, was equated with the idea of "critically informed practice." *Praxis* requires reflection on three levels: the exact nature of the action as conducted (and as it is perceived and understood by practitioners), the impact or consequences of the action, and its context. This reflection is meant to transform the knowledge base in order to guide further action. In short, praxis is in essence building "theories of understanding" from practice for social transformation.

Another important dimension to praxis is its guidance by a moral predisposition to act for the enhancement of truth and justice, a disposition labeled "phronesis" by the Greeks. Without such a moral imperative, one was left with technique and the possibility of perpetuating self-deception and injustice (Grundy, 1987).

It is the *praxis* dimension of action research that distinguishes the latter from applied social science. An applied science is normally the counterpart to basic science, and the applied scientist is typically seen as one who puts into practice the principles uncovered by basic scientists. Argyris, Putnam, and Smith (1985) have argued that "this division of labor reinforces a pernicious separation of theory and practice" (p. 5). What action research emphasizes instead is the importance of practical knowledge, the knowledge of the practitioners or the community of individuals with whom the researcher interacts, and the need for harnessing this knowledge to inform social theory and to achieve social change.

In looking at action research, we drew from earlier work by John Dewey and Kurt Lewin. Dewey's (1910) writing in the educational context suggested that a philosophy isolated from the rest of life was sterile, and that social practice was an important focus of scientific inquiry.

The social scientist most often associated with action research is Kurt Lewin (1946), who invented the term *action research* to describe a process whereby social scientists worked collaboratively with a group, an organization, or community. His vision of action research embodied a dynamic relationship between knowing and doing. He has in mind the process of improving understanding in dialectical relationship with the process of improving action: "Research that produces nothing but books will not suffice" (p. 34).

For Lewin, action research "consisted in analysis, fact-finding, conceptualization, planning, execution, more fact-finding or evaluation; and then a repetition of this whole circle of activities; indeed, a spiral of such circles" (p. 947). Such a plan was geared toward a program of social action, and participants in the community or group were to be involved in every stage of the action research cycle. Learning within the group was dependent on everyone's participation in formation-seeking and diagnosis; moreover, freedom of choice was imperative for the selection of and engagement in new kinds of action.

Clearly, Lewin was impelled by the principles of knowledge sharing, of rational analysis, and of democratic participation. He further believed these values to be compelling for the social actors involved in the process of focusing on the amelioration of some social problem. He also recognized that "expertise" and the capacity for learning were resident in *both* the researcher and the group.

Finally, Paulo Freire was a significant influence on our thinking about action research and communication. We summarize his ideas in terms of four concepts: thematic investigation, dialogue, co-intentional education, and codification.

Thematic investigation is an educational pursuit for the investigators, a process of "cultural action" for the purpose of obtaining a deeper and sympathetic understanding of the cultural context. It involves rigorous observations of the *"moments* of the life of the area,"* requiring detailed note keeping of varying social contexts (Freire, 1970, pp. 102-103; emphasis in original). This base is necessary before investigators are able to engage in dialogue.

Occurring in what Freire (1970) has called "thematic investigation circles" (p.110), the dialogic process involves exploration of ideas, problem-posing, and challenge. Through problem posing, facilitators and group members, teacher and students, learn to question answers rather than just respond to questions. It is through this critical dialogic process that *conscientization* occurs. In the process, both facilitators and community members become part of the transformation engendered by co-intentional education: "Teachers and students (leaders and people), co-intent on reality, are both subjects, not only in the task of unveiling that reality, and thereby coming to know it critically, but in the task of recreating that knowledge" (p. 56).

Finally, the process of codification involves choosing appropriate channels of communication for the activities undertaken. In this sense, although Freire uses "communication" in what we consider to be a limited context, his insistence on situating learning, education, communication, and codification in the experiences of every-day life democratizes and makes accessible the means of communication.

These major Freireian themes conjoins theory and practice in transformative fashion and brings theory into the realm of social practice.

How did these ideas, in conjunction with our development practices, contribute to our theoretical conceptions about communication? We thought it useful to present four levels of analysis on communication: First, it is useful to think in terms of communication as a social right. This arena for looking at communications and development reflects action research's concerns for issues of information availability, information accessibility, ownership of information and knowledge, and knowledge validity. It surrounds such questions as knowledge for what, knowledge for whom, and whose knowledge?

Second is the level of communications as social practice. This requires a full understanding of the cultural context within which communications take place and the forms of communication practices within a community so that these might serve as a base for information sharing or knowledge dissemination (what Freire refers to as the "codification" process). An outcome of this understanding has been the greater reliance on indigenous modes of communication already prevalent over the last decade (Casey, 1975). Part of this task of understanding communications as social practice involves preparing a book of basic data or an accounting of all the known traditional media in a particular community.

Third there is the level of communications as dialogue. As a process of exchange, dialogue is a form of and a forum for participation. The "rules" for this type of exchange need to be worked out among the group members, and the assessment of the effectiveness of the process needs to be taken into account as much as the need for assessing the group's success in achieving its agreed-on goals.

Finally, we started to think about communications as the instrument for community. In observing the evolution of various groups within the community through their dialogic encounters, we were also witnessing and participating in furthering the sense of community. Communication presupposes some sense of shared meanings, and these shared meanings and experiences are intrinsically related to "community." We are not describing an evolution from no sense of community to the growth of one; rather, we are referring to the heightening sense of "community" by means of participation in the processes of reflection and action in defining problems and in the pursuit of common goals. This common will and development of greater "social consciousness" are the essence of community.

In theorizing about communications in the context of these four levels of analysis, we can begin to explore its full potential as a tool for social transformation.

REFERENCES

Argyris, C., Putnam, R., & Smith, D. (1985). *Action science.* San Francisco: Jossey-Bass.

Armstrong, W. (1991). *Development beyond dole-outs—entitlement to food: A systemic approach* (Occasional Paper Series, Food Systems Development Project). Iloilo, Philippines.

Casey, R. (1975). Folk media in development. *Instructional Technology Report, 12*(1).

Dewey, J. (1910). *Essays on philosophy and education.* Carbondale: University of Southern Illinois.

Fals-Borda, O., & Rahman, M. A. (1991). *Action and knowledge: Breaking the monopoly with participatory action research.* New York: Apex Press.

Freire, P. (1970). *Pedagogy of the oppressed.* New York: Herder and Herder.

Grundy, S. (1987). Three modes of action research. *Curriculum Perspectives, 2*(3), 23-24.

Habermas, J. (1970). On systematically distorted communications: Towards a theory of communicative competence. *Inquiry, 13.*

Hall, B. (1979). Knowledge as a commodity and participatory research. *Prospects, 9*(4), 393-408.

Lewin, K. (1946). Action research and minority problems. *Journal of Social Issues, 2*(4), 34-36.

Servaes, J. (1989). *One world, multiple cultures: A new paradigm on communication for development.* Leuven, Belgium: Acco.

Part ▪ **II**

Freire and Pedagogy

INTRODUCTION

This section is concerned with what might be described as the heart-land of Freire's work: his pedagogy and its implications for emancipation through learning. The chapters in this section highlight Freire's influence on pedagogic practices in a wide range of contexts and in so doing offer a reassessment of the relevance of Freire's theoretic and conceptual contributions in a modern global context.

A central question driving his work is why do curricular and teacher practices fail so many learners? Freire's answer is that conventional institutionalized learning, based on the depositing of knowledge through a teacher-centered narrative within a hierarchical teacher–learner relationship, his now famous "banking" concept, is both static and oppressive. The authors of chapters in this section explore some of the implications of Freire's alternatives to "banking" education, for example, those that seek to resolve teacher contradictions through dialogue, and those that encourage individuality and the transformation of reality through Freire's widely known process of conscientization.

Freire's writing in general is extensively cited by educationalists and theorists engaged in a wide range of work. This fact alone makes a strong case for reassessing his arguments and theoretical apparatus in a changing global context, but there are other reasons for undertaking the enterprise: one is the relevance of original context to contemporary debates. For example, Freire's discussions of cultural action are generally elaborated on by reference to Latin American societies, and there has certainly been some questioning of their relevance to other contexts. Therefore, as well as the important contributions that draw on experience in Latin America, the section also includes significant examples from South Africa and Malaysia.

In addition to the issue of context is the question of Freire's continuing theoretic relevance and the resolution of apparent discontinuities in his arguments. For instance, in Freire's important elaboration of the economic and cultural dominance practiced by a metropolitan society on a dependent society, society is sometimes presented as a being in itself, and yet at other times as being concerned with class relations within societies in general and not restricted to the metropolitan-dependent relations of specific Latin American societies. This matters, because for Freire transformation is the outcome of cultural action, particularly but not exclusively through education projects executed by radical thinkers who themselves are positioned as the motive force of history. But equally, history, according to Freire, has its own motive force, which suggests that his radicals are not strictly needed. In Freire's teleological conception of history, explicit cultural action is nevertheless necessary because other forms of action, acting in the interest of the oppressors, hold back the forces of history.

Although these dominant forms have had significant expression in contemporary educational systems, according to Freire, other new questions suggest themselves. Do these forms change and develop new characteristics over time? Are they also found in other types of institutions and structures? If so, who are the "new" oppressors, perhaps not just "banking" teachers? Answers to these types of questions and insights into the issues that underpin them can be sought in the following chapters.

Chapter ▪ 8

Freirean Pedagogy and Higher Education: The Challenge of Postmodernism and the Politics of Race

Peter McLaren

> I remember when young people rebelled all around the world in 1968 without intentionally coordinating their actions. In 1968, students in Mexico were not telephoning young people at Harvard, or in Colombia, in Prague, in Brazil; nevertheless, they carried out more or less the same movement, it was impressive. I also remember that communication between world universities was nonexistent and it was unbelievably easy for dominant classes to repress world movements.
> —Paulo Freire (1994, pp. 126-127)

We are living the hallucinatory wakefulness of nightmare reason. It is a time in which U.S. culture and history threaten the autonomy of the human spirit rather than exercise it. Henri Lefebvre (1975) warns that during this present historical conjuncture we are suffering from an alienation from alienation, that is, from a disappearance of our consciousness that we exist in a state of alienation.

Educators and cultural workers in the United States living in this twilight of reason are facing a crisis of democracy. The democratic aspiration of U.S. schooling and social, cultural, and institutional practices in general have been carried forth to an unheralded present moment in what retrospectively appears to have been an act of bad faith. The consequences of such an act for future generations are only faintly visible and are bathed in an ethos eerily reminiscent of earlier swindles of hope. The "democratizing" imperatives of private enterprise, wage labor, free trade, and other fundamental axes for the new capitalist world system ushered in by the third industrial revolution of computer technology have shrouded individuals in a web of promotional logic patterned by the conquering dynamism of Eurocentrism. Colonization has gone transnational and corporatist (Miyoshi, 1993). As Jacques Attali (1991) warns, "From Santiago to Beijing, from Johannesburg to Moscow, all economic systems will worship at the altar of the market. People will sacrifice for the gods of profit" (p. 120). We live in an age in which desires, formerly tilted inward, are now constructed on the surface of bodies like pathologically narcissistic tattoos that reflect lost hope and empty dreams— forfeited identifications turned into grotesqueries, unable to escape the circuit of deceit and despair constructed out of capitalist relations and rationalizations. Mark Olssen (1996) notes that the shift from classical liberalism to neo-liberalism involves a change in the subject position from "homo economicus" (individuals detached from the state who operate out of self interest) to "manipulatable man" (individuals created by the state who are encouraged to be "perpetually responsive") in order that citizens are encouraged to make a "continual enterprise" of themselves (p. 340).

Capitalism carries the seeds of its own vulnerability and frailty, even though its cunning appears inexhaustible and its mechanisms of production and exchange irreproachable and unchallenged. Its vulnerability is, ironically, the most steadfast and dangerous precondition for its further development. So long as it has bourgeois universal reason and the epistemic privilege of science as its spokesperson and Eurocentrism as its cultural anchor, and whiteness as its foundation of cultural calculability, its very constitution as a discourse of power within an increasingly homogeneous "world culture" needs to be challenged by popular movements of renewal within a polycentric cultural milieu.

Educators in the United States have no special immunity to these conditions but bear a signal responsibility to understand them and, in turn, help their students to do the same. Students are particularly vulnerable in these dangerous times as they are captured in webs of social and cultural meaning not of their own making, motivated to remember in specific ways, and silently counseled through advertisements, the media, and religious and political "others" to respond to the logic of commodity fetishism as if it were a natural state of affairs. Exchange values that encode the practical relations between people are misunderstood such that they appear as fantastically transhistorical relations between things. The result is functionally advantageous to the capitalist class. Teachers and students together face New Right constituencies of all types and stripes, in particular, fundamentalist Christians and political interest groups, who are exercising an acrimonious appeal to a common culture monolithically unified by a desire for harmony in sameness.

The forms of ethical address that have been constructed by the sentinels of our dominant political, cultural, and educational systems—even under cover of abstract endorsements of diversity—are bent on draining the lifeblood out of difference by installing an invisible ideological grid through which appeals to normalcy, decency, and citizenship may be filtered and differences extorted into reconciliation. They are effectively limiting the range of meanings that are being stockpiled in the name of democracy. E.D. Hirsch (1987) wants to drain culture of nuance and complexity in order to ontologically and epistemologically fix the relationship between citizenship and language so that "real Americans" will not be bothered anymore by the babel of foreign tongues. Educational reformers under the sway of marketplace logic are implored to get youth off the streets and into the declining job markets, where they can then be conscripted into the corporate wars with Germany and Japan.

Insinuated into grand narrative of progress, these contestable sets of assumptions and social practices effectively reproduce the systems of intelligibility that further the interests of the privileged and powerful.

Against the backdrop of the global underclass, the growing influence of neo-conservatism and neo-liberalism in political life in general and education in particular, and the struggle for democracy exists the legacy of Paulo Freire, one of the great revolutionaries of this and any other generation. It is important to make clear that Freire's work cannot be articulated outside the diverse and conflicting registers of indigenist cultural, intellectual, and ideological production in the Third World. The *Third World* is a term that I use most advisedly after Benita Parry (1993) and Franz Fanon to mean a "self-chosen phrase to designate a force independent of both capitalism and actually existing socialism, while remaining committed to socialist goals" (p. 130). As such, it offers a starting point for a critique of the empire of capital and "retains its radical edge for interrogating the Western chronicle."

Of course, one of the powerful implications surrounding the distinction between First and Third Worlds involves the politics of underdevelopment. Andrew Ross (1989) describes the classic model of underdevelopment as one that benefits the small, indigenous elites of Western developed nations. Foreign markets such as those in Latin America provide a consumption outlet for the developed nations of the First World for absorbing the effects of a crisis of overproduction in the core economy. According to Ross, the peripheral economy (Latin America) underproduces for its domestic population. He reports that "The Economic surplus which results from peripheral consumption of core products is appropriated either by core companies or by the domestic elites; it is not invested in the domestic economy of the peripheral nation" (p. 129). Of course, what happens as a result is that the domestic economies of Latin America and foreign capital certainly does encourage peripheral economies to develop, but such development—if you can call it that—is almost always uneven. Consequently, such contact forces the peripheral economy to undevelop its own domestic spheres. Witness the current struggle of the Zapatistas in Chiapas, Mexico.

When there is economic dependency, cultural dependency often follows in its wake. However, the capitalist culture industry is not simply superstructural but constitutive in that the masses—both in First and Third Worlds—do not simply consume culture passively as mindless dupes. There is often resistance at the level of symbolic meaning that prevents the culture industry from serving simply as a vehicle of a repressive homogenization of meaning (Martin-Barbero, 1992; McLaren, 1992). According to Ross (1989), the elites of the peripheral nations are the first to acquire access to Westernized popular culture, but because of the limited access of the indigenous population to the media, the media generally serve to encourage affluent groups to adopt the consumer values of the most developed countries. The elites basically occupy a supervisory capacity when it comes to the cultural consumption of the indigenous peasantry. However, the continuing ties of the peasantry to their own ethnic cultures does help them become less dependent on Western information. Foreign mass-produced culture is often interpreted and resisted at the level of popular culture, and we must remember that First World cultural values can also be affected by its contact with the cultures of less developed countries. Furthermore, not everything about contact with Western culture is to be shunned, although the emergence of a new, transnational class appears to have all the ideological trappings of the older, Western bourgeoisie. While the Western bourgeoisie is not all of one piece and is less united as some might claim, its current practices of uneven development, enforced by the World Bank and the International Monetary Fund, ensures the continuing reproduction of the existing international division of labor despite the increasing militancy and organizational strength of workers in Asia and other sites experiencing economic crises.

The image of Freire that is evoked against this recurring narrative of the decline and deceit of Western Democracy and the cultural hegemony of developed nations is a distant voice in a crowd, a disturbing interloper among the privileged and powerful—one who bravely announces that the emperor has no clothes. Ethically and politically Freire remains haunted by the ghosts of history's victims and possessed by the spirits that populate the broken dreams of utopian thinkers and millenarian dreamers—an individual whose capacities for nurturing affinities among disparate social, cultural, and political groups and for forging a trajectory to moral, social, and political liberation exceeds the disasters that currently befall this world.

Freire's internationally celebrated praxis began in the late 1940s and continued unabated until 1964, when he was arrested in

Brazil as a result of a literacy program he designed and implemented in 1962. He was imprisoned by the military government for 70 days and was exiled for his work in the national literacy campaign, of which he had served as director. Freire's 16 years of exile were tumultuous and productive times: a five-year stay in Chile as a UNESCO consultant with the Chilean Agrarian Reform Corporation, specifically, the Reform Training and Research Institute; an appointment in 1969 to Harvard University's Center for Studies in Development and Social Change; a move to Geneva, Switzerland in 1970 as consultant to the Office of Education of the World Council of Churches, where he developed literacy programs for Tanzania and Guinea-Bissau that focused on the re-Africanization of their countries; the development of literacy programs in some postrevolutionary former Portuguese colonies such as Angola and Mozambique; assisting the governments of Peru and Nicaragua with their literacy campaigns; the establishment of the Institute of Cultural Action in Geneva in 1971; a brief return to Chile after Salvador Allende was assassinated in 1973; the provocation of General Pinochet to declare Freire a subversive; and his eventual return to Brazil in 1980 to teach at the Pontifica Universidade Católica de São Paulo, the Universidade de São Paulo, and the Universidade de Campinas. These events were accompanied by numerous works, most notably, *Pedagogy of the Oppressed* (1970b), *Cultural Action for Freedom* (1970a), and *Pedagogy in Process: Letters to Guinea-Bissau* (1978). Little did Freire realize that on November 15, 1988, the *Partido dos Trabalhadores* (Workers Party or PT) would win the municipal elections in São Paulo, Brazil, and he would be appointed Secretary of Education of the city of São Paulo by Mayor Luiza Erundina de Sousa.

Relentlessly destabilizing as *sui generis* and autochthonous mercenary pedagogy—that is, spontaneous pedagogy wantonly designed to stimulate the curiosity of students yet imposed in such a bourgeois manner so as to "save" those who live in situations of domestication only when they are reinitiated into the conditions of their own oppression—Freire's praxis of solidarity, that is, his critical pedagogy, speaks to a new way of being and becoming human. This "way of being and becoming" constitutes a quest for the historical self-realization of the oppressed by the oppressed themselves through the formation of collective agents of insurgency. Against the treason of modern reason, Freire aligns the role of the educator with that of the organic intellectual. Freire's positioning of the educator as a revolutionary social agent brushes against the grain of what could be called "the educational uncanny," a modality of bourgeois anxiety surrounding the questioning of axiomatic assumptions related to prevailing epistemologies and pedagogical practices. It should come as no surprise then that contrary perspectives generated in the metropolitan epicenters of education designed to serve and protect the status quo, Freire's work has, even today, been selected for a special disapprobation by the lettered bourgeoisie and epigones of apolitical pedagogy as a literature to be roundly condemned, travestied, traduced, and relegated to the margins of the education debate. That Freire's work has been placed under prohibition, having been judged to be politically inflammatory and subversive and an inadmissible feature of academic criticism, is understandable given the current historical conjunction. But it is not inevitable.

It is not the purpose of this essay to address the often egregious misrepresentations of Freire's work by mainstream educators, nor to simply situate Freire unproblematically within the context of First World efforts to ground liberation struggles in pedagogical practices. I intend merely to elaborate on one of the central themes of Freire's work, which is the role of the educator as an active agent of social change.

CRITICAL PEDAGOGY VERSUS THE ACADEMY

Although their political strategies vary considerably, critical educators of various stripe (many of whom have been directly influenced by Freire's work) generally hold certain presuppositions in common that can be summarized as follows: pedagogies constitute a form of social and cultural criticism; all knowledge is fundamentally mediated by linguistic relations that inescapably are socially and historically constituted; individuals are synecdochically related to the wider society through traditions of mediation (family, friends, religion, formal schooling, popular culture, etc.); social facts can never be isolated from the domain of values or removed from forms of ideological production as inscription; the relationship between concept and object and signifier and signified is neither inherently stable nor transcendentally fixed and is often mediated by circuits of capitalist production, consumption, and social relations; and language is central to the formation of subjectivity (conscious and unconscious awareness). Furthermore, certain groups in any society are unnecessarily and often unjustly privileged over others, and as the reason for this privileging may vary widely, the oppression that characterizes contemporary societies is most forcefully secured when subordinates accept their social status as natural, necessary, inevitable, or bequeathed to them as an exercise of historical chance. In addition, oppression has many faces and focusing on only one at the expense of others (e.g., class oppression vs. racism) often elides or occults the interconnection among them; an unforeseen world of social relations awaits us, and that power and oppression cannot be understood simply in terms of an irrefutable calculus of meaning linked to cause-and-effect conditions, which means that an unforeseen world of social relations awaits us; domination and oppression are implicated in the radical contingency of social development and our responses to it; and mainstream research practices are generally and unwittingly implicated in the reproduction of systems of class, race, and gender oppression (Kincheloe & McLaren, 1994).

Freire's work certainly reflects this list of assumptions to different degrees, and although his corpus of writing does not easily fall under the rubric of poststructuralism, his emphasis on the relationship among language, experience, power, and identity certainly give weight to certain poststructuralist assumptions. For instance, Freire's work stresses that language practices among individuals and groups do more than reflect reality, they effectively organize our social universe and reinforce what is considered to be the limits of the possible while constructing at the same time the faultlines of the practical. To a large extent, the sign systems and semiotic codes that we use are always already populated by prior interpretations because they have been necessarily conditioned by the material, historical, and social formations that help give rise to them. They endorse and enforce particular social arrangements because they are situated in historically conditioned social practices in which the desires and motivations of certain groups have been culturally and ideologically inscribed, not to mention overdetermined. All sign systems are fundamentally arbitrary, but certain systems have been accorded a privileged distinction over others, in ways that bear the imprint of race, class, and gender struggles (Gee, 1993). Sign systems not only are culture-bound and conventional but also are distributed socially, historically, and geopolitically (Berlin, 1993). For U.S. educators, this implicates our language use in Euro-American social practices that have been forged in the crucible of patriarchy and White supremacy (Giroux, 1993; McLaren, 1995, 1997).

Knowledge does not, according to the view just discussed, possess any inherent meaningfulness in and of itself but depends on the context in which such knowledge is produced and the purpose to which such knowledge is put. If there is no preontological basis for meaning that is extralinguistically verifiable, no philosophical calculus that can assist us in making choices, then we can come to see language as a form of power that teaches us to adopt particular ways of seeing and engaging the self and others, which, in turn, has particular social consequences and political effects (McLaren & Leonard, 1993). Few educators have helped us judge the political effects of language practices as much as Paulo Freire. And few educators have been as misused and misunderstood. Clearly, Freire does not see individuals and groups to be agentless beings invariably trapped in and immobilized by language effects. Rather, human beings are politically accountable for their language practices, and as such agency is considered immanent (McLaren & Lankshear, 1994). Freire's position reflects Gramsci's notion that the structural intentionality of human beings needs to be critically interrogated through a form of *conscientization* or conscientização (this Portuguese word is defined by Freire as a deep or critical reading of commonsense reality).

THE EDUCATIONAL INSTITUTION AS A MORAL AGENT

When Egas Moniz was chosen to perform the first medical lobotomy (a procedure that, it may be recalled, won him the Nobel Prize and that led reactionary advocates to consider lobotomies for individuals opposed to good citizenship practices), it was inconceivable at that time to think that such an act of cerebral terrorism could be achieved at a cultural level more effectively and much less painfully through the powerful articulations of new and ever more insidious forms of capitalist hegemony. The emancipatory role of university and public intellectuals has been greatly diminished by this process, as well as the function of the organic intellectual. In fact, emancipatory praxis has been largely orphaned in our institutions of education as educators are either unable or refuse to name the political location of their own pedagogical praxis. Part of the problem is that postmodern traditions of mediation have become simulacra whose ideological dimensions cannot easily be identified with or organically linked to the most oppressive effects of capitalist social relations and material practices.

The redoubled seduction of new information technologies not only rearticulates a submission to multinational financial strategies, but creates possibilities for a resignification of, resistance to, and popular participation in the politics of everyday life. The fact that relationships between the specific and the general have become blurred by these new electronic forces of mediation has intensified the reorganization and liberation of difference but has also posed a danger of further cultural fragmentation and dissolution limiting the struggle for strategic convergences among sites of intellectual production, the formation of new moral economies, and the expansion of new social movements. This disaggregation of public spheres and the massification of *mestizaje* identities makes it difficult to establish the solidarities necessary for developing liberating idioms of social transformation (Martin-Barbero, 1992; McLaren, 1992). It is to a deeper understanding of the relationship between the role of hegemony in the formation of public intellectuals and the function of the university itself in the context of wider social and political formations that Freire's work needs to be engaged. Part of this engagement necessitates an engagement with postmodernist criticisms.

Freire's work has not explicitly addressed current political debates surrounding the pedagogy and politics of postmodernism. What can be loosely described as postmodern social theory has been influential in, among other things, offering criticisms of material and economic causality and the Cartesian notion of subjectivity by placing an emphasis on reading social reality as a text, on language as a model of representation that helps "construct" social reality, on power as both a condition and effect of discourse, on world construction as an interplay of signifying relations, and on unmasking Enlightenment conceptions of truth as the aesthetic effectiveness of the rhetoric of reading and writing practices. Yet such criticisms have also tended to obscure the relationship among discourse production and the wider social relations of production linked to the international division of labor (McLaren, in press).

Recently Sande Cohen (1993) has from a postmodern perspective offered a forceful challenge to the timid and frequently

duplicitous role that university intellectuals have assumed in relation to the sociality of capital and the "catastrophe of socialized
expectations." Following the persistent contentions of Baudrillard,
Nietzsche, and others, Cohen maintains that objectivity can no
longer hide or deny its subjectively based interests—a situation that
has serious implications for the role of the intellectual in contemporary North American society. According to Cohen:

> It is suggested that our texts and objects now fail to connect
> with everything but *our own simulacra, image, power, forma-
> tion of exchange.* In doubting and negating everything, in
> affirming and consecrating everything, intellectuals remain
> prisoners of the futile role of the subject-in-consciousness
> and enforce the pretense that our efforts translate and repre-
> sent for the truth of others, the reality of the world. (p. 154;
> emphasis in original)

For Cohen, as for Freire, the dilemma of the intellectual lies in the
failure to forcefully challenge the perils of capitalism. In response to
this dilemma, Cohen mounts an articulate and vigorous attack on
the U.S. professoriate. University discourse and practices are condemned as mobilizing the academicization and domestication of
meaning through a modernist process of historicization—a process
that, in effect, amounts to creating various self-serving theologies of
the social that enable professors to speculate on the future in order
to justify their social function as intellectuals. Resulting from this
process are acute forms of anti-skepticism leading in many instances
to a debilitating cynicism. According to Cohen, universities and their
academic gentry operate as a discursive assemblage directed at creating a regime of truth, a process that fails to undertake the important task of "inventing systems independent of the system of capital"
(p. 3). In this instance, academic criticism is crippled by its inability
to break from conventional categories such as "resemblance."
Critical languages forged in the theoretical ovens of the academy
simply and regrettably pursue their own hegemony through the production of pretense and the desire for power. Furthermore, in the
face of the cultural logic of late capitalism, "the category of the intellectual is disengaged from any possible antimodernist argument" (p.
68). This situation recenters "high-status" knowledge within the liberal tradition of therapeutic discourse. According to Cohen, "universities cannot speak to their own participation in the destruction of
events without undoing their 'need' and control structures" (p. 114).

Even Habermas's now popular appeal for a rational means of
resolving differences and restoring democratic social life in the ideal
speech situation is described as "psychologically based moral economy" (Cohen, 1993, p. 67), in which "intellectuals are empowered so
long as they stay in the precut grooves of providing resocialization
with concepts, theory, sophistication, the seductions, one might say,

of bureaucratic integration" (p. 70). With this dilemma in mind, Cohen asserts:

> Why isn't capitalism—which makes mincemeat of real argumentation by its homogenization of signifiers, accomplished, for example, by the media's ordinary excessive displacement of analysis or the marginalization of unfamiliar cultural and social voices—rendered more critically? . . . Why is the economic mode so accepted in the first place as an unalterable form of social relation? Why is criticism so often an opposition that acts under the identity of a "loyal opposition"? (p. 70)

In order to escape the inevitability under capitalism of a modernist historicist recoding of knowledge, Cohen astutely adopts Lyotard's notion of "dispossession." Dispossession is recruited in this context in terms of "the dispossession of historicizing, narrating, reducing, demanding" (p. 72). More specifically, it refers to a form of "uncontrolled presentation (which is not reducible to presence)" (p. 73). It also points to the suspension of identification—including negative identification. Cohen also conscripts into the service of a critique of capitalism Hannah Arendt's concept of "active critique" of ends and goals "that never identif[ies] with time valuations which are, unavoidably, always already atrophied" (Cohen, 1993, p. 113). We are advised here to "strangify"—a term he employs in tandem with an unyielding commitment to resubjectification—to making subjectivity different outside the acts of negation and opposition through the creation of insubordinate signifiers that loosen and "neutralize . . . the Platonic control on the power to select" (p. 118). To strangify is to engage in a nonreduction of meaning that terrorizes all forms of equational logic, both positive and negative.

Cohen's project of strangification—a type of postmodern extension of Freire's term of conscientization—is directed at destabilizing and decentering the monumentalization of the already known and the militarization of existing sign systems established by the academic gentry and mandarins of high-status knowledge, whose participation is aimed at the legitimization of their own power. Along with smashing through the Western arcs of destiny—those supposedly unassailable narratives of individual freedom arching to Disneyland, Aztecland, Inca-Blinka, San Banadov, or Gangsterland—strangification unsettles foundational myths that anchor meaning in a sedentary web of contradictory appearances and precodes the world in such a way that entrance to the world of "success" depends on the imprimatur of one's cultural capital and the potential for earning power.

A number of questions are raised by Cohen's analysis for those who are developing Freirean-based pedagogical work. These questions include, among others:

- Of what importance does "postmodern theory" and "resistance postmodernism" have for the Brazilian sociopolitical context?
- The recent thesis on "the death of the subject" advanced by many poststructuralists (the individual is constituted by discourse or is simply a position in language, systems of signification, or chains of signs) has called into question the feasibility of historical agency of political praxis. How can we think of agency outside of a transhistorical and prediscursive "I" and yet not fall into the cynical trap that suggests that individuals are simply the pawns of the interpretive communities in which they find themselves? If the subject has been aestheticized and reduced to simply a "desiring machine," how are we to address the concepts of morality and ethics and multidimensional forms of agency?
- How are we to react to those who proclaim the "death of History" thesis that decries the metanarratives of the Enlightenment as a misguided belief in the power of rational reflection? If we are to reject "grand theories" that essentialize others and speak for their needs from a perspective that refuses to critically interrogate its own ideological constitutiveness, then are we simply left with a micropolitics of local struggles? In other words, is it possible to build global alliances in the postmodern era that do not produce the same forms of technocratic capitalism that are part of the problem?
- If master narratives are colonizing practices that repress differences and the recognition of multiple identities, and if it is virtually impossible to represent the real outside the constraints of regimes of representation, how should we begin to rethink and practice liberation?
- Although postmodern theorists have developed new understandings of desire as a means of criticizing the disabling effects of instrumental reason, how can we address pragmatically the project of human freedom?

Postmodern critiques of educational institutions such as those advanced by Cohen can be helpful to Freirean educators in placing social and educational critique within a wider contemporary problematic. But they also have their limitations.

THE NOCTURNAL ACADEMY AND THE POLITICS OF DIFFERENCE

Western intellectuals need to further understand that even though affirming the experiences of subaltern groups is exceedingly important within a praxis of liberation, it is a highly questionable practice to render the "other" as transparent by inviting the other to speak for herself. Freire and other critics make this point very clear. As Gaurav Desai (1993) notes (following Gayatri Spivak, Lata Mani, and Partha Chattergee), the position of permitting the other to speak for him- or herself is uncomfortably "complicitious with a Western epistemological tradition that takes the conditions of the possibility of subaltern counterinvention for granted without engaging in a critique of the effects of global capitalism on such counterinvention" (p. 137). Because the oppressed speak for themselves within a particular sign structure, the language of critique adopted by the insurgent intellectual needs to be able to analyze the embeddedness of such a sign system in the larger episteme of colonialism and White supremacist, capitalist patriarchy. Insurgent intellectuals must apply the same critique to their own assumptions about the other as they do to the other's self-understanding. In fact, critical educators need to counterinvent a discourse that transcends existing epistemes.

Jim Merod (1987) poses the challenge of the intellectual as follows: "The critic's task is not only to question truth in its present guises. It is to find ways of putting fragments of knowledge, partial views, and separate disciplines in contact with questions about the use of expert labor so that the world we live in can be seen for what it is" (p. 188).

The problem, as Merod sees it, is that there exists within the North American academy no political base for alliances among radical social theorists and the oppressed. According to him:

> North American intellectuals need to move beyond theory, tactics, and great dignified moral sentiments to support, in the most concrete ways possible, people harmed or endangered by the guiltless counterrevolutionary violence of state power. . . . The major intellectual task today is to build a political community where ideas can be argued and sent into the world of news and information as a force with a collective voice, a voice that names cultural distortions and the unused possibilities of human intelligence. (p. 191)

One important counterintuitive task of the critical educator is to translate cultural difference. This is certainly the challenge for Freirean educators. The act of translation is, in Bhabha's (1990) terms, "a borderline moment" (p. 314). As Walter Benjamin pointed out, all cultural languages are to a certain extent foreign to themselves, and from the perspective of otherness it is possible to interrogate the contextual specificity of cultural systems (Bhabha, 1990). It is in this sense, then, that "it becomes possible to inscribe the specific locality that apprehension of difference, to perform the act of cultural translation" (p. 314).

All forms of cultural meaning are open to translation because all cultural meanings resist totalization and complete closure. In other words, cultural meanings are hybrid and cannot be contained within any discourse of authenticity or race, class, and gender essences. Bhabha (1990) describes the subject of cultural difference as follows:

> The subject of cultural difference is neither pluralistic nor relativistic. The frontiers of cultural differences are always belated or secondary in the sense that their hybridity is never simply a question of the admixture of pre-given identities or essences. Hybridity is the perplexity of the living as it interrupts the representation of the fullness of life; it is an instance of iteration, in the minority discourse, of the time of the arbitrary sign—"the minus in the origin"—through which all forms of cultural meaning are open to translation because their enunciation resists totalization. (p. 314)

The subaltern voices of minority cultures constitute "those people who speak the encrypted discourse of the melancholic and the migrant" (p. 315). The transfer of their meaning can never be total. The "desolate silences of the wandering people" (p. 316) illustrate the incommensurability of translation, which confronts the discourse of White supremacist and capitalist patriarchy with its own alterity.

As translators, critical educators must assume a transformative role by "dialogizing the other" rather than trying to "represent the other" (Hitchcock, 1993). The site of translation is always an arena of struggle. The translation of other cultures must resist the authoritative representation of the other through a decentering process that challenges dialogues that have become institutionalized through the semantic authority of state power. Neither the practice of signification nor translation occurs in an ideological void, and for this reason educators need to interrogate the sign systems that are used to produce readings of experience. As Joan Scott (1992) notes, "experience is a subject's history. Language is the site of history's enactment" (p. 34). It is due to Freire's particular strength that he has developed a critical vernacular that can help to translate both the other's experience and his own experience of the other in such a way that ideological representations may be challenged. The challenge here is to rethink authorative representations of the other in a critical language that does not simply reauthorize the imperatives of First World translation practices. To do otherwise would open translation to a form of cultural imperialism. Experiences never speak for themselves, even those of the oppressed. Freire is careful to make sure his language of translation provides the oppressed with tools to analyze their own experiences, while at the same time recognizing that the translation process itself is never immune from inscription in ideological relations of power and privilege.

Although Freire's dialogue does not centrally address the politics of race, his message can, nonetheless, be elaborated through an engagement with the work of Black insurgent intellectuals. Cornel West blames what he perceives as a decline in Black literate intellectual activity on the "relatively greater Black integration into postindustrial capitalist America with its bureaucratized, elite universities, dull middlebrow colleges, and decaying high schools, which have little concern for and confidence in Black students as potential intellectuals" (hooks & West, 1991, p. 137). He is highly critical of "aspects of the exclusionary and repressive effects of White academic institutions and humanistic scholarship" (p. 137) and, in particular, "the rampant xenophobia of bourgeois humanism predominant in the whole academy" (p. 142). West sketches four models for Black intellectual activity as a means of enabling critical forms of Black literate activity in the United States. The bourgeois humanist model is premised on Black intellectuals possessing sufficient legitimacy and placement within the "hierarchial ranking and the deep-seated racism shot through bourgeois humanistic scholarship" (p. 138). Such legitimation and placement must, however, "result in Black control over a portion of, or significant participation within, the larger White infrastructures for intellectual activity" (p. 140).

The Marxist revolutionary model, according to West, is "the least xenophobic White intellectual subculture available to Black intellectuals" (p. 140). However, West is also highly critical of the constraints Marxist discourse places on the creative life of Black intellectuals in terms of constructing a project of possibility and hope, including an analytical apparatus to engage short-term public policies. According to West:

> The Marxist model yields Black-intellectual self satisfaction which often inhibits growth; also highlights social structural constraints with little practical direction regarding conjunctural opportunities. The self-satisfaction results in either dogmatic submission to and upward mobility with sectarian party or pre-party formations, or marginal placement in the bourgeois academy equipped with cantankerous Marxist rhetoric and sometimes insightful analysis utterly divorced from the integral dynamics, concrete realities, and progressive possibilities of the Black community. The preoccupation with social structural constraints tends to produce either preposterous chiliastic projections or paralyzing, pessimistic pronouncements. (hooks & West, 1991, p. 141)

It is important to point out amidst all this criticism that West does recognize the enabling aspects of the Marxist revolutionary model in its promotion of critical consciousness and its criticisms of dominant research programs within the bourgeois academy (however in my view he does not mine the possibilities of this model nearly enough).

The Foucaultian postmodern skeptic model invoked by West investigates the relationship among knowledge, power, discourse, politics, cognition, and social control. It offers a fundamental rethinking of the role of the intellectual within the contemporary postmodern condition. Foucault's "political economy of truth" is viewed by West as a critique of both bourgeois humanist and Marxist approaches through the role of Foucault's specific intellectual. The specific intellectual, according to West:

> shuns the labels of scientificity, civility, and prophecy, and instead delves into the specificity of the political, economic, and cultural matrices within which regimes of truth are pro- duced, distributed, circulated, and consumed. No longer should intellectuals deceive themselves by believing—as do humanist and Marxist intellectuals—that they are struggling "on behalf" of the truth; rather the problem is the struggle over the very status of truth and the vast institutional mechanism which account for this status. (hooks & West, 1991, p. 142)

West summarizes the Foucaultian model as an encouragement of "an intense and incessant interrogation of power-laden discourses" (p. 143). But the Foucaultian model is not a call to revolution. Rather, it is an invitation to revolt against the repressive effects of contemporary regimes of truth.

Selectively appropriating from these three models, West goes on to propose his own "insurgency model," which posits the Black intellectual as a critical, organic catalyst for social justice. His insur- gency model for Black intellectual life recovers the emphasis on human will and heroic effort from the bourgeois model; highlights the emphasis on structural constraints, class formations, and radi- cal democratic values from the Marxist model; and recuperates the worldly skepticism evidenced in the Foucaultian mode's destabiliza- tion of regimes of truth. However, unlike the bourgeois model, the insurgency model privileges collective intellectual work and commu- nal resistance and struggle. Contrary to the Marxist model, the insurgency model does not privilege the industrial working class as the chosen agent of history, but rather attacks a variety of forms of social hierarchy and subordination, both vertical and horizontal. Furthermore, the insurgency model places much more emphasis on social conflict and struggle than does the Foucaultian model. Although Freire's critique of domesticating forms of pedagogy pro- vides a specifically Latin American context for the development of the insurgent intellectual, West's own typology extends some central Freirean themes in order to deepen its engagement with issues of race.

bell hooks describes an intellectual as "somebody who trades in ideas by transgressing discursive frontiers . . . who trades in ideas in their vital bearing on a wider political culture" (hooks & West, 1991, p. 152). However, hooks argues that White supremacist capi- talist patriarchy has denied Black women, especially, "the opportunity to pursue a life of the mind." This is a problem that is also firmly entrenched in the racist White university system that involves "persecution by professors, peers, and professional colleagues" (p. 157). hooks rightly notes that "any discussion of intellectual work that does not underscore the conditions that make such work possible misrepresents the concrete circumstances that allow for intellectual production" (p. 158). She further elaborates:

> Within a White supremacist capitalist, patriarchal social context like this culture, no Black woman can become an intellectual without decolonizing her mind. Individual Black women may become successful academics without undergoing this process and, indeed, maintaining a colonized mind may enable them to excel in the academy but it does not enhance the intellectual process. The insurgency model that Cornel West advocates, appropriately identifies both the process Black females must engage to become intellectuals and the critical standpoints we must assume to sustain and nurture that choice. (p. 160)

I have employed criticisms of the academy by West, hooks, and Cohen because concerns dealing with postmodern social conditions and theory and those of race and gender help to widen Freire's criticisms by situating his insights more fully within the context and concerns of North American liberation struggles, specifically as they address struggles of the poor, women, and people of color. Of course, there is room to broaden the context even further in relation to the struggles of indigenous peoples, gays and lesbians, and other cultural workers within and outside of university settings. Freirean-based educators need to raise more questions related to race and gender so that these issues are given a more central focus in the struggle for social transformation. These include:

- In what ways have pedagogical practices been colonized by racialized discourses?
- What is the relationship between racial differentiation and subordination and dominant discourses about race and ethnicity? How are these relationships reproduced by White supremacist discursive regimes and communicative practices?
- Although the struggle for racial and gender equality is deemed worthwhile, those who struggle on behalf of this worthy goal are often deemed deviant when they step outside of the legitimating norms of what is considered to be the "common culture." How is race and gender inequality reproduced within liberal humanist discourses?
- If there is no necessary racial teleology within the educational practices of most U.S. schools, how does the

> reproduction of racist discourses occur in most school sites?

- How does the hypervisibility of White cultures actually hide their obviousness in relations of domination and oppression?
- How does race constitute a boundary constraint on what is considered normal and appropriate behavior?
- In what ways are the conditions within the dominant culture for being treated justly and humanely predicted on utilitarian forms of rationality and the values inscribed and legitimated by bourgeois, working-class, and elite forms of White culture? How do these forms of rationality work within the episterne of a larger discourse of colonialism?

Despite these absent discourses, Freire's work remains vitally important in the current debates over the role of universities, public schools, and educational sites of all kinds throughout North America. Freire warns educators that the activity of reading the world in relation to the social world has been regrettably pragmatic rather than principled. In other words, schooling (in relation to both universities and public schools) revolves around the necessity of differentially reproducing a citizenry distinguished by class, race, and gender injustices. The challenges of educators in both First and Third World contexts is to transform these reproductive processes. I will try to nuance this idea in what follows. Freirean pedagogy is set firmly against what Kristin Ross (1993) calls "the integral 'pedagogicizing' of society," by which she refers to the "general infantilization" of individuals or groups through the discourses and social practices of "the nineteenth-century European myth of progress" (p. 669).

Ross conceives of critical pedagogy through what she refers to as the "antidisciplinary practice" of cultural studies. Drawing on the revisionist theories of allegory of Walter Benjamin, Paul de Man, and others, Ross moves away from the essentialist conceptions of cultural identity informed by a symbolic (mimetic and synechdochical) model of experience and representation in which one part timelessly and ahistorically reflects the whole. According to this model, the plight of White women in New York reflects the plight of Black women in the Southern United States. Rather than viewing this relationship as an unmediated one in which the plight of Black women constitutes an authentic reflection of the plight of White women, Ross prefers to see this and similar relationships as allegorical rather than mimetic. According to Ross,

> Allegory preserves the differences of each historically situated and embedded experience, all the while drawing a relationship between those experiences. In other words, one experience is read in terms of another but not necessarily in terms of establishing identity, not obliterating the qualities particular to each. (p. 672)

Because it is impossible to represent every cultural group in the curriculum, the task of critical pedagogy, in Ross', terms, is to construct cultural identity *allegorically*—for each group to see his or her cultural narrative in a broader and comparative relation to others and within a larger narrative of social transformation.

For students to recognize the historical and cultural specificity of their own lived experiences allegorically—that is, in allegorical relations to other narratives—is especially urgent, especially, as Ross puts it:

> at a time of growing global homogenization [in which] the non-west is conceived in two, equally reductive ways: one whereby differences are reified and one whereby differences are lost. In the first, the non-West is assigned the role for the repository for some more genuine or organic lived experience; minority cultures and non-Western cultures in the West are increasingly made to provide something like an authenticity rush for blase or jaded Westerners, and this is too heavy a burden for anyone to bear. In the second, non-Western experiences are recorded and judged according to how closely they converge on the same: a single public culture or global average, that is, how far each has progressed toward a putative goal of modernization. (p. 673)

An emancipatory curriculum cannot present First and Third World cultures in the context of binary oppositions as relations of domination and resistance as this move usually permits the First World perspective to prevail as the privileged point of normative civilizations (Ross, 1993). Although Freire's work calls attention to the danger of a reductive dichotomization of First and Third World cultures, his interpreters often attempt simply to transplant Freire's perspective into First World contexts as a fortuitous equivalence or natural counterpart to subaltern resistance without recoding Freire's arguments sufficiently in terms of First World contexts. This leads to an unwitting embrace of pedagogy as a Western "civilizing" practice. And as we have learned from recent NATO alliance bombing raids in Iraq and Yugoslavia, the West often civilizes alien groups by killing them.

As a teacher, Freire has provided the pedagogical conditions necessary to understand that Enlightenment humanism and its specifically Eurocentric (and Euro-American) "voice of reason" has not always been insightful or even reasonable in exercising its transcontinental thinking in the service of truth and justice. Freire's work helps further confront this issue as well as many others of concern to educators and cultural workers.

The perspectives of Freire can help deepen the debate over the role of the university in contemporary North American culture and, by extension, can also help situate the struggle of Latin American educators within the concerns of postmodern and insurgent criticisms of the academy as exemplified by the perspectives of West, hooks, and Cohen.

In a world of global capitalism we need global alliances through cultural and political contact in the form of critical dialogue. Samir Amin (1989) notes that we collectively face a problem that "resides in the objective necessity for a reform of the world system; failing this, the only way out is through the worst barbarity, the genocide of entire peoples or a worldwide conflagration" (p. 114).

In attempting to develop a project premised on the construction of an emancipatory cultural imaginary that is directed at transforming the conditions that create the victims of capitalist expansion, educators need to go beyond simply severing their arterial connections to the forces of production and consumption that defraud them through the massification of their subjectivities. Rather, they need to create new alliances through a politics of difference and political transformation. Otherwise, they face the prospect of becoming extensions of multinational corporations within the larger apparatus of capitalist expansion in the service of unequal accumulation and further underdevelopment in the peripheral and semi-peripheral countries of Latin America. In short, what is needed to accompany resistance to and transformation of capitalist relations of exploitation is a politics of radical hope. Hope needs to be conjugated with some aspect of the carnal, tangible world of historical and material relations in order to be made a referent point for a critically transformative praxis.

While postmodernist readings of Freire can help to deepen Freire's approach to questions of subjectivity and identity, it is important to prevent Freire's work from being domesticated by the voguish apostasy and fashionable insurgency that characterizes much of the field of postmodern criticism. Whereas postmodernists legitimate their politics on the basis of "experience," Freire links such "experience" to an object economic analysis and historical materialist view of consciousness that does not divorce the "subject" from the social and material relations in which he or she is embedded. Freirean pedagogy stipulates as its aim the transformation of the means of production into the means of emancipation. While, postmodern criticism can often tragically expose the illusion of democracy and the ruse of capitalist progress, in the end such *faux* radicalism is functionally advantageous to ruling class interests and biased in favor of capitalist stability (i.e., through reactivating existing power relations). For Freire, social relations are always historical—materialist relations arising from the specific conditions under which surplus labor is extracted from the direct producers. Freirean pedagogy points beyond harmonizing the social order fractured by capital's internal contradictions or serving as an apologia for social stability. It is fundamentally agonistic.

Freirean pedagogy argues that pedagogical sites, whether they are universities, public schools, museums, art galleries, or other spaces, must have a vision that is not content with adapting individuals to a world of oppressive social relations but is dedicated to transforming the very conditions that promote such relations. This means more than simply reconfiguring or collectively refashioning subjectivities outside of the compulsive ethics and consumerist ethos of flexible specialization or the homogenizing calculus of capitalist expansion. It means creating new forms of sociality, new idioms of transgression, and new instances of popular mobilization that can connect the institutional memory of the academy to the tendential forces of historical struggle and the dreams of liberation that one day might be possible to guide them. This is a mission that is not simply Freirean but immanently human.

Rather than ground his pedagogy in a doctrinal absolutism, Freire's attention is always fixed on both the specific and generalized other. Categories of identity, when confronted by Freire's practice of conscientization, are vacated of their pretended access to certainty and truth. What has endeared several generations of critical educators to Freire, both in terms of a respect for his political vision and for the way he conducts his own life, is the manner in which he has situated his work within an ethics of compassion, love and solidarity.

To disentangle hope from the vagaries of everyday life, to disconnect human capacity from the structures of domination and then to reconnect them to a project in which power works as a form of affirmation and a practice of freedom is, these days, to invite more cynical critics to view Freire's work as a nostalgic interlude in a world whose modernist dream of revolutionary alterity has been superseded by the massifying logic of capitalist accumulation and alienation. Yet Freire's work cannot be so easily dismissed as an anachronistic project that has failed to notice history's wake-up call from recent postmodernist critiques. Many, but not all, these critiques have relegated human agency to the dustbin of history, along with modernist projects of emancipation including those, like Freire's, that continue to be informed by socialist and humanistic ideals. To argue in this climate of the simulacrum, as does Freire, that freedom can be both true and real is to instantly arouse skepticism and in some quarters to provoke derision.

For both the oppressed and nonoppressed alike, Freire's life and work have served as a life-affirming bridge from private despair to collective hopefulness to self- and social transformation. Insofar as he addresses individuals as more than the capricious outcomes of historical accident, or exceeding the abstract boundaries of metaphysical design, Freire's work presupposes a subject of history and points towards a time when a transcendence (Aufhebung) of class struggle is finally accomplished in the forging of socialist democracy.

At a time in U.S. culture in which history has been effectively expelled from the formation of meaning and hope has been quarantined in the frenetic expansion of capital into regions of public and private life hitherto unimaginable and unthinkable, Freire's pedagogy of liberation is one we dismiss at our peril.

REFERENCES

Amin, S. (1989). *Eurocentrism.* New York: Monthly Review Press.

Attali, J. (1991). *Millennium.* New York: Random House.

Berlin, J. (1993). Literacy, pedagogy, and English studies: Postmodern connections. In C. Lankshear & P. McLaren (Eds.), *Critical literacy: Politics, praxis, and the postmodern* (pp. 247-270). Albany: State University of New York Press.

Bhabha, H. K. (1990). *Nation and narration.* London and New York: Routledge.

Cohen, S. (1993). *Academia and the luster of capital.* Minneapolis: University of Minnesota Press.

Desai, G. (1993). The invention of invention. *Cultural Critique, 24,* 119-142.

Freire, P. (1970a). *Cultural action for freedom.* Harmondsworth: Penguin.

Freire, P. (1970b). *Pedagogy of the oppressed.* New York: Continuum.

Freire, P. (1978). *Pedagogy in process: The letters to Guinea-Gissau.* New York: Seabury Press.

Freire, P., with Escobar, M., Fernández, A. L., & Guevara-Niebla, G. (1994). *Paulo Freire on higher education: A dialogue at the National University of Mexico.* Albany: State University of New York Press.

Gee, J. (1993). Postmodernism and literacies. In C. Lankshear & P. McLaren (Eds.), *Critical literacy: Politics, praxis, and the postmodern* (pp. 271-296). Albany: State University of New York Press.

Giroux, H. (1993). *Border crossings.* New York: Routledge.

Hirsch, E. D., Jr. (1987). *Cultural literacy: What every American needs to know.* Boston: Houghton Mifflin.

Hitchcock, P. (1993). *Dialogics of the oppressed.* Minneapolis: University of Minnesota Press.

hooks, b., & West, C. (1991). *Breaking bread: Insurgent black intellectual life.* Boston: South End Press.

Kincheloe, J., & McLaren, P. (1994). Rethinking critical theory and qualitative research. In N. K. Denzin & Y. S. Lincoln (Eds.), *Handbook of qualitative research* (pp. 138-157). Newbury Park, CA: Sage.

Lefebvre, H. (1975). *Metaphilosophie.* Frankfort: Suhrkamp.

Martin-Barbero, J. (1992). *Communication, culture, and hegemony: From media to mediation.* London: Sage.

McLaren, P. (1992). Collisions with otherness: Multiculturalism, the politics of difference, and the enthographer as nomad. *The American Journal of Semiotics, 9*(2-3), 121-148.

McLaren, P. (1995). *Critical pedagogy and predatory culture.* London and New York: Routledge.

McLaren, P. (1997). *Revolutionary multiculturalism.* Boulder, CO: Westview Press.

McLaren, P. (in press). *Che Guevara and Paulo Freire: An introduction to the pedagogy of revolution.* Boulder, CO: Rowman and Littlefield.

McLaren, P., & Lankshear, C. (Eds.). (1994). *Politics of liberation: Paths from Freire.* London and New York: Routledge.

McLaren, P., & Leonard, P. (Eds.). (1993). *Paulo Freire: A critical encounter.* London and New York: Routledge.

Merod, J. (1987). *The political responsibility of the critic.* Ithaca, NY: Cornell University Press.

Miyoshi, M. (1993). A borderless world? From colonialism to transnationalism and the decline of the nation-state. *Critical Inquiry, 19,* 726-751.

Olssen, M. (1996). In defense of the welfare state and publicly provided education. *Journal of Educational Policy, 11,* 337-362.

Parry, B. (1993). A critique mishandled. *Social Text, 35,* 121-133.

Ross, A. (1989). *No respect: Intellectuals and popular culture.* New York and London: Routledge.

Ross, K. (1993). The world literature and cultural studies program. *Critical Inquiry, 19,* 666-676.

Scott, J. W. (1992). Experience. In J. Butler & J. W. Scott (Eds.), *Feminists theorize the political* (pp. 22-40). New York and London: Routledge.

Chapter ▪ 9

Discourses of Discipline in South Africa: Rethinking Critical Pedagogies in Postmodernity*

Roger Deacon

INTRODUCTION

The fields of video production, rural development, history writing, and education in South Africa have long been dominated by stale orthodoxies in South Africa underpinned by conservative political and commercial interests. However, since at least the 1970s in some cases, and increasingly during the 1980s, these fields have become battlegrounds on which a multiplicity of new critical discourses have asserted themselves in support of alternative pedagogical and cultural visions and interventions. Although this proliferation of discourses was not for the most part deliberately orchestrated, their emergence and consolidation was in each case conditioned by apartheid and the struggles against it. More specifically, alternative discourses have explicitly defined themselves in opposition to what they criticize as the authoritarianism and instrumentalism of orthodoxies, against which they advocate and implement more democratic and participatory means and ends. Five such discourses are examined in the first

*My appreciation to Costas Criticos, Dienie Nel, Ben Parker, and Jane Skinner for comments on a earlier version of this chapter which appeared in *Discourse and Studies in the Cultural Politics of Education*, 17(2), 227-242, August 1996.

section of this chapter, contrasted with their respective orthodoxies, and with particular attention being paid to educational alternatives: social history, community video, sustainable rural development, People's Education, and critical pedagogy. Implicit in this examination is a critique of some of their specific modernist effects and limitations. The second section makes the form and basis of the critique more explicit, on the basis of a reconceptualization of discourse in terms of the concepts of power, knowledge, and the figure framed between them: the modern subject. The focus then returns to the five discourses, now identified as historically specific regimes of power-knowledge, and the disciplinary effects of their rationalist procedures, which, it is argued, vitiate their democratic and participatory ideals. The fourth section analyzes the subjection of intellectuals within and in relation to these modernist discourses of discipline. Finally, an attempt is made to draw out the import of the preceding analyses and critiques, arguing in particular that our implication in modern relations of power and knowledge must be acknowledged and strategically exploited in multidimensional and mutable ways.

CHALLENGES TO ORTHODOXIES IN SOUTH AFRICA

Criticisms directed at the orthodox approaches from the side of alternative discourses have always been strongly principled and often quite sophisticated and self-reflective, although in no field has an existing orthodoxy been entirely supplanted. In film and television production, standard documentary approaches and Americanized soap operas reflecting the near monopoly of the state-aligned South African Broadcasting Corporation far outweigh committed political, humanist or participatory productions, whereas the purview of the "alternative press" is insignificant in relation to the business-aligned and -owned mainstream. In pedagogy, the orthodox "educational science" of Fundamental Pedagogics prevails in White Afrikaans-speaking and historically Black universities and teacher-training institutions, as well as in the school system itself, and thus far has been nearly impervious to an eight-year-old People's Education movement and various critical pedagogies. Afrikaner nationalist historiographical orthodoxy as well as its 1960s liberal and 1970s structuralist Marxist critics were only partially displaced by and co-exist alongside the social history of the 1980s. Finally, despite the manifest failure of official "betterment" schemes and the recent exposure of corruption in numerous government departments, including that of development aid, alternative rural development projects remain localized and have yet to shrug off their Cinderella status.

In each of the fields just mentioned, the orthodox discourses are underpinned by broadly similar assumptions. The subject that communicates (a person, a symbol, or a text) is constituted as the active, authoritative catalyst of the process of instrumentally transmitting information. The recipients (an audience, learners, those under research or surveillance or being targeted for development) are constituted relationally as passive and reified as objects; their role is to submit to certain prescribed norms. The knowledge or techniques being transmitted, as well as the communicative mechanisms, are treated unproblematically as neutral and effective: their legitimacy or truth claims are unquestionable and require little reflection and no critique. Social inequalities are considered to be natural and even desirable, and priority is given to order, stability, and the preservation of tradition. In reality this translates into autocratic and often technicist directives, the uncritical dissemination and consumption of information preselected by experts, social engineering in the "general interest," the provision of few, if any, alternatives, and strict discipline. On the basis of various presumptions about the deficiences, inadequacies, and subordinate status of the target audience, they are treated as having neither the capacity nor the right to speak for themselves. Strong pressures impel agents to orthodoxy and away from alternatives: under repressive circumstances, with limited resources, and in contexts in which either the medium of communication is a foreign language or agent and target speak different languages, orthodoxy offers at least a coherent survival strategy if not a sense of security and, by constituting recipients as passive and dependent subjects, prevents the exposure of agents' inadequacies.

As is often the case when conventional wisdoms are challenged, alternative discourses initially emphasize their distance and difference from the orthodox, but tend to become more tolerant to the extent to which their tenets become more widely accepted. Although it can be said that the five alternative discourses to be examined here collectively contribute to the conventional wisdoms of the Left in South Africa, the only one of these discourses to have entered the main-stream itself is social history (Saunders, 1991); community video projects, sustainable rural development schemes, and critical pedagogies have seldom been recognized outside of the academies and the terrain of nongovernmental organizations. The People's Education movement, subjected to years of severe repression, has the smallest institutional base and takes up the most confrontational stance. The concept of People's Education was the product of the National Educational Crisis Committee (NECC), formed by parents, teachers, and activists during the turmoil of the 1984–86 uprising. Amidst fears that widespread student-led boycotts of schools threatened to undermine not only the legitimacy and authority of the state but also that of the family, the liberation movements, and education itself, the NECC advocated a strategy of taking–over and using the schools as bases for counterhegemonic organization and alternative instruction.

People's Education was thus conceived from the outset as both a strategic weapon and a vision of the future (Kruss, 1988). In common with other oppositional discourses, it sought to enlighten specific populations, in this case, students, teachers, parents, and workers, about the structures of oppression and exploitation and about the wider context of the struggle and to prepare them for orga-

nized, collective, active, and critical participation in a future nonra-
cial democracy (Mashamba, 1990; Mkatshwa, 1986). However,
repression, coupled with a lack of resources, alternative materials,
trained teachers, and a significant institutional base, has meant that
despite the establishment of research-oriented Education Projects
Units at some universities, and the formation of national youth, students', and teachers' organizations and Parents-Teachers-Students
Associations, its efforts to date have either been frustrated or outmoded by the rapid turn of events since the South African government and the liberation movements began negotiating a way out of
the political and strategic impasse. Nevertheless, the discourse of
People's Education added important if indirect weight to a growing
tendency within progressive educational circles and emerging critical
pedagogies, in particular, to significantly rethink education.

     In contrast to orthodoxy, People's Education can be described
as a vanguard discourse in that it seeks not to reproduce but to challenge and transform the status quo along the lines of a specific vision
of the future. Like orthodoxy, a vanguard discourse constitutes the
intellectual (whether researcher, producer, developer, or teacher) as
the legitimate purveyor of knowledge and enforcer of rules. But unlike
orthodoxy, it allows its target group a degree of autonomy, partly
because it favors the leveling of political and economic hierarchies in
society, and partly because knowledge is not assured but requires
scientific validation. Authority is premised either on the intellectual's
alleged access to science or objective truth or on common ideological
interests. Both forms of justification invest those authorized as the
vanguard with the right to speak for and on behalf of those being
taught, researched, or developed, either because of their common
interests or because the latter are perceived as lacking a sufficient
degree of political awareness. Nevertheless, the fact that knowledge
and authority are problematized, even if only slightly or in a positivist
manner, encourages reflection and active discussion, thus creating a
(circumscribed) space for hitherto silenced voices, and reconstituting
the target group as potential agents (whose tasks, however, are
defined in advance). It is this space for critique and agency that is
progressively expanded, up to a certain point, by the more reflective
discourses of social history, community video, sustainable rural
development, and critical pedagogy.

     Social history seeks to recover "the lives of ordinary people"
by writing "history from below" and recreating the experiential self-
generation or "making" of the subordinate classes of society.
Sympathetic to earlier attempts by local Africanists to bring to light
the submerged histories of diverse Southern African societies before
their conquest and subjugation by imperialism and colonization,
social history defined itself in opposition to the structuralist,
Poulantzas-influenced Marxist historiography of the 1970s. Its dominance in South African studies has been increasingly institutionalized since 1978, through successive history workshops modeled on
British social history. It has been at the forefront of attempts to
democratize the history profession by emphasizing community

involvement and the importance of oral evidence and by popularizing its work in the quasi-vanguardist form of "people's history," which aims to provide "an intellectually challenging revision of the common past of *all* South Africans, regardless of their present-day affiliations" (Bozzoli, 1987, p. xvii; emphasis in original; see also Deacon, 1991a).

Recent community video projects in South Africa display similar concerns, although they dispense with vanguardism (Criticos & Quinlan, 1991; Deacon, 1992). Instead, they emphasize participatory democracy, the social construction of knowledge, and critical reflection on practice. For these projects, the relationship between producer-cum-researcher and community must be conceptualized as a mutually enriching, nonhierarchical experience, a "dialogic relationship . . . in which learning is a collaborative task" or "a process in which both anthropologist and subject mutually construct shared meaning about various aspects of the society inhabited by the latter" (Criticos & Quinlan, 1991, pp. 50-51). Critical reflection on one's practices, in order "to see beneath the external layers of reality," is aimed at realizing a "critical consciousness" among participants and revealing "opportunities for constructive community and individual intervention in that world" (pp. 50-51).

In the field of rural development, alternative discourses also emphasize that the "basic needs" of communities themselves must be taken into account, not ignored or overridden by an impersonal development "plan," and that only through negotiation and direct community representation and participation in and control over the development process could developers succeed in attaining their ideals of empowerment: "Rural people need to be empowered to decide for themselves what their development priorities will be and how they will be achieved" (Tapson, 1990, p. 565); they must be allowed "to become the subject, not the object, of development strategies" (Taylor, 1992, p. 257). Grassroots control in turn requires the implementation of literacy programs and community training in the technological, organizational, and administrative skills necessary to reproduce their livelihood and overcome dependence. A common focus in rural development discourses are work-study programs and what is called "education for production," in which communities can benefit both materially and politically in terms of diversifying their income, developing skills that can be locally practiced, and being made aware of opportunities within the wider context (Nasson, 1990). Aside from a handful of parastatals that tend to lack legitimacy, nongovernmental organizations provide most of the institutional bases for rural development, and in South Africa local and international funding for such projects is rapidly drying up. If rural development "is a question of sustaining development through local self-management" (Spivak, 1992, p. 26), and if possible replicating it, then not only have its successes been limited but, more ominously, the discourse of sustainable development is itself being echoed by institutions as orthodox as the World Bank (Mackenzie, 1992).

Critical pedagogy (also referred to as action or participatory research) has been confined to the historically "White liberal" universities and the projects of a myriad nongovernmental organizations, and its impact on educational practices in South Africa has been negligible. Yet its institutional location coupled with its affinities to the ideals of People's Education make it extremely influential at the policy-making level, at which it constitutes the unspoken consensus underlying the recently completed two-year ANC-initiated National Education Policy Investigation (NEPI, 1993). Like community video and sustainable rural development, critical pedagogy is acutely aware of the different identities of, and asymmetries of power between, teacher (and/or text) and learner. As a consequence it shys away from the instrumentalism perceived to inhere in the orthodox and vanguard approaches and seeks instead to attain its ends by building them into its classroom and teaching practices. Knowledge is no longer conceptualized as guaranteed or scientific but as mutually and democratically constructed, and learner self-understandings are deemed to be as important as teacher knowledge. The expansion in the realm of students' voice, reflection, agency, and control over the process is taken as mitigating teacher–learner inequalities and as empowering learners to speak and act for themselves, either directly or indirectly through the medium of the teacher. The relationship between teacher and learner is thus reconceptualized as an egalitarian, reflective, and empowering collaboration. In South Africa, however, the implementation of critical pedagogy has been largely impeded by the predominance of the orthodox approach, peer pressure, inexperience, fear of change, deprived material conditions and lack of resources, time and syllabus constraints, student expectations, and the lack of recognition or reward.

THE MARKS OF MODERNITY

The similarities between each of the alternative discourses previously discussed, as well as the differences between orthodox and alternative discourses, are readily apparent. The manner in which a vanguardist alternative like People's Education aims to attain the democratic ideals professed by the alternative discourses through the instrumentalism associated with orthodoxy has also been noted. What is less often remarked on are the fundamental assumptions that underpin *both* the orthodox *and* the alternative discourses, or the ways in which each and every one of these discourses bears the characteristic marks of modernity. The Enlightenment bequeathed to modernity a faith in the power of knowledge or the capacity of reason to illuminate, transform, and improve nature and society. In obedience to this faith, each of the discourses referred to earlier centers itself around rational-speaking subjects in the process of searching for truth, representing and intervening in the world, and lacking or possessing power in relation to a fixed and essential reality. In the first place, *the subject* is conceived of as self-present (conscious and hence identifiable), coherent (hence unified and discrete) and autonomous; second, *knowledge* is conceptualized as reason directed at discovering the truth inherent in reality by representing it to consciousness via the referential medium of language; finally, *power* is treated as negative, homogeneous, and centralized, something external to and tending to distort knowledge, the intentional product of a sovereign subject who possesses and exercises it in a top-down and repressive fashion over (relatively) powerless others.

The subject is the usually unacknowledged but always presumed hinge that links the will to power with the will to truth, the transformation of nature and society with the quest for knowledge. The myriad dichotomies that have infested philosophy since its beginnings, and that the Enlightenment provided with an historical gloss and centered around the rationalist and humanist concept of "Man," manufacture our understanding of ourselves and our societies by according value to and hierarchically ordering and effectively empowering social relations through specific reference to a mythical ideal subject: the modern, Western, urban, middle-class, educated White male, heterosexual individual (Deacon & Parker 1993). No less powerful for being mythical, the subject is the condition for and manifestation of the modern obsession with truth and power, knowledge and transformation. This section attempts to reconceptualize and set out in greater detail the connections between the subject, knowledge, and power, in order to provide a theoretical backdrop to an analysis, first, of the specific modernist effects of alternative discourses in South Africa, and second, of the proselytizing role of intellectuals in relation to these discourses.

The "power of human reason," which in its capacity to illuminate the true nature of the world permits its possessors to fashion a better society, is one way of summing up the linkages among modern subjects, forms of knowledge, and relations of power. Derrida (1983), in a dense paragraph that invites closer examination, offers a different summation:

> The modern dominance of the principle of reason had to go hand in hand with the interpretation of the essense of beings as objects, an object present as representation [*Vorstellung*], an object placed and positioned *before* a subject. This latter, a man who says "I," an ago certain of itself, thus ensures his own technical mastery over the totality of what is. The "re-" of *repraesentatio* also expresses the movement that accounts for—"renders reason to"—a thing whose presence is *encountered* by *rendering* it present, by bringing it to the subject of representation, to the knowing self. (pp. 9-10; emphases in original)

Rational, objective analysis of reality is inseparable from the interpretation of beings as objects, which objectifies or reifies some beings in relation to others. In interpreting beings as objects, reason (re)presents them fourfold—as *objects* in relation to a subject, as objects represented or *portrayed*, as objects represented or *spoken for*, and as objects *placed and positioned* before a subject. The objects of reason are accounted for (made known) and encountered (as if discovered) by literally rendering them present, constituting them in a form available for analysis and mastery. The subject of reason and representation, the knowing self, is invested with the power to position or represent another, to render it present in order to know and master it, or to master reality. The dominance of reason is thus bound up with a process in which beings are both objectified and subjected, both produced as objects of knowledge to be mastered and as subjects who reify and master. In this process of interpreting beings as objects, however, the being that interprets, represents, knows, and masters—the rational, self-present, and autonomous "being-before"—is so taken for granted as to be rendered invisible (and hence itself not available for interpretation): "The principle of reason installs its empire only to the extent that the abyssal question of the being that is hiding within it remains hidden, and with it the question of the grounding of the ground itself" (Derrida, 1983, p. 10).

In these terms, the "power of human reason" subscribed to by modernist discourses could be more fruitfully described as sets of interlocking grids of knowledge and power relations, at the interstices of which are constituted beings that are both—and simultaneously—the targets of discourses (their objects) and the vehicles of discourses (their subjects). The modern subject, on which reason grounds itself, and which the process of objectifying others conceals, is thus exposed as an unstable, potentially contradictory, and multiple (but equally objective) effect of discourses.

Subjects are thus artifacts, constituted as objects, embodied, inscribed or "in-formed" by knowledge and relations of power: "Information does not inform merely by delivering an information content, it gives form. . . . It installs man in a form that permits him to ensure his mastery on earth and beyond" (Derrida, 1983, p. 14).

The constitution of the subject, "the entire process of subjectivation, of assuming different subject-positions" (Zizek, 1990, p. 253), always takes place intersubjectively, through and in relation to others (including one's self), who may either be objects for oneself or subjects for whom one is an object. As Hegel (1977) pointed out in his discussion of the dialectic between Lord and Bondsman, "self-consciousness . . . exists only in being acknowledged" (p. 111). One's "intuitive" sense of oneself as a self-present, coherent, and autonomous agent paradoxically depends on being recognized as such by another (Mahoney & Yngvesson, 1992). Subjects thus constitute themselves in relation to others, in the dual sense of being "subject to someone else by control and dependence, and tied to his own identity by a conscience or self-knowledge" (Foucault, 1982, p. 212; see also Althusser 1971; Foucault, 1977).

It follows that discourses, which constitute subjects, are neither simply "theories" nor "practices," but more accurately produce the very dichotomy between "theory" and "practice," as well as that between "thought" and "reality." Neither of these dichotomies has any meaning outside of specific discourses, and neither does that between truth and power, another effective myth that tends to occult all that is positive, internal, dispersed, heterogeneous, productive, and provocative about power (and all that is constraining about truth). The relations of power that operate through discourses are not simply "harmful" (repressive) but are also "helpful" (producing truth and normalizing subjects): "We are subjected to the production of truth through power and we cannot exercise power except through the production of truth" (Foucault, 1986, pp. 229-230).

Hence, discourses are not means by which we decipher the world but forms of subjection, the "power to constitute domains of objects" (Foucault, 1984, p. 133); they are mechanisms by which an order or a meaning is violently imposed on things (Foucault, 1984; Heidegger, 1969; Laclau & Mouffe, 1985). To study discourses is also to study ourselves, for constituted as different kinds of subjects, we participate in the production, operation, and dissemination of discourses.

DISCOURSES OF DISCIPLINE

Discourses in South Africa, whether orthodox or alternative, can be analyzed as historically specific and mutating regimes of "power-knowledge" (Foucault, 1979, pp. 27-28) or "discourses of discipline," which through local or global networks of more or less institutionalized power relations, relays of communication and forms of knowledge differentially embody, discipline, and effect innovative or habitual (re)inscriptions of subjects. No less than their authoritarian orthodox counterparts, alternative discourses determine who has the right or the authority to speak or act, what must, may, and may not be said or done, when and where and to whom, and which rituals are prescribed as well as their supposed effects, legitimate responses, and limitations. On this basis subjects (as objects) are constituted, distinguished, and unequally empowered, bound together or segregated and excluded. Modernity is indelibly stamped on the attempts by alternative discourses in South Africa to liberate others or to represent them in a responsible and accountable fashion. It is ingrained in their commitment to various rationalist procedures and especially evident in their criteria and processes of evaluation. It is latent in the way in which they conceive of others, whether as groups or individuals, and in their understanding of the relationship between themselves and others. Finally, it is implicit in their (ironically often uncritical) reflections on themselves.

The escalating struggles against apartheid over the past two decades crystallized into various new discourses that represented themselves as a response to and a catalyst of the demands, needs, and struggles of diverse subjects, from students, teachers, and parents to workers, women, rural and urban communities, and subordinate groupings in general. Often displacing (but mostly unable to replace) the orthodox positions in their respective fields, and also tending to displace and modify each other, they attempted to emancipate oppressed and marginalized groups from the totalitarianism of orthodox discourses by revaluing oral evidence, subjective experience, popular knowledge, and the self-understandings of local communities or individual learners. In this context two overlapping discursive trends emerged. Community video and sustainable rural development projects subscribed in part to what Bourdieu and Passeron (1990, p. 24) call a "'culture for the masses' programme of 'liberating' the dominated classes by giving them the means of appropriating legitimate culture as such; empowering a community through literacy programs, or involvement and direct training in video production techniques" (Deacon, 1992, p. 42). In addition, most alternative discourses favored "the populist project of decreeing the legitimacy of the cultural arbitrary of the dominated classes as constituted in and by the fact of its dominated position, canonizing it as 'popular culture'" (Bourdieu & Passeron, 1990, p. 24). People's Education and critical pedagogy affirmed both that the masses must be provided with the means to emancipate themselves, and that mass culture or learners' beliefs must be built into the educational process, although the former lays stress on the first and the latter on the second.

However, in many cases these subjugated discourses were, perhaps unavoidably, "no sooner brought to light, accredited and put into circulation, than they were re-codified and re-colonized" (Foucault, 1987b, p. 206). The oral traditions of diverse groups, written down and canonized as "people's history," have become a thriving academic trade, in the same way that the conceptual development of People's Education has been monopolized. The landscape has been colonized by development projects of all sorts. More generally, the alternatives that promised empowerment or emancipation were often themselves variants of other orthodoxies such as Marxism, thus simultaneously imposing new constraints and carrying out more surreptitious functions. For example, the formation of the National Education Crisis Committee and the discourse of People's Education also signified a renewed attempt by certain forces of discipline—parents, teachers, leaders, and adults in general—to reestablish their authority over the youthful "shock troops of the revolution." The attempt, which contributed to the demobilization of the youth but was unable to enlist them in any more disciplined crusade, coincided with wider efforts to stem a strong anti-intellectual mood that swept the liberation struggle in the mid-1980s. Even intellectuals with close affinities with liberation organizations were forced to close ranks and to reconstitute themselves, their work, and their relationship with the rest of society. Only if intellectuals "come to see themselves as ordinary people with definable interests," it was argued, "will community folk come to see them and their precious university as a useful resource for struggle and social progress" (Muller & Cloete, 1986, p. 23).

By reconstituting intellectuals as "ordinary people" and by displaying impeccable democratic credentials, the "power of human reason" (manifest in all modernist discourses) seeks to conceal what orthodoxy asserts so boldly: the privileged positioning of the intellectual, whether alternative or orthodox, in relation to power and knowledge. The inequalities in the relationship between teachers, researchers, or developers, on the one hand, and those being taught, researched or developed, on the other, which are usually ignored by a vanguard alternative discourse such as People's Education (and then justified in scientific or normative terms if challenged), are claimed to have been transcended by the other alternative discourses. Critical pedagogy is a case in point: By emphasizing the identification and equal consideration of all viewpoints and the mutual construction of knowledge, it sets in motion discursive mechanisms that regulate conflict and the power to speak, constitute participants as equal subjects (in the process concealing real inequalities between learners and between learners and teachers), and obliges them to speak under the disciplinary gaze of reason (Ellsworth, 1989; Spivak, 1992). More generally, alternative discourses (People's Education excepted) cannot overcome the contradiction between their aversion to technocratic manipulation and their impulse to intervene strategically on behalf of the oppressed (Touraine, 1988), or the paradox inherent in some subjects "making" others autonomous without directing them (Ellsworth, 1989). In Freirean pedagogy, teachers and learners are "together, but not equal," and it is left up to teachers to determine whether the pedagogical relationship will be democratic or authoritarian (Freire & Shor, 1987), or what measures they might take to earn their supposed status of "first among equals" from learners (Alexander, 1989).

The effect of these mechanisms that authorize the intellectual as the ultimate guardian of truth is to problematize all invocations of democratic and participatory procedures and decision making. In the event of an altercation between "people's history" and its object, for example, the ultimate arbiter is not the people but history as defined by intellectuals. As a prominent intellectual spokesperson for the History Workshops put it, "people's history" explicitly entertains a "universalist ambition" that does not fit into the interpretive straitjackets demanded by specific political movements (Bozzoli, 1987, p. xvii), and is thus in itself a potential barrier to its own endeavours to empower the dispossessed. In one of the community video projects, despite painstaking efforts to intimately involve all concerned in decision making, it was the researchers who pieced the oral testimonies together into a continuous narrative, filled in historical gaps, and even deviated from the community-approved and -refined "final" version of the script, if only in apparently innocuous and minor ways (Criticos & Quinlan, 1991). Similarly, pressures of time and inadequate grassroots organization dictated that the principles guiding the National Education Policy Investigation, originally meant to be democratically generated through an Education Charter campaign that would broadly and vigorously canvass the educational demands of "the people," were ratified only by the academics and activists involved (Parker 1993; Taylor, 1991).

That alternative discourses differentially and unequally constitute or inform the subjects who are to be their targets (a community, learners, the people, in short, others), under the guise of equally distributing, or relinquishing any special claim to, power and knowledge, was an explicit finding by the community video projects referred to here. After discovering that the communities in question could be rendered "fit" for analysis and participation in the projects only through an initial "education" or groundwork, Criticos and Quinlan (1991) concluded that "our projects have created community rather than begun with identifiable communities" (pp. 52-53). The other is not inert and "out there," passively awaiting the discovery of its essential nature; rather, as noted earlier, it is "*encountered* by *rendering* it present" (Derrida, 1983 pp. 9-10; emphasis in original). What we know of the other, what truth we produce in knowing the other (by extorting truth or provoking action), is conditional on the forms in and relations of power and knowledge through which we constitute it, and actually reveals more of ourselves than of the other (Bauman, 1987). "The subaltern cannot speak" (Spivak, 1988, p. 308): the other is always the other *for us*, never the other *as* other ('in itself') because the latter is effaced and muted in the very process by which meaning, identity, or voice is inscribed upon it.

To attempt to know or give voice to the other is literally to forge that knowledge or voice and the subject represented by it, to produce an artificial and counterfeit representation of the other that subordinates it even in the process of empowering it. Despite the fantasies of oral history, there is no "authentic" popular voice: some subjects speak for others as much as theory speaks for the facts. However, subjection is not an entirely one-sided process: subjects are constituted discursively, relative to different contexts, by being presupposed as objects predisposed to a particular form of subjection (Bourdieu & Passeron, 1990). Thus, the emancipatory projects of alternative discourses depend, paradoxically, on first constituting subjects as "uneducated," "un(der)developed," or "dominated," and hence available for potential "education," "development," or "liberation." As Illich and Sanders (1989) put it, the body of the subject is a "layer cake of superimposed texts, each 'text' lettered by a different profession to define a separate set of needs that only that profession can meet" (p. xi).

DISCIPLINE AND THE INTELLECTUALS

Discourses do not only constitute those who are subjects to intervention in the name of research, development, or education; they also subject, and are perhaps first applied to, the intellectual vehicles of power and knowledge, those who direct these interventions (Foucault, 1981). Such discipline promotes the integration of the latter (Bourdieu & Passeron, 1990, p. 35) as much as it literally empowers both vehicles and targets and generates direct material and intellectual benefits (Deacon, 1992; Deacon & Parker, 1991). A recent evaluation of a rural education discourse in the remote Maputaland region of Kwazulu-Natal, which seeks to overcome the acute shortage of school books by operating a mobile library, concluded that even though pupils were benefiting, teachers benefited even more—and not because of improved educational materials but due to their greater personal mobility and flexibility given by their access to a motor vehicle (Salmon 1992)! In educational discourses, "teaching aids" are both instruments for constituting particular kinds of learning subjects and "instruments of control tending to safeguard . . . orthodoxy . . . against individual heresies" (Bourdieu & Passeron, 1990, p. 58). The rites of initiation into the mysteries of knowledge that all intellectuals undergo—ordeal (asceticism and hard work), taboo and purification (objectivity and institutional isolation), and possession (the dedicated and professional pursuit of the truth)—proclaim, explain, and justify their separation from and elevation above the layman; present "the resultant relationship of domination as one of service and self-sacrifice" (Bauman, 1987, p. 13); and operate as a set of internalized constraints. Ironically, these constraints are exercised most effectively by the technique championed by alternative discourses as the surest path to liberation: critical self-reflection. To reflect on oneself critically involves treating one's self as one's object; to seek to emancipate the self in this way is simultaneously to police the self and bind it with responsibilities.

Intellectuals occupy specific and pivotal positions in this normalizing epoch of modernity:

> The judges of normality are present everywhere. We are in the society of the teacher-judge, the doctor-judge, the educator-judge, the "social worker"-judge; it is on them that the universal reign of the normative is based; and each individual, wherever he may find himself, subjects to it his body, his gestures, his behaviour, his aptitudes, his achievements. (Foucault, 1977, p. 304)

The subject position of the intellectual is closely associated with two mechanisms that discipline with a minimum of direct coercion: confession and examination. The confession—"the formidable injunction to tell what one is" (Foucault, 1981, p. 60)—is a ritual of discourse that, having achieved scientific status as a therapeutic operation, has discernible effects of power: truth is corroborated by the ordeal of relating it, which "produces intrinsic modifications in the person who articulates it" (Foucault, 1981, p. 62). Whereas confession is present in all alternative discourses that seek to oblige others to speak either in their own voices or by giving them voice, the examination is more closely (although not exclusively) aligned with institutionalized educational discourses. The examination, supported by hierarchical observation and normalizing judgment, subjects those perceived as objects and objectifies those who are subjected (Foucault, 1977). It permits particular features of the subjects under observation or analysis to be reported, classified, assessed, and utilized and functions both to produce and to discipline because it not only authenticates an acquisition of knowledge, but extorts from the other an immense tactical knowledge reserved for the intellectual (Foucault, 1977).

The proselytizing power of the intellectual is "bent on converting its subjects from one form of life to another," avowedly superior, form (Bauman, 1987, p. 49). It is not that alternative discourses aim at remolding others in the image of their specific intellectuals, thus dissolving the difference between each mode of life; rather, each seeks "the recognition by its subjects of the superiority of the form of life it represents and derives its authority from" (p. 49). In accepting this superiority, which is the condition for their salvation, the subjects "may well solidify and eternalize the gap between the power holders and their subjects instead of bridging it" (p. 49). In South Africa's rural areas, despite, or perhaps because of, the paucity of educational provision, schooling retains its modernist image of providing access to the urban economy and to the more general values of the Enlightenment. This image may lose some of its luster, but none of its force, however, even when it is shown to have dubious advantages for local development (depriving the homestead of labor power in both the short and long term, seriously threatening its stability by generating and exacerbating inequalities in status and bargaining power, fostering dependency between literate and illiterate members, and encouraging gender discrimination) (Deacon & Parker, 1993). Modernity's discourses are not premised on their capacity to deliver their professed goods, but on the disciplining of subjects, and it is only by perpetuating the perceived imperfections or differences of those compelled to be taught, researched, or developed that a whole series of privileged subjects, including those categories alleged to be able to overcome these imperfections or bridge these differences (intellectuals, among others), can be reproduced.

> The spread of normalization operates through the creation of abnormalities that it then must treat and reform. By identifying the anomalies scientifically, the technologies of biopower are in a perfect position to supervise and administer them. (Dreyfus & Rabinow, 1982, pp. 195-196)

Hence, the near-perpetual crises in education the world over, or the litany of failures of development, or even the widespread disillusionment with modernity itself, all further justify the need to refine the technologies of power and knowledge within discourses—the less they succeed, the more they become necessary (Smart, 1985).

GRASPING THE NETTLE

Implicit in the preceding critique of the power of modern human reason as it manifests itself in alternative discourses in South Africa is
a reconceptualization of modernity, its discourses, relations of power
and knowledge, subjects, processes of subjection, and the role of
intellectuals. Several important issues, such as the question of postmodernity and its relation to modernity, the nature of critique, politics and social change, and more specifically the form, location, and
objectives of struggle demand attention, but this chapter can do little
more than make some of the implications more explicit. It is possible
to state, however, that an appropriate strategic response to these
issues must necessarily include an account of the subject. Its future
may be precarious: An "invention of recent date," it is like "a face
drawn in sand at the edge of the sea" (Foucault, 1970, pp. 385-387);
nevertheless, until the turn of the tide, the subject will remain an
object of intense study and extensive controls, as well as a vehicle for
purposive-rational power. Given this, Foucault (1982) indicates what
our task might be:

> Not to discover what we are, but to refuse what we are . . . to
> imagine and build up what we could be . . . not to try to liber-
> ate the individual from the state, and from the state's institu-
> tions, but to liberate us both from the state and the type of
> individualization which is linked to the state . . . [to] promote
> new forms of subjectivity. (p. 216)

Captured in this statement by Foucault are five elements usually
associated with more conventional accounts of politics and change:
analysis, critique, struggle, vision, and transformation. In order to
refuse and criticize what we are, we must at least in a minimal sense
have both discovered what we are or how we are constituted and
have imagined or invented what new kinds of subjects we could be.
On this basis, an appropriate strategy for social change under conditions of modernity would involve engaging in what Foucault (1987a)
calls practices of freedom, games of truth, or powerplays that are
aimed at discursively *reconstituting* or re-in-forming subjects in particular historically and culturally proposed or imposed patterns.

    If modernist discourses are conceptualized not as represen-
tations of reality but as strategic simulations that constitute reality,
the possibility exists that these games of truth and power could be
turned against themselves and each other and outplayed. Modernity
and its discourses are not homogeneous or monolithic but incomplete and in constant danger of disintegration. Although their tendency is to totalization, unremitting efforts to reaffirm and reinforce
this tendency are required: Modern societies may be disciplinary, but
they are not disciplined (Smart, 1985). The order of modern discourses is not imposed from without but practiced from within,

through internal struggles that (re)inscribe traces of the past on the present akin to the manner in which the "tradition of all the dead generations lays like a nightmare on the brain of the living" (Marx, 1977, p. 300). What is called postmodernism is one of those struggles: Because modernity can only be criticized from within, postmodernism in effect is modernity (re)thinking itself. This is the nettle that must be grasped; our implication in relations of power and knowledge must be acknowledged—and exploited.

Derrida, Foucault, and Spivak have developed some of the implications of a strategy that seeks to exploit from within the indeterminacy and fragility of modernity, its discourses, and its overdetermined subjects: "multiple sites, a stratified terrain, postulations that are undergoing continual displacement, a sort of strategic rhythm" (Derrida, 1983, p. 17). This strategy no longer posits unity as either prerequisite or objective of struggle, but engages inequalities of power and knowledge simultaneously on the individual, local, and global levels and on a number of fronts (state apparatuses, corporations, trade unions, schools, universities, homes, prisons, armies, asylums, courts, the media, political parties, hospitals, churches, and institutions and organizations of all kinds). It is a strategy that takes cognisance of a terrain stratified by race, gender, class, status, geography, education, sexuality, and age, among other differentiations; a strategy whose postulations are never fixed but which mutate and proliferate, and are always temporary, particular, partial, partisan, and perpetually cooptable. Persistent informed critique is integral to this strategy. A "constant questioning of identity defers identity even while presupposing it" (Oliver, 1991, p. 194). What Derrida (1981) has claimed for the relation between grammatology and science is equally applicable to the relation between a postmodern strategy and modernity: "it *inscribes* and *delimits* science; . . . it *marks* and at the same time *loosens* the limit which closes classical scientificity" (p. 36; emphasis in original). Delimitation suggests that, in modernity as in mime, it is possible to make a departure while remaining in place (Ulmer, 1985), to shift the boundaries of modernity even while enforcing them, thus permitting the production of new and the modification of existing subjectivities in its interstices. Similarly, it has been argued that "when [Foucault] shows that the practices of our culture have produced both objectification and subjectification, he has already loosened the grip, the seeming naturalness and necessity these practices have" (Dreyfus & Rabinow, 1982, p. 203). Finally, a strategy that seeks to exploit the contradictions of modernity could be called homoeopathic, in that it gives modernity a taste of its own medicine: By constituting modernity as its object, it reenacts the archetypical modernist maneuver.

The objectification of modernist discourses facilitates the recognition and questioning of their characteristic features and provides one with a strategic purchase from which to subvert and reverse the hierarchies and inequalities they establish and perpetuate (Derrida, 1981). But it would be simplistic (and modernist) to assume that by reversing hierarchies, and accentuating difference, multiplicity, discontinuity, or particularity instead of identity, unity, continuity, and universality, one has prepared the ground for a new, nonphallogocentric, postmodernist discourse: This is to do no more than resuscitate a liberal pluralism and to repeat and reinforce modernity. Reversal must be supported by displacement, by exposing the mechanisms by which these hierarchies and the discourses based on them are produced, produce, operate, and mutate (constituting subjects through games of truth and power). Any attempt to subvert modernist discourses will be incomplete, temporary, and strategic and hence should aim not at the replacement and repetition of modernist discourses but their displacement and reinscription, not at transcending binary oppositions but at exploiting the tensions between them. It has been shown how attempts in South Africa to transcend rural inequalities, to revalue popular experience, or to empower and emancipate through alternative education come with modernist strings attached and are ultimately unrealizable: The alternative is to highlight differential and contradictory relations of power in order to destabilize and perpetually oppose their tendency to coalesce into global forms of domination disguised by consent and legitimated as reasonable or natural.

CONCLUSION

The objective of this chapter has been to deconstruct alternative discourses in South Africa by exposing the relations of power and knowledge that underpin them and demonstrating how the premises, practices, and presence of these discourses—their reflexivity, participatory democratic procedures, and representations of themselves and others—are effects of, and depend on, that which they deny, marginalize, or claim to transcend: their will to truth and power, their constitution and reification of subjects, and their effacement of the intellectual. Inherent in this deconstruction is the fuzzy outline of a different way of conceptualizing and intervening in the modern world. Elements of such a strategy have been parasitic on and yet critical of modernity since its origins (in the work of Rousseau, Marx, Nietzsche and Wittgenstein, among others) and are proliferating rapidly; for example, Derrida's deconstruction, Foucault's genealogy, Rorty's pragmatism, Laclau and Mouffe's hegemony, as well as developments in feminist, post-Marxist, and postcolonial discourses. Although it has only been over the last 30 years that the 2,000 year-long philosophical marathon has begun to show clear signs of exhaustion, a long haul remains: charting the direction(s) in which modernity and its discourses are likely to move, working out the possibilities for reconstituting subjects, and, in general, rethinking our understandings of education, development, communication, research, politics, and change—and ourselves.

REFERENCES

Alexander, N. (1989). Liberation pedagogy in the South African context. In C. Criticos (Ed.), *Experiential learning in formal and nonformal education* (pp. 1-14). Durban, South Africa: Media Resource Centre, University of Natal.

Althusser, L. (1971). *Lenin and philosophy and other essays*. London: New Left Books.

Bauman, Z. (1987). *Legislators and interpreters: On modernity, postmodernity and intellectuals*. Cambridge: Polity.

Bourdieu, P., & Passeron, J.-C. (1990). *Reproduction in education, society and culture* (2nd ed.). London: Sage.

Bozzoli, B. (Ed.). (1987). *Class, community and conflict*. Johannesburg, South Africa: Ravan.

Criticos, C., & Quinlan, T. (1991). Community video: Power and process. *Visual Sociology, 6*, 2.

Deacon, R. (1991a). Hegemony, essentialism and radical history in South Africa. *South African Historical Journal, 24*, 166-184.

Deacon, R. (1991b). *Power, knowledge and community video in South Africa* (Media Working Papers No. 8). Durban, South Africa: Media Resource Centre, University of Natal.

Deacon, R. (1992). Power, knowledge and community video revisited. *Visual Sociology, 7*, 2.

Deacon, R., & Parker, B. (1991). Preliminary reflections on an education project. In W. Flanagan (Ed.), *Teachers and their work: Case studies of in-service education in African primary schools* (pp. 106-120). Cape Town, South Africa: Primary Education Project, University of Cape Town.

Deacon, R., & Parker, B. (1993). The curriculum and power: A reconceptualization with a rural dimension. In N. Taylor (Ed.), *Inventing knowledge: Contests in curriculum construction* (pp. 127-142). Cape Town, South Africa: Maskew Miller Longman.

Derrida, J. (1981). *Positions*. London: Athlone.

Derrida, J. (1983). The principle of reason: The university in the eyes of its pupils. *Diacritics, 13*, 3-20.

Dreyfus, H., & Rabinow, P. (1982). *Michel Foucault: Beyond structuralism and hermeneutics*. Brighton, UK: Harvester.

Ellsworth, E. (1989). Why doesn't this feel empowering? Working through the repressive myths of critical pedagogy. *Harvard Educational Review, 59*, 3.

Freire, P., & Shor, I. (1987). *A pedagogy for liberation*. London: Macmillan.

Foucault, M. (1970). *The order of things: An archaeology of the human sciences*. New York: Random House.

Foucault, M. (1977). *Language, counter-memory, practice: Selected essays and interviews* (D. F. Bouchard, Ed.). Oxford, UK: Blackwell.

Foucault, M. (1979). *Discipline and punish: The birth of the prison*. Hammondsworth, UK: Penguin.

Foucault, M. (1981). *The history of sexuality: An introduction.* Harmondsworth, UK: Penguin.

Foucault, M. (1982). The subject and power. In H. L. Dreyfus & P. Rabinow (Eds.), *Michel Foucault: Beyond structuralism and hermeneutics* (pp. 208-226). Brighton, UK: Harvester.

Foucault, M. (1984). The order of discourse. In M. Shapiro (Ed.), *Language and politics* (pp. 108-138). Oxford, UK: Blackwell.

Foucault, M. (1986). Disciplinary power and subjection. In S. Lukes (Ed.), *Power* (pp. 229-242). Oxford, UK: Blackwell.

Foucault, M. (1987a). The ethic of care for the self as a practice of freedom—An interview with Michel Foucault. *Philosophy and Social Criticism, 12*(2/3), 112-131.

Foucault, M. (1987b). The juridical apparatus. In W. Connolly (Ed.), *Legitimacy and the state* (pp. 201-221). London: Blackwell.

Hegel, G. (1977). *Phenomenology of spirit.* Oxford: Clarendon.

Heidegger, M. (1969). *Kant and the problem of metaphysics* (J. S. Churchill, Trans.). Bloomington: Indiana University Press.

Illich, I., & Sanders, B. (1989). *The alphabetization of the popular mind.* New York: Vintage.

Kruss, G. (1988). *People's Education: An examination of the concept.* Cape Town, South Africa: Centre for Adult and Continuing Education, University of the Western Cape.

Laclau, E., & Mouffe, C. (1985). *Hegemony and socialist strategy.* London: Verso.

Mackenzie, F. (1992). Development from within? The struggle to survive. In D. Taylor & F. Mackenzie (Eds.), *Development from within: Survival in rural Africa* (pp. 1-32). London: Routledge.

Mahoney, M., & Yngvesson, B. (1992). The construction of subjectivity and the paradox of resistance: Reintegrating feminist. *Anthropology and Psychology, 18,* 1.

Marx, K. (1977). The eighteenth brumaire of Louis Bonaparte. In D. McLellan (Ed.), *Karl Marx: Selected writings* (pp. 300-325). Oxford: Oxford University Press.

Mashamba, G. (1990). *A conceptual critique of the People's Education discourse.* Johannesburg, South Africa: Education Policy Unit, University of the Witwatersrand.

Mkatshwa, S. (1986). Keynote Address to the first National Consultative Conference. In *Proceedings of the First National Consultative Conference* (pp. 5-15). Johannesburg, South Africa: University of the Witwatersrand.

Muller, J., & Cloete, N. (1986). The white hands: Academic social scientists and forms of popular knowledge production. *Critical Arts, 4,* 2.

Nasson, B. (1990). Education and poverty. In B. Nasson & J. Samuel (Eds.), *Education—from poverty to liberty* (pp. 88-108). Cape Town, South Africa: David Philip.

National Education Policy Investigation (NEPI). (1993). *The framework report.* Cape Town, South Africa: Oxford University Press/National Education Consultative Committee.

Oliver, K. (1991). Fractal politics: How to use "the subject." *Praxis International, 11*, 2.

Parker, B. (1993). NEPI: Intellectuals and education system change. *Perspectives in Education, 14*, 2.

Salmon, C. (1992). *Understanding the educational needs of rural teachers: A case study of a rural education innovation in KwaNgwanase* (M.Ed. Research Report). Durban, South Africa: University of Natal.

Saunders, C. (1991). Radical History—the Wits Workshop version—Reviewed. *South African Historical Journal, 24*, 160-165.

Smart, B. (1985). *Michel Foucault.* London: Routledge.

Spivak, G. (1988). Can the subaltern speak? In C. Nelson & L. Grossberg (Eds.), *Marxism and the interpretation of culture* (pp. 271-313). London: Macmillan.

Spivak, G. (1992). *Thinking academic freedom in gendered post-coloniality* (T.B. Davie Memorial Lecture). Cape Town, South Africa: University of Cape Town.

Tapson, D. (1990). Rural development and the homelands. *Development Southern Africa, 7*, 561-581.

Taylor, D. (1992). Development from within and survival in rural Africa: A synthesis of theory and practice. In D. Taylor & F. Mackenzie (Eds.), *Development from within: Survival in rural Africa* (pp. 214-258). London: Routledge.

Taylor, N. (1991, March). Early days for NEPI. *UDUSA News*, pp. 4-5.

Touraine, A. (1988). *Return of the actor.* Minneapolis: University of Minnesota Press.

Ulmer, G. (1985). *Applied grammatology: Post(e)-pedagogy from Jacques Derrida to Joseph Beuys.* Baltimore: Johns Hopkins University Press.

Zizek, S. (1990). Beyond discourse-analysis. In E. Laclau (Ed.), *New reflections on the revolution of our time* (pp. 249-260). London: Verso.

Chapter ▪ 10

Cultural Action and the Limits to Solidarity and Participation*

Costas Criticos

INTRODUCTION

South Africa's first democratic national elections in 1994 anticipated the end of 300 years of dispossession, silence and social engineering in which democracy has been both violently suppressed and pursued. Apartheid, which according to some, is the logical outcome of the European enlightenment and colonial adventure, has been erased from the new constitution. Notwithstanding the beginning of the end of apartheid, the promise of an election was heralded by an escalation of violence and intolerance that supposedly claimed more lives than the Vietnam War.

Will difference continue to separate or can it contribute to a plural democracy? What can we expect of cultural action in this post-colonial period? What are the similarities between our experience and those of other countries undergoing national reconstruction? Which

*This chapter draws substantially on an earlier produced work, Criticos, C. (1993). Experiential learning and social transformation for a post-apartheid learning future. In D. Boud, R. Cohen, & D. Walker (Eds.), *Using experience for learning* (pp. 157-168). London: Open University Press.

I am indebted to my colleagues, Jeanne Prinsloo and Roger Deacon, who gave critical comments on the early drafts of this chapter.

voices will be heard in the postcolonial and postelection South Africa? For how long will the master voice of apartheid endure? Can postmodern sensibilities protect us from the excesses of the modern project?

This chapter just scratches at the surface of these questions. I introduce a new metaphor for talking about borders of difference in the hope that this will give a way of discussing some of the principal concerns of emerging democracies. These discussions are important as we enter a period of national reconstruction in which the central authoritarian state has been weakened by the emergence of an increasing number of political nodes.

In South Africa, which has large variations in the provision of basic life resources and political power, we are starting to see features that are commonly associated with the postmodern era in the West. Particularly in the urban areas, we see cultural forms, practice, dress, and architecture reflecting the tension of nostalgia and irony that is the usual hallmark of the modern project running dry. Politics is becoming decentered, and we are part of the global information and consumer market—Volkswagen South Africa exports large numbers of cars to China; Nelson Mandela wears a New York Yankees peak cap; teenagers wear American Basketball team T shirts and peaks; some White teenagers sport African hairstyles and Malcolm X peak caps; Peter Mokaba, president of the ANC youth league, who is famous for his support of the chant "Kill the Boer Kill the Farmer," runs a chain of salons that specialize in straightening hair; CNN and SKY are offered as round-the-clock broadcasts; and in the predominantly Black student residences on our campus, meals and student meetings are scheduled around the broadcast time of the U.S. soap, "The Bold & The Beautiful." These manifestations are partly due to the modern project losing its tight grip on certainty, partly because of our international media diet and partly because South Africa is in the global market. These few signs notwithstanding, the modern project is not exhausted, in some parts of South Africa and some fields the project is still the central organizing principle. This is particularly the case in development work that is still locked in to a modernization paradigm. The South African corporate world sees modernization as central to development. Apart from our election date of April 27, April 1 is described in the business press as a historical date, "the great cellular switch-on," the day on which "South Africa will look far from foolish as it joins many other countries in a new phase of modernity" (*Daily News*, 1993).

The new South African Constitution has already given us a foretaste of the future—it represents a startling number of compromises and weakening of the old pillars of apartheid. The ANC policy of a command economy is replaced by a mixed economy, women are guaranteed one third of the ANC's political posts, and there will be limited regional autonomy and nine official languages. None of these outcomes had been anticipated of the ANC and the Nationalist Party; their demands were initially poles apart and irreconcilable. Understanding difference and cultural action within and across borders of difference is essential in a new society with so many voices.

APARTHEID SOCIETY

South Africa and other countries struggling to escape oppression and poverty seem to have a deep understanding for education that liberates. Emancipatory education in these settings becomes a defense against oppression and a preparation for a future free of the constraints and practices that had disempowered citizens. This education attempted to release the stranglehold of apartheid education constructed by the present government that reinforced the myth that most South Africans were inferior and in need of special (segregated and inferior) treatment. Society was segregated so that each race group had its own curriculum, schools, homes, hospitals, and even prisons. These ghettos of differential privilege and oppression ensured that people did not engage in conversation or encounter experiences that would contradict the myth of apartheid.

Apartheid, as explained by Nationalist Party propaganda and later school textbooks, is a policy of "self-determination" (an argument for self determination has also been advanced by the Zulu [IFP] and Afrikaner [CP] nationalists in opposition to the multiparty constitutional talks). This explanation stands in strong contrast to certain theological and political science perspectives that explain apartheid as racist oppression. Two of the most important institutions in South Africa that challenged apartheid and allowed conversations to continue are certain churches and universities. Some of these were, however, instruments of the state that gave theological and academic support to policies of oppression.

EDUCATIONAL FOUNDATIONS

The revolutionary climate of resistance in South Africa created a popular interest in an education that advanced democracy in contrast to the domesticating education, which maintained the status quo of oppression. At the heart of this emancipatory education is an alternative view of knowledge itself: Knowledge is not something fixed that is transferred to learners. The epistemology of emancipatory education is a perspective that regards knowledge as being constructed by learners. Learners in emancipatory education are constructors rather than consumers of knowledge. The debate about epistemologies is not a peripheral interest, but rather a central issue that impacts on the way we teach, learn, and view our role in the process of development and education.

According to Palmer (1990):

> the way we know has powerful implications for the way we live. Every epistemology tends to become an ethic, and every way of knowing tends to become a way of living. The relation

established between the student and the subject, tends to become the relation of the living person to the world itself. Every mode of knowing contains its own moral trajectory, its own ethical direction and outcomes. (p. 107)

Most of us engaged in cultural action are faced with two major competing epistemologies. The epistemology that underpins mainstream education and development is an analytical and objective way of knowing; it does not tolerate experiential learning, action research, participatory video, holistic medicine, and other alternative ways of knowing and working.

Tim Stanton (1986, private communication), Stanford University academic and experiential learning advocate, explains why the work he does is necessarily marginal in traditional higher education:

> The dominant epistemology of knowledge which informs higher education is based on a sense that replicability is the final test of truth, that knowledge is analytical, abstract and logical. The task of education is the distribution of knowledge, or the "banking" method of education. Random experience is inadequate as a means of knowledge. We are taught to distrust personal experience as a guide, to identify universal truths from logical, preorganized, abstractions.

In contrast to an objective knowing, emancipatory education has an alternative epistemology that is based on a connected knowing. This is an education that is generative not consumptive, concerned with perception not reception, searching not researching. In such a system intelligence is a process not a product, and intelligence equals intelligent behavior (Stanton, 1986, 1990).

Habermas's (1972) theory of how fundamental human interests influence the social construction of knowledge is a valuable contribution to this examination of the foundations of education. He rejects the dominant view of knowledge that is separate and discovered by the individual in favor of a knowledge that is constructed in communal action. He posits three ways of knowing—empirical-analytical, historical-hermeneutic, and critical. Habermas's critical way of knowing would be associated with what I described earlier as an epistemology of connected knowing and is concerned with emancipatory cognitive interests. This interest, according to Grundy (1987) is:

> The ability of individuals and groups to take control of their own lives in autonomous and responsible ways. . . . At the level of practice the emancipatory curriculum will involve the participants in the educational encounter, both teacher and

pupil, in action which attempts to change the structures within which learning occurs and which constrains freedom in often unrecognized ways. (p. 19)

In South Africa, these emancipatory interests were suppressed; the structures of education were designed specifically to constrain freedom. Education was divided on racial lines, and the curricula were designed to reinforce the myth of White supremacy. Whites were prepared for positions of management, whereas Blacks were prepared for positions of service. In addition to school texts that perpetuated the myth of apartheid the type of education that was typical in most schools did not give pupils opportunities to be critical of their own learning. Teaching styles in these classrooms is typical of what Paulo Freire (1972) has called "banking education"—the depositing of knowledge into the heads of passive learners.

Opposition to apartheid was waged in a low-level civil war of armed resistance on South African borders, townships, and industrial settings. In parallel to armed resistance there was oppositional activity in educational settings. Black schools became sites of struggle as "banking education" that disempowered through its contents and methods was rejected. In the place of "banking education," emancipatory alternatives such as "People Education" was popularized by the National Education Crisis Committee and other groups that sprung up following the education-focused protests. Educational authorities and the police tried to control this resistance through harassment and imprisonment of education activists.

PAULO KICKS UP STORM

In the 1970s, Paulo Freire's ideas kicked up a storm in South Africa. Freire's (1972) *Pedagogy of the Oppressed* was picked up as a theoretical framework to challenge oppression. His writing seemed to be directly addressing the South African situation, and it offered liberation through education. The security forces were not slow to realize the danger that Freire's writing presented, so Freire's books were banned. The interest in Freire's work was spread through the University Christian Movement and from there to the South African Students Organization.

As a student I remember Freire being revered as a prophet—part of the attraction was that he was banned. Students reasoned that he must be worthwhile if the authorities had banned his works. In my own university library Freire's writings were kept in a locked room containing banned literature. Students were allowed into this room for the private study of one book at a time. There was no possibility of photocopying these materials or browsing the shelves. These concessions were only extended to postgraduate students who had permission from the Minister of Education's office to study banned literature essential to their research.

South African educationist, Neville Alexander (1989), imprisoned for his political beliefs, examines the history of emancipatory education and the central role played by the works of Paulo Freire:

> Although the government banned Freire's works, about 500 or more copies of Pedagogy of the Oppressed made the rounds at the "bush colleges" (segregated universities established in the 'homelands' as part of grand apartheid) and were eagerly studied by the young activists of the Black Conscious Movement. In Freire's works, they saw the mirror image of that which they rejected in the Bantu-Education system as well as the possible way out of the cul-de-sac. (p. 6)

He cites four key reasons why Freire's ideas were so readily received. A summary of these are:

- Freire's anti-capitalist social theory concurs with analyses of educationists in South African liberation movements.
- The context in which Freire's pedagogy was formed was similar to that of oppression in South Africa.
- Freire linked education with conscientization.
- The demand for and interest in democratic by grassroot organizations reinforced the interest in Freire.

Alexander, like many other political activists, was imprisoned on Robben Island, the high-security prison for political prisoners. In the film, "Robben Island: Our University," three ex-prisoners—Neville Alexander, Fiks Bam, and Max Kwedi—discuss the reasons why they regard the island as the university of the liberation struggle. The island was the place where some of the prisoners encountered African history for the first time—their school history spoke only of colonial conquests. They were a community of intellectuals who held discussions and tutorials in the midst of their work details in the rock quarry or during exercises. The principal texts were their own life experiences and their common purpose to liberate South Africa. In addition to the political debates and discussions many prisoners studied for higher degrees through UNISA, the distance education university in South Africa. (The materials supplied by UNISA are traditional correspondence study guides that usually invite no discursive engagement with the issues presented.) These students formed discussion groups with prisoners who were leaders in their own fields, such as Neville Alexander for History, Nelson Mandela for law, and Denis Brutus for english.

The prisoners had a high regard for the island because they took control of their own learning, they constructed knowledge out of their personal and collective experience. An important lesson I learned from this film and my discussions with Alexander is that the learner is responsible for making every experience educative. It was intended that Robben Island should constrain the prisoners—instead they grew more powerful!

Emancipatory education that attempts to make all experience educative, has a price—a price that many students who have internalized the banking education tradition are not prepared to pay (Shor, 1993).

A local research project revealed a disturbing statistic that, unlike the Robben Island prisoners, many students resist classroom activities that make demands on critical skills. The students who brought education to a standstill and marched with banners proclaiming "NO DOMESTICATING EDUCATION" and "PEOPLE'S EDUCATION FOR PEOPLE'S POWER" have not welcomed the demands of an emancipatory education. The research by Gilmour (1988) showed in a sample of over 1,000 teachers and high school students that:

> There is a deep-seated individualism amongst students in the sense less of personal assertion, and more in terms of the internalization of values consistent with capitalist ideology. These include an instrumental view of education in the sense of preferring goals that are extrinsic to the learning process itself, a belief in meritocracy as manifested initially by a downplaying of the goal of equality, and further by the ways in which success and failure are perceived. The lack of concern with syllabus changes as a major task of reform, and the low ranking of independent learning, illustrate an instrumental view of knowledge that is reinforced by both examination, illustrate an instrumental view of knowledge that is reinforced by both examination orientation and teachers' behavior. (p. 21)

Even leadership at the vanguard of these struggles seems unable to carry the political slogans through to action. The National Education Coordinating Committee (NECC, successor to the National Education Crisis Committee), which has been at the forefront of the school resistance campaign, is now using familiar capitalist strategies. At the founding conference of the NECC in 1985, Father Smangaliso Mkatshwa addressed People's Education:

> The theme of this conference is "Peoples' Education for Peoples' Power." This theme makes it clear that we dod not want just any type of education. Peoples' education is a devastating indictment of Apartheid slave education. The call is now for education for liberation, justice and freedom. It is a demand for full participation in all social structures. (quoted in Criticos, 1989, p. 210)

The conference then went on to pass a number of resolutions that defined the character of the struggle for People's Education. Two of these us a glimpse of the features of this education

- Elimination of capitalist norms of competition
- Encouragement of collective input, critical thinking, and analysis

In 1993, however, the NECC fought the South African educational crisis in a most uncharacteristic manner. They announced the Top Students Awards initiative in an effort "to encourage positive attitudes towards education" (*Daily News*, 1993). With the support of the non-racial South African Democratic Teachers Union and the radical student movement COSAS (Congress of South African Students), a competition was established to reward the country's top Black school students. With all the glitter of a TV game show, the top 10 students were offered a scholarship for tertiary education studies, a computer, and a holiday trip. This competition was established in response to a year in which general-secretary James Maseko said the "crucial culture of learning and teaching has been seriously eroded." It is surprising that the culture of capital was called in to rescue the culture of learning.

Education is not the only quarter in which we have witnessed remarkable contradictions. The organizers of the Miss South Africa beauty pageant negotiated a deal with ANC Youth League President, Peter Mokaba. If it had been successful the pageant organizers would have established a $100,000 trust for training beauty pageant organizers and models in exchange for an ANC endorsement. The ANC deal advocates who claimed this as "a major breakthrough for the oppressed masses of our people" did not anticipate the wrath of the ANC executive or the reaction of the ANC Women's League. Women's League secretary-general Baleka Kgositsile said "We really have to ask ourselves why we as an organization should be involved in this kind of activity. If one is looking for projects to help build-esteem and self-confidence, there are much better ways of doing so. It's time that looks became less important than inner strengths" (*Weekly Mail*, 1993).

The examples of the student competition and the beauty pageant show the fragility and limitation of political rhetoric. The rally calls for noncompetitive education and nonsexist policies that challenged apartheid structures and practice are drowned in a competitive and sexist market. Without the challenge of civil movements and the women's movement in particular we might have seen the first "politically correct" beauty pageant. Civil society that was crucial in the anti-apartheid struggle must be maintained and strengthened to sustain a democratic society and avoid the excesses and limitations of the powerful.

CIVIL SOCIETY

Civil society is made up of those voices that are peripheral to government and that represent a wide array of interests and variation of support or resistance to central powers. In the last years of apartheid many oppositional organizations were connected in alliances and collaborative networks. These groups were also actively supported by the international community in the common goal of transformation of apartheid society.

Part of the apartheid government's strategy of survival was to harass resistant civil society. Social action groups were closed down and their officers harassed or imprisoned. In an effort to turn off foreign support for local groups the government introduced a number of bills including The Affected Organizations Act and The Disclosure of Foreign Funding Act. Although the government argued that these bills were designed to protect the public from exploitation in the name of charity, the acts were used for political control. The most notable example of this was the declaration that FOSATU, the federation of trade unions that preceded COSATU, was an "affected" organization and therefore could no longer receive public funds.

Because of these limitations of freedom, many service and research organizations committed to social transformation relocated themselves on the progressive university campuses. The university like the cathedral and mosque was sacred ground—authorities were more reluctant to intrude there than elsewhere.

Now that a democratic society is held tantalizingly in front of our eyes, there is a perception that civil society can take a holiday. Civil society's work, however, is not over; its principal value is in nation building and not just as society's watchdog. The many agencies, organizations, unions, and movements provide a means for citizens to act our their social responsibilities.

According to South African philosopher, Mala Singh (1993), the current debate on civil society in South Africa has negative and positive dimensions that coincide with liberal and Gramscian interpretations.

The negative function of civil society pertains to its "watchdog" role as a check against the claims of the state to monopolize decision making in an authoritarian way, in other words, to make the state more accountable. The positive dimension of the idea of civil society as employed within the South African debate pertains to the fact that although the individual's right of free association may be the basis of traditional liberal conceptions of civil society, civil society could also foster solidarity, communitarian values, and an associational ethos that leads citizens to achieve social goals together.

Earnest work is presently underway to convince constitutional negotiators that South Africa needs an "Enabling Environment for NGOs" to foster growth and viabililty of civil society. The first demand is for the removal of the present controls and a simplification of procedures for establishing and operating a civil organization (DRC, 1993).

THE ELASTIC BORDER

Apartheid South Africa destabilized civil society because it expressly gave support to the victims of apartheid. Civil society grew to address the limitations and excesses of the state—its principal interest being citizens who have been ignored or victimized by the state. Paradoxically, the growth of civil society is dependent on the state's limitations, while, at the same time, it operates within the framework and control of state provision.

An understanding of difference is essential for an understanding of oppression. Oppression is not just a process of weakening, it is also a process of maintaining weakness. Oppressors construct borders that restrict the social freedom of the oppressed. These borders are usually rules that describe limits of freedom differentially to people on either side of the border. Sometimes these rules are enforced by physical borders that demarcate the territorial range of the rules—a prison is an obvious example of this. On a bigger scale, South Africa has constructed these borders in the homeland system and Black townships that are distant and concealed from the central (White) residential and business areas.

The modernist project constructs borders based on crude categorizations of class, race, and gender in order to reproduce existing power relations of domination. It is precisely on the questions of inflexible borders that modernism is being challenged.

Postmodernism constitutes a general attempt to transgress the borders sealed by modernism, to proclaim the arbitrariness of all boundaries, and to call attention to the sphere of culture as a shifting and historical construction (Giroux, 1992).

In this postmodern period the broad simplified borders that delineate the subject and object of master narratives are under threat. At one level the master narratives themselves are challenged, but more importantly multiple new political and narrative nodes have emerged in which new borders of micropolitics weaken the master narrative and the power of macropolitics. Critical postmodern citizens occupy those "borderlands," which are at the intersections of these multiple borders.

Discourses of apartheid were engineered to construct and maintain borders—borders that were expressly designed to signal difference and to limit solidarity between people within borders and across borders. Alexander's (1989) account of the prisoners on Robben Island, who became increasingly stronger as a community of intellectuals and activists, bears testimony to the limitations of oppressive borders. Borders designed to weaken by isolating and limiting freedom of communities may in the end strengthen their political resolve to collaborate and share resources.

BORDER PEDAGOGY AND BORDER DEVELOPMENT

Giroux's (1992) book, *Border Crossings*, makes a valuable contribution to our understanding of critical pedagogy, which he has extended to what he calls *border pedagogy*. In such a pedagogy he incorporates an acknowledgment of difference, with the central theme being education as a process of crossing borders. As educators this means that we negotiate learning events in which students are encouraged;

> to cross ideological and political borders as a way of furthering the limits of their own understanding in a setting that is pedagogically safe and socially nurturing rather than authoritarian and infused with the suffocating smugness of a certain political correctness. (p. 33)

Critical perspectives of education reject the simplistic assumptions of culture as common experience and the individual as principal unit of social analysis. Giroux challenges these assumptions and writes difference and power into an augmented critical pedagogy:

> Reading in opposition to these assumptions, the notion of difference has played an important role in making visible how power is inscribed differently in and between zones of culture, how cultural borderlands raise important questions regarding relations of inequality, struggle, and history, and how differences are expressed in multiple and contradictory ways within and between different groups. (p. 169)

What Giroux and others do not tell us is that these borders are not just lines drawn in the sand that we step over. In his book *Border Crossings* he implies that the border offers little resistance to crossing: "*Subordinated cultures push against and permeate* the alleged unproblematic and homogenous borders of dominant cultural forms and practices" (Giroux, 1992, p. 169; emphasis added)

I agree with Giroux that these borders are problematic and heterogeneous, but I disagree that the border crosser who pushes against a border will permeate through the border like a spiritual being passing through a material barrier. In my opinion we need a new metaphor to describe the complexity of border crossing.

When I use the notion of border to explain transformation in South African society I find the picture of a fence, a wall, or a line drawn in the sand not helpful. These metaphors make border crossing appear all too easy. Moreover, they do not accommodate the internalization of a border (some refer to this as baggage) that is dragged along with the border crosser. My science background came to my rescue with a more useful metaphor to explain and describe complex border transformation and crossings.

My picture of a border is of a continuous membrane that surrounds people in an envelope or bubble of difference. This border describes the "rules of behavior" and migration of groups on either side of the border. The border behaves like an elastic material—resisting change and springing back to its original constructed shape when stresses are removed.

BORDER OF DIFFERENCE

The border is a border of difference. The border may be imposed or accepted as practice, such as the case of ethnic groups who choose to live together for solidarity. Eventually these traditional borders become universally accepted, and they operate as effectively as borders imposed by force to control and exclude. From a different perspective, borders may also empower and include.

A community—that is, a community of common "struggle," common needs, common fears, and so on—is not a community of homogenous people without difference. Within such a community or school classroom, difference cannot be abandoned or ignored, nor should it be used as a justification to separate; it is rather a valuable resource for development. So within this community we will have many and varied borders of difference. Furthermore, these differences ought not to be seen as inherent characteristics but rather as relational differences.

ELASTIC BORDERS

Some borders are more resistive to change than others. Until a border is tested or challenged, its strength is unknown; until tested all borders appear equally resistive. The border behaves like an elastic material—it has memory. Although it has memory, it does not differentiate between the push-and-pull forces—a similar force on either side of the border will yield the same result. When a border is put under stress so as to cause some transformation and the stress is removed, the border springs back elastically back to its original form.

Rules are bent in institutions for special cases—these are associated with temporary memory lapses that are soon restored. If these special cases increase the frequency of stretching the border, the elastic properties start to weaken and the border suffers memory loss.

Paradoxically borders are strengthened during initial crossings. In some cases a border is not fully mature—its elastic properties not yet realized. Providing the crossings are limited (limited stress), then the border is enabled and strengthened. If a new teacher introduces rules in a classroom—provided there is not wholesale transgression—one or two transgressions serve the interests of the teacher to demonstrate the effectiveness of the border and advance its elastic properties.

PLASTIC DEFORMATION

When a border comes under large and continual stress either from frequent crossings or from the collective action from people on either side of the border, the border experiences memory loss that prevents it from returning to its constructed shape. In physics, this border would be said to have tone beyond the elastic limit, and from then on the material behaves in a plastic manner. This means that any deformation is more or less permanent. Given the right conditions (environment), however, it is possible to recover memory and reconstitute the elastic properties of a border.

Although border crossings transform or shift borders so that there is little correspondence between current and past borders, the past borders remain as virtual borders an afterimage or trace memory imprinted or learn by individuals during crossings. These trace memories or histories are part of the complex biographies of people that contradict broad classification into static categories of difference such as "working class."

BORDER ENVIRONMENTS

The environment of a border influences the elastic properties of a border in the same way as elastic materials are temperature dependent and become plastic under high temperature. In a similar way institutional borders are influenced by social and political environments.

In my own university I have seen borders of access to the university becoming more flexible in the changing political environment. There are now alternative routes of access for students who have been denied an adequate school foundation, whereas in the past a rigid and unyielding requirement was a minimum performance in the final secondary school examination.

Political strategists who able to read the environmental conditions apply force on the border at its most flexible moment. Moreover they push collectively and with collaborators who pull from the other side of the border.

In December 1993, the new vice-chancellor of our university was chosen. As a result of tensions that led to the resignation of our previous vice-chancellor, the social pressure for democratic processes, and the increasing power of student bodies and trade unions in the university community, applicants were nominated in an exhaustive process of consultations. The two candidates who were shortlisted were then scheduled to give public lectures on their vision for the university to allow all interested people to examine the candidates and then submit recommendations to senate. The border, or traditional practice of appointment, had yielded to the synergistic demands of student, academic, worker, and community bodies for a democratic and transparent selection process. These changes would not have occurred without the political environment in 1993 that had made the rules (border) more pliable.

DEVELOPMENT IN PRACTICE

Whether one is in education, agricultural development, or development communication, there is a politics of difference that operates to define relations between oneself and the learners, listeners, or farmers. Radical practice in development work acknowledges difference and proceeds in a way that causes the borders to yield. In other words, we need to broadcast in ways in which the models of broadcasting are subject to transformation, or teach in ways that the process of teaching is itself subject to scrutiny and change.

This is not an impossible challenge. There are already trailblazers. Narrowcasting and open learning are examples of transformed practice in which the role of broadcaster/listener and teacher/learner are redefined.

A local South African agency, The Bophuthatswana Agricultural Department, has not met this challenge. In an effort to promote conservation in rural areas it has initiated a video-supported development program with all the rhetoric of participation and emancipation. The program is called Project Inspire, which the organizers claim is "environmental education by video to inspire vital action to conserve" (Project Inspire, 1993, p. 3).

The claims and guidance offered in the fieldworkers manual on the use of the video looks promising, the authors suggest an approach that seems beyond the directive of a modernity paradigm of development:

> People already have concepts, attitudes and views about their environment. These are the starting point of the development process and it is important to be able to reveal and work with these concepts, attitudes and views. For example: you may find litter offensive, but a child who has always been surrounded by litter will probably consider it a normal part of the environment. (Project Inspire, 1993, p. 3)

In the end local understandings are not accommodated. Viewers are simply told what to do by the urban expert through the mediation of electronic media. The claim of interaction is supposedly realized by frequent signals to stop the VCR and discuss the issues raised by the presenter. The presentation, however, limits the possibility of any meaningful dialogue. The presenter has identified the problem and already told the viewers how to deal with the problem.

In response to the presenter of that video I present a testimony from Kate Sihlangu who spoke at a recent environment conference on her experiences in rural Sekhukhuneland:

> It is wrong for anybody to dump their wastes on our living grounds. We are not dirty people. Our women clean the environment, remove tins and plastics that come from industry, dig trenches and bury them. We recycle these wastes in several ways. And we are not ignorant about the environment. (quoted in Aburge, 1993, p. 9)

As a contrast to the environmental education video of the expert instructing, there is a video recording of an agricultural activist who simply tells her life story. The woman in the video is Tshepo Khumbane, a worker in the Environmental Development Agency, who challenged development policy and practice that was framed by the apartheid modern narrative. After a few years in voluntary exile, to escape the attention of the security police, Khumbane is now back at her work of agricultural development. A recent development has been the recognition of her grounded understanding of agricultural development and rural experience. Khumbane is one of the new members of the SABC Board, which is critical and representative of diverse interests and needs in broadcasting in South Africa.

PRACTICING PARTICIPATION

Participation (a form of border crossing that challenges the subject/object border) is an interest that extends beyond education to other disciplines such as anthropology, history, geography, and others that have accepted participatory action research as an alternative to traditional experimental research. My own training as an educational television producer equipped me to be creative as an individual and to make executive decisions about the "texts" that I created. As I became involved in working with community organizations I was influenced by their democratic styles of working. I found my expert and directive style of working to be inappropriate. My training gradually yielded to participatory approaches that were consistent with the democratic interests of the organizations and unions that I was serving. Initially, this yielding was simply satisfying a "customer's whim." Very soon, however, I embraced this approach. In addition to the moral imperative for participation there is a different quality to the work. Although there is no technical advantage in this approach, the distorted power relationship between producers and subjects is addressed.

Working in a participatory manner, founded on an epistemology of connected knowing and democracy, is not something that can be picked up as one of the tricks of the trade. It is rather an overriding way of working (and living). Instead of approaching a subject with a shooting script, we establish production collectives made up of production workers and members who are the subjects of the video. This way of working demands that we collectively determine the outcomes of the video (form and content) in a dynamic and collaborative manner.

"Hanging Up The Nets," a video on the history of the Durban Bay fishing community, produced by the Media Resource Center, was an important production that has given me and our practice considerable maturity. The production process revealed contradictions in our practice and showed us the potential of new ways of working.

The documentary was initiated at a meeting of 70 descendants of an Indian fishing community. The fishermen and their families were no longer actively fishing because a variety of council and national (apartheid) rulings had moved them away from the traditional fishing sites. The meeting had been prompted by a few fishermen, who expressed an interest in documenting their struggle to maintain a viable fishing community.

As is usual in our work, we requested that a meeting be called to consider how we ought to proceed. In the past this has been a meeting of the production workers of the Media Resource Centre and representatives of the organization that has commissioned the production. In this case, we held a public meeting in a local temple where the researchers showed samples of previously produced work and the preliminary interviews of the fishermen, who had invited us to produce a documentary. The fishing families and the descendants of the pioneer fishermen brought photographs, newspaper cuttings and letters illustrating their lives as a fishing community.

It was at this meeting that the first discourse that had been established by the researchers was challenged in the face of their commitment to the principles of community video. Initially, some of the fishermen and their descendants were cautious about the project. In the past they had been filmed by commercial companies without their consent and without any knowledge of the purpose of the filming. The initial distrust led to fishermen withholding information. The public showing of these preliminary interviews at the meeting resulted in the fishermen being more critical of themselves and the researchers. For instance, one fisherman rejected the footage of his interview accusing me of having "got it all wrong"; "why did you only ask part of the story?"; "why didn't you ask me about my experience when I was a child?" The error of asking "only part of the story" lay in the attempt to extract certain answers about the community's history, based on our previous research, rather than to arrive at an understanding of this history through dialogue.

Nevertheless, the meeting proved to be crucial to the success of the project. It established a collective intent to produce a video, and it served to rekindle interest among the descendants of the pioneer fishing community that they were a "community" with a "history." It was here that the "community" was revitalized and, through dialogue with the researchers, the conditions of the project established. A production collective that included a social geographer, two members of the fishing community, and myself was formed. The meeting gave us both a mandate to proceed and some specific directives—the granddaughter of one of the famous pioneer fishermen was nominated to be the narrator. The narrator had no professional training, which added to the many educational demands that are part of any participatory approach.

Keep in mind what we learned from the meeting, we continued to record oral testimonies. When we had completed the bulk of the interviews we put together a draft film in the form of a continuous chronological narrative of the oral history. The draft film and a full transcript of the interviews and the narrator's text was presented to the community representatives and others for comment. Once the script was returned to us we completed the sound recording and started to edit the film.

The completed video was then shown to representatives of the community. They requested minor changes such as editing and caption errors, which we then corrected in a revised version of the video. The completed video was then shown to the community at a meeting held in a local library, where it was discussed and where it received the support of the fishing community.

The video is now being circulated to schools to present an alternative account—a history from below—that has not been featured in the history lessons in South African schools. The video was also instrumental in convincing the Durban City Council to guarantee the fishing rights of this community and to promote the video through the museum and library services of the city.

Apart from the role of the video as an educational and political tool, the process of production was itself extremely valuable. The fishing community developed an understanding of the production processes of video. Some of the community with direct production roles, such as the narrator, developed specific production skills. I expect them to be more assertive and less intimidated by the demands of commercial film crews in the future. With the fishing fleet reduced to a single boat operated by part-time fishermen, the community is no longer united in the common interest of fishing. The production, which took three years to complete, reconstituted the community in their common interest to document their history.

Although we had used meetings in previous productions, this was the first production in which we used large public meetings. The principal value of these meetings was the animation of community interest and involvement of people that smaller meetings might have missed.

Wherever possible, I now attempt to use this approach to encourage collective reflection, public scrutiny, and accountability.

CONCLUSION

The examples I have given of the documentary production show some ways in which a whole community and external animators may learn. Furthermore, collective learning and cultural action by civil society enable groups to challenge, cross, and transform borders that limit understanding, conversation, and power within those borders or across borders. There are easy ways of working and learning in which borders are not left unchallenged and unaltered; every time a learner crosses a border the border and the learner change.

I conclude with a question that flows out of this book's theme: Has the critical edge of liberation theology and emancipatory education gone, or does it have a new form in postmodern critique? Freire and others have given us the language to challenge borders; postmodern and feminist critiques, however, reveal borders as more complex and varied. I have attempted at a very superficial level to sharpen our examination of borders by proposing a new metaphor that releases us from the old metaphors that have held our imaginations captive.

REFERENCES

Aburge, C. (1993). What's green? Perspectives on the Earthlife Conference. In D. Hallowes (Ed.), *Hidden faces, environment, development, justice: South Africa and the global context* (pp. 8-14). Pietermaritzburg, South Africa: Earthlife Africa.

Alexander, N. (1989). Liberation pedagogy in the South African context. In C. Criticos (Ed.), *Experiential learning in formal and non-formal education* (pp. 1-14). Durban, South Africa: Media Resource Centre, University of Natal.

Criticos C. (1989). Media, praxis and empowerment. In S. Weil & I. McGill (Eds.), *Making sense of experiential learning* (pp. 206-220). London: Open University Press.

Daily News. (1993).

Development Resources Centre (DRC). (1993). *The independent study into an enabling environment for NGOs.* Johannesburg, South Africa: DRC.

Freire, P. (1972). *Pedagogy of the oppressed.* Harmondsworth, UK: Penguin.

Giroux, H. (1992). *Border crossing: Cultural workers and the politics of education.* London: Routledge.

Gilmour, D. (1988, October). *Shortages of skills or skilled shortages? A comparison of employer, pupil and teacher expectations of education.* Paper presented at the Kenton Conference, Cape Town, South Africa.

Grundy, S. (1987). *Curriculum: Product of praxis?* London: Falmer Press.

Habermas, J. (1972). *Knowledge and human interest* (2nd ed.). London: Heinemann.

Palmer, P. J. (1990). Community, conflict and ways of knowing: Ways to deepen our educational agenda. In J. Kendall (Ed.), *Combining service & learning* (Vol. 1). Raleigh: NSIEE.

Project Inspire. (1993). *Guidelines and suggestions for showing an interactive video* (Manual, No. 2). Mmabatho, South Africa: Agricor & Bop Parks.

Shor, L. (1993). Freire's critical pedagogy. In P. McLaren & P. Leonard (Eds.), *Paulo Freire, A critical encounter*. London: Routledge.

Singh, M. (1993). The role of civil society in promoting democratic development: Some aspects of the South African debate. In A. McKinstry-Micou & B. Lindsnaes (Eds.), *The role of voluntary organizations in emerging democracies*. New York: Danish Centre for Human Rights & Institute of International Education.

Stanton, T. (1990, July). *Think piece: Field Experience and Liberal Arts Education*. Paper presented at the 1990 NSIEE conference in Boulder, CO.

Chapter ▪ 11

Questioning the Concept of Globalization: Some Pedagogic Challenges

Michael Richards

This chapter has three main aims. First, to argue that certain developments in worldwide mass media, the so-called globalization process, can reinforce the claims of the dominant paradigm of development and overstate the potential of Western media products to sustain ideological practices of domination in developing countries. The second aim is to challenge simplified notions of globalization and to situate some Freirean ideas relating to, for example, the questioning of the nature of society, power and knowledge, control, consciousness and pedagogy within this debate. From this, the final aim is to propose a perspective on communications education capable of contributing to an understanding of the role of the mass media in a developing context.

THE IDEA OF GLOBALIZATION

Changes have taken place affecting broadcasting systems around the world that are often taken as leading to the threat, and perhaps the reality, of the globalization of television in spite of whatever local cultural context may obtain. Among these are the increasing number of channels, the increasing length of television schedules, changing patterns of global ownership, the increasing wealth potential of local television markets, the increasing massification of television markets, the changed economic base of broadcasting systems, changes in the technology of reception and pressure on established regulatory regimes. These changes are often taken to signify a process called globalization.

The globalization debate provides a framework for the study of East–West media relations. A forerunner of the issue was the media imperialism debate, the main aspects of which have been discussed by Wells (1974), Tunstall (1977), Katz and Wedell (1978), Golding and Elliot (1979), among others. It has continued as the new technologies of cable and especially satellite have, on the one hand, offered new opportunities to use mass communication to solve the problems of underdevelopment and, on the other hand, to increase the dependence of less wealthy countries on the rich by virtue of an imbalance in the control of the new technologies.

During the 1970s and 1980s, many viewers in developed and then in developing countries found themselves receiving new television channels and experienced an overall increase in the number of conventional television channels, video channels, and channels provided by cable, whether from near neighbors or via satellite from faraway locations. This increase in channels and the number of hours of transmission available usually led to an increase in the proportion of U.S.-originated content in television schedules. This was often taken as evidence that there was a Western imperialist policy to dominate global markets, irrespective of the effects on local and national cultures (see Cruise O'Brien, 1974; Hartmann, Patil, & Dighe, 1989; Schiller, 1969).

However, Tunstall and Palmer (1991) suggest that that there is little evidence of a U.S.-led media industry because, although popular channels in Europe and the Far East required extra advertising revenue, both popular viewer demand and regulatory pressures persuaded those channels to invest in domestic programming. Indeed, they argue that during 1980s there was an increasingly complex relationship of media levels beyond the national, such as the local, the regional, the city-urban, and the community, all of which cast doubt on a simple model of global media penetration by the West.

Earlier in 1977, Tunstall had argued that the television imperialism thesis was both too strong and too weak. The thesis was too strong because it accepted the optimistic rhetoric of U.S. television promotional campaigns. Also proponents of the thesis have noted that in poor countries only the rich can afford television sets, yet television is said to subvert the whole nation. The thesis is at the same time too weak because it ignores the tendency of television, wherever programs may have originated, merely to repeat a previous pattern of Western-dominated practices in radio and feature films.

Support for the view that the media imperialism thesis is too strong also came from Katz and Wedell (1978), who suggested that it takes too little account of radio and of the differences within and between countries. In their study of the history of radio and television in the African, Asian, and South American countries, the tendency of mere repetition of Western media practices and structures was challenged. Katz and Wedell pointed to phases of institutionalization, in which the direct transfer or adoption of a metropolitan model of broadcasting was followed by a period of adapting the system to the local society. Following this phase, a new sense of direction was introduced, removing at least direct foreign ownership and therefore some potential influence.

A further limitation of the media imperialism thesis is its assumption that media imperialism equals cultural imperialism and therefore that "authentic" national cultures will be swamped by imported Western cultures. More specifically, the thesis claims that these cultures are undermined by the dumping of Western culture via slick media products. There are two problems with this argument: first, many programs are bought cheaply and are old, dated, and relatively unsophisticated. They were made for a different audience at a different time in television history and therefore may appear to be inappropriate and unreal. Second, cultural identity is only part of a national identity, and many countries have an ambiguous national identity. When there are multiple languages, religions, ethnic groupings, further complicated by social class and social status differences, then the existence of any simple national and cultural identity is difficult to imagine. If it does not exist, it cannot be subverted. In any case, the different elements in multivariant societies respond differently to outside media sources whose products can be "read" against the prevailing local culture and identity. Culture is a multilayered phenomenon, the product of local, tribal, regional, or national dimensions, which is anything but the product of a simple international culture.

A further weakness of the thesis is that media imperialism fails to recognize that there are strong regional exporters of television programs other than the United States. For example, Mexico and Argentina have a tradition of exporting media to near neighbors and to Hispanic countries, whereas Indian films and records are distributed to many countries in Africa and Asia. However, it should be noted, countries that are strong "regional exporters" of media tend themselves to be heavy importers of U.S. media (Tunstall, 1977). This suggests that in addition to rejecting some of the tenets of a simple media imperialism thesis, it would be wise also to recognize that there are "open" and "less open" markets for media products. The door that is opened to allow exports out also allows imports to pass through it.

Finally, as Hartmann et al. (1989) in their intriguing study of the impact of the mass media on village in India and the implications for development have pointed out, assumptions about the influence of media on day-to-day life often ignore social structure and structural conflict, treating audiences as an amorphous mass. In addition, there is a tendency in the received wisdom about development and the mass media to regard consumers as essentially passive. This leads to particular assumptions about media effects work and therefore misleading privilege research paradigms and methodologies that operate within an effects or effectiveness framework. As these authors and many others have noted, "in most respects mass communications are far less important sources of information and influence than interpersonal communication" (p. 259).

Globalization can be considered in terms of three distinct categories: First, in its corporate form, as supranational business organizations with a structure of ownership and control organized to operate on a global basis. Included within this are the organizational activities of governments and intergovernmental organizations that provide the operative conditions under which supranational business can function. Second, globalization can be seen as corporate ideology, not in the sense that its basis lies only in the corporations, but that an ideology has been established that serves the interests of the corporations and that sets the terms of the debate, such that the growth of global culture is accepted as a given. It may be fought against, but it is a real process that sets the terms within which action and debate has to take place. More than this, the globalization process is something that has the force of inevitability behind it and will only not come to fruition if held off by the actions of resistance movements fighting the tide of history. In this sense the globalization ideology is subscribed to by many opponents of the globalization process just as strongly as by those who support the corporate forms of globalism. The third dimension of globalization is as a process with an empirical dimension—in other words, as a process that can be observed. Globalization is often characterized by major social, cultural, and institutional change, whose token persuasiveness demands investigation.

Globalization emphasizes the break-up of the nation-state as a major unit of world order, coupled with the growth of the multinational corporation, which through industry, trade, and communication technologies, has the power to transcend national boundaries. Globalization is not a new, sudden, or overnight phenomenon, but a new concept to explain the changing nature of global media. It is perhaps a panic-like intellectual response to a phenomenon that has been gaining pace throughout the 1980s.

Ferguson (1992) has challenged some of the assumptions about globalization. Globalization is fundamentally about change and reordering; it is a concept for evaluating "a particular series of developments concerning the concrete structuration of the world as a whole" (Robertson, 1990, p. 20), in which we become part of "the whole earth as the physical environment, everyone living as world citizens, consumers and producers with a common interest in collective action to solve global problems" (Albrow, 1990, pp. 8-10). Postmodernists, for example, Baudrillard (1985) and Jameson (1984), have tended to emphasize the coming of a common culture of style and consumption. Nevertheless, a common feature of discussions of globalization is a concern with the empirical reality of a world system that consigns national concerns to a world stage.

Ferguson's (1992) analysis focuses on the myths of globalization, arguing that the meaning of the concept, the evidence for its processes and actions, and the evolution of the concept are befuddled by seven myths about globalization: the myth that big is better, that more is better, that time and space have disappeared, that a global cultural homogeneity has arrived, that globalization has masked the real issues in saving the planet, that democracy can be exported via U.S. television, and that there is new world order. As she points out, the categorization of globalization as myth demands a critical approach to globalization, particularly in "an examination of the resurgent economic determinism at the heart of the globalization rhetoric emanating from postmodernists, media imperialists and corporate publicists alike" (p. 87).

Massey (1991) has examined the nature of mobility in the era of globalization and what this means for our sense of place—the phenomenon of time–space compression. Her point is that despite advances in new communication technologies and global transportation, time–space compression does not happen for everyone in all spheres of social and economic activity. Different social groups and different individuals are situated in various ways in relation to international flows and interconnections, which has to do with power. Different social groups have distinct relationships to mobility, and some are more in charge of these relationships than others. The ones distributing films, controlling the news, selling television programs, are really the ones in charge of time–space compression. This group, Massey argues, can also include Western teachers, academics, and journalists, those who write and talk most about time–space compression.

Some aspects of these debates about the nature and existence of globalization were captured in a paper written nearly 25 years ago by Peter Golding (1974). He argued that orthodox theories of modernization used "the characteristics of Western European and North American society as goal states from which calibrated indices of underdevelopment can be constructed" (p. 30). This orthodoxy, he suggests, denies the complex histories of developing countries and imposes a set of values deemed to be crucial to development that are no more than ideological representations of free enterprise. Thus, in one sense, development equals liberation, a freedom created by outside influences (see also, Ferguson, 1992).

This diffusion approach focuses on the part played by the mass media in social change. Rogers (1963) argues that media exposure is the key intervening variable, along with education, between major socioeconomic variables and attitudes and knowledge to development. Indeed, he is anxious that the media should "enable officials to reach mass audiences with rapid, standardized and accurate messages about development." This position takes an unsophisticated view of the media, ignoring its content and the use made of it. It assumes that because the mass media are an important feature of advanced societies, then mass media in traditional societies will promote development, in particular a form of development that emphasizes identification with the goals, aspirations, and values of a middle-class Western lifestyle (see Lerner, 1963; Pool, 1963; Schramm, 1964). Researchers who have in fact only examined media content have been criticized for ignoring the action frame and the role of communications media in defining broad types of forms of action that are "open" rather than "closed" and that offer multiple interpretations (see Peacook, 1969). An important task for social analysts is to chart and understand cross-border identifications (see Collins, 1990; Hebdige, 1982; Schlesinger, 1991). Over a considerable period it is possible that discrete national cultures will be eroded. The globalizing pressures of transnational media distribution and the impact of new communication technologies, plus developments in commercial and transportation systems, suggest the creation of image spaces. However, we must be careful not to argue a simple case of technological determinism and must situate work in empirical investigations of local consumption contexts. Indeed, some aspects of globalization can, according to some authors (see Hall, 1992), produce a strengthening of localized ethnic and cultural identities. Put another way, academic research has begun to recognize the importance of the circumstances in which television is watched and what meanings or pleasures are created when television is consumed (see Silverstone, Hirsch, & Morley, 1991; Morley, 1991).

Insights into local resistance have been provided by Negus (1993), who focuses on processes of globalization in the music industry, in which locally produced music is usually depersonalized in favor of material produced by artists from Britain and the United States. When local state and community interests attempt to support musical activity, they are in opposition to that of the major entertainment corporations. Negus shows how transnational policies practiced by music companies create local tensions and reactions, and how a complex series of nationstate, market, and zonal relationships and reactions mediate processes of globalization as global intentions are translated into local activities. In that globalization is concerned with the organization of production and the exploitation of markets on a world scale, it signifies the continuation of a trend the concentration of capital and attempts by capitalist organizations to expand by breaking down geographical and political boundaries. However, Robins (1991) has argued that globalization fractures the association between cultural and geographical territory with the potential for creating new identities. Although the ability to receive and act on these new identities is dependent on access to the appropriate technologies of reception, globalization nevertheless makes the relationship between culture and geographical territory more significant when products and messages are perceived as coming from the outside. In this case, as Hall (1991) has suggested, globalization increases the awareness of local territories and their characteristics.

Ali Mohammadi (1990) has argued a similar case for the potential to resist global media in a case study of Iran. Acknowledging that national cultures of the Third World may be threatened by Western cultural imperialism, with media at the cutting edge of the process, he demonstrates that Iranian experience leads us to question the powerful media/powerful effects model of communication. He argues that in prerevolutionary Iran, the Shah could control all the media but could not procure political legitimacy, and that Iranian viewers, although exposed to a lot of U.S. programming, preferred their own values to those portrayed in these programs. But, more importantly, the case study also showed that even though cultural identity may be an important appeal against the forces of Westernization, it alone does not guarantee broader progressive social values such as freedom and justice.

Sahin and Aksoy (1993) demonstraté how "the Turkish media scene was swept by powerful winds of technological change and globalization with profound implications for national and cultural identities." The opening of the media floodgates, such as that experienced by Turkey in the late 1980s and early 1990s has, according to Sahin and Aksoy, expanded the range of ideological debate and contributed to the dissolution of official dogma and the relativization of Turkish culture. Thus, operating outside the official ideology, global stations such as the Magic Box brought issues such as ethnicity, religion, language, and group aspirations to the fore, and in so doing have helped to redefine the national culture and identity of Turkey.

In addition, there were the negative aspects of globalization, and the importation of cheap U.S. and Latin American series, largely quiz shows and comedies. Global media also helped to shape the format of programs produced in Turkey, in which professional style and production values became Westernized. Sahin and Aksoy suggest that global media have played a significant part in breaking up a unitary national culture by feeding the so-called small worlds of real Turkey into the larger world of imagined Turkey, while at the same time homogenizing differences and creating imagined communities. In this new cultural landscape "identity by choice" (see Schlesinger, 1991) is created, in which new types of communities, based on shared values such as consumption, ethnicity, religion, or gender, are created. In this new landscape individuals can choose their own identities and the communities to which they wish to belong. Thus with greater transnational communication the identities of individuals may be determined more by economic, political, or cultural communities than by nations. Appadurai (1990) suggests that these communities are able to subvert the imagined worlds of the official discourse.

However, choosing identities through global media is not problematic, for the choices may become progressively more limited when market forces of production and distribution operate in a deregulated, even delegalized, environment, and when untrammelled competition is the norm.

This "tour" of some of the issues discussed in the context of the nature and consequences of globalization has inevitably been selective in order to serve the overall argument of this chapter. However, it is clear that globalization as a concept is open to challenge. Evidence for it is partial, sometimes contradictory, yet at the same time it remains powerful. A legacy of the globalization debate is to encourage the promotion of the idea of freedom from dominant ideologies through media and to rediscover the importance of the action frame of reference. Such a position recognizes the value of that work on audiences and media that identify the capacity of audiences to act on and utilize media in a variety of ways, ways that could not be "read" from a text or from a producer source (see Morley, 1991; Silverstone et al., 1991).

SOME LINKS WITH FREIRE

I now turn, in a selective fashion, to some of the ideas of Freire and to link them, as heuristic devices, to the preceding discussion in an attempt to propose a pedagogy of communications and media education that recognizes the opportunities for action arising from the globalization debate.

Freire's writings are of course central to the debate because they are concerned with forms of cultural action. Using a similar argument to the "globalists" in terms of the relation of the West to the East, or of the center to the periphery, Freire's work asserts that economic and cultural dominance is practiced by a metropolitan society on a dominated society. Education becomes an important site of domination by the metropolitan society, an instrument of oppression that limits the development of societies dependent on metropolitan society.

Freire's critique of the educational process highlights the interpersonal relationship between teacher and pupil. Teachers engage in a form of action on behalf of oppressors, a domination characterized by narration. The narrative process is an instrument of oppression in which teachers are the conscious or unconscious instruments of oppression, and, through these forms of cultural action, a form of ideological consciousness is secured within which the oppressed are absorbed.

Thus Freire's social pedagogy situates education as a set of processes that help to construct both the individual and society. But education is a process of social action that can either domesticate students or empower them. Domesticity is achieved in traditional classrooms in which students develop authority dependence listening to teachers telling them what to do and what things mean (see Shor, 1993).

Education is a cultural process; cultural in the anthropological sense that culture is the result of the actions of humans in society and what they contribute to the world in which they find themselves. Culture is what ordinary people do every day, and as such everyone has and makes culture. An anthropological definition of culture, situated in the experiences of everyday life, democratizes pedagogy because the curriculum is built around the conditions of peoples' lives. Freirean educators emphasize the need to study their students to discover conditions and habits central to their experiences. From this material they identify generative words and themes that are familiar words, experiences, and situations that are represented to students as something to reflect on. In this way they gain some critical distance from their immediate experiences and generate what Freire calls an "epistemological relationship to reality," that is, becoming a critical examiner of experience. By contrast, traditional education presents its themes, language, and materials from the top down: invoking a culture and languages that are unfamiliar to most students.

Freire's conception of the process of education echoes that of globalization. Both are concerned with domination, oppression, cultural hegemony, and the denial of the possibility of social action and of actors' abilities to reconstitute forms of knowledge handed down. Both warn against the values of the "other."

A crucial legacy of Freire's work is the opportunity it provides to develop a pedagogy of media education that can both inform those who will study globalization and, at the same time, provide insights for understanding processes of local resistance to and transformations of the globalization of the media by ordinary people in their everyday lives.

Freire's work as an academic commodity cannot be utilized for all times and places without some self-evaluation (see Giroux, 1993). First, the specific forms of privilege that are dominant in the language of Western educators and cultural producers must be acknowledged. Perhaps the most important are those that sustain maleness, whiteness, property, competition, and the market as dominant forces. Second, ways in which Western knowledge is encased in particular historical and institutional societies that both privilege and exclude particular forms of authority, values, representations, and social relationships must be· made visible. Third, the complex nature of human agency and the multiple discourses and cultural resources available must be acknowledged.

TOWARD A COMMUNICATIVE PEDAGOGY OF GLOBALIZATION

What then should a pedagogy for globalization address? What is it that students and consumers of global products alike should be enabled to understand and develop, and how can this be achieved? It may be tempting to think that globalizing the communications curriculum means producing more textbooks outside the United States or Western Europe, or better, the need for courses to include material on a wider variety of national and international contexts. Both of these responses miss the point. A pedagogy of globalization must be a response to the new cultural environment in which students in Asia and in developing countries are being educated (see Holaday, 1992). In these contexts, the curriculum has been Westernized, Asianized, and now must be globalized. Of course, there have been attempts to assert Asian values against the imbalance of cultural and informational flows from the West. These approaches have tended to look for Asian values and philosophical assumptions to underpin teaching and research in communication (see Dissanayake, 1988). As a specific instance of this, Mahmoud Abu-Said (1993) has argued that "a Muslim researcher who wishes to write about any behavioural science from an Islamic point of view must follow a method that relies upon Islamic philosophy . . . which is the ideal that determines the aim of life and the motive for every action" (p. 16).

However, it is not content, nor the source of material, nor even the philosophical underpinnings of arguments, but a conceptual framework accessible to both students of communication and consumers of communication that will permit an understanding of globalization and thus empower users to engage with it. Building on Shor (1993), I suggest that the pedagogy should have the following points of focus.

1. Power. Information and knowledge are an ever-increasing part of the formula of power, and the role of information itself can transform the relationships of power. Traditional concepts of power, following Weber, see it as the use of qualities and possessions in a direct way to attain goals or end-states, that is, to achieve objectives at the expense of others. Thus, there are those who have power and those who are powerless. However, power can also be seen as a dynamic process, sometimes asymmetrical, as writers such as Foucault (1980) and Giddens (1984) have pointed out, an understanding that societies can be constituted through human social action and by organized groups. Knowing who exercises power, and how it is organized, constitutes an important first step for social action. Although there is a flow of information from the center to the metropolitan center of the periphery, rarely is there more than a trickle of indigenously produced information in the opposite direction. The flow of media material should be understood in terms of the difficulties that less developed countries have in combating information flow and strategies that can be developed to redress this imbalance.

2. Critical awareness. Developing analytical habits of thinking go beneath surface impressions and beyond traditional myths, understanding the social context and meaning of events for those who are the objects of study and the consumers of cultural goods. For example, assumptions about flow patterns tend to assume a passive audience which receives rather than responds to a text. Critical awareness of media products is also particularly important in a context in which a substantial part of the broadcast diet is material produced in another culture and with another culture in mind. In this case Freire's method of conscientization is particularly important, in which individuals are enabled to understand

their condition through critical reflection and participation and in so doing can break through the culture of silence.

3. Resources. Just as the domination of Western media products should be resisted, so should the exclusive use of Western-generated critiques be eschewed. Course material should be situated in the thought, language, and material conditions of those who are the recipients of globalization.

4. Self awareness. Students should question what we know about globalization, how we know what we know, and how we can learn what we still need to know. Students should reflect on their own knowledge, language, and experiences in relation to the subject matter and interrogate their own processes of coming to know. Whatever the content and nature of national cultures, language is crucial in maintaining cultural difference. Language of origin is an important factor in the establishment of global communities, thus those whose first language is not English, Spanish, Russian, or Portuguese—the four most widely spoken European languages—may feel that they are not part of a linguistically determined world order.

5. Problem raising. Issues on globalization should be generated from the inside, from the "periphery," from the "oppressed," not just from concerns by Western scholars who themselves contribute to the process of the globalization of knowledge. That the culture of nondominant groups should be as rich a driving force for the pedagogy as that of the dominant groups. For example, the perpetuation of particular organizational structures, often derived from an imported model, can be sustained by the nature of professionalism. Professionalism in broadcasting may produce resistances to change, arguing that change may lower standards. But training and education for the media in developing countries must be considered in the context of national priorities and needs. Educational broadcasting often commands a low priority in terms of talent and effort in many national broadcasting organizations in the West. This need not apply in a developing context: Recruitment and career structures in both education and broadcasting could be coordinated for the better use of talent.

6. Research-orientated. Pedagogy should encourage research and expect students to be researchers into their own conditions and those of others and into their relationship to existing academic material. Any research project must be self-reflective and determine which actors, which interest groups may be enabled to engage more critically with "global media" as a result of the research project, while at the same time identify the

structural constraints to the exercise of "freedom" that
may still exist and what local strategies are possible.

7. Active. A communications pedagogy should encourage
action outcomes, to relate knowledge to power, to enable
people to act on knowledge, and to utilize knowledge to
enable students and consumers alike to become change
agents. Knowledge must be accessible to consumers,
and a reflexive relationship to television use encouraged.

8. Policy-oriented. The capacity of broadcasting to assist the
incorporation of communities and groups into societies—
that is, to reverse the marginalization of underprivileged
and underrepresented groups—should be pursued. The
capacity of a broadcast system to respond to the needs of
different groups highlights its effectiveness as a two-way
process rather than a one-way process of control. An
awareness of external constraints and a positive attempt
to maintain national control for national purposes
requires an understanding of its internal goals, an ability
to relate organizational policies to national policies.

CONCLUSIONS

Freire's work has provided guidance and inspiration, but, as he
acknowledges, his ideas and methods should be reinvented as a
basis for a liberating education in our own situations. Freirean principles can be applied to education in general and the study of television in particular. Television is a powerful educational force, a significant source of orientations, and one to which we may be more
receptive than we are to education. Because the "inspiration" it provides does not come from the classroom, it is all the more reason to
educate for television, to educate for freedom, to use television, and
not to be used by it. Communications and media education has
tended to pay insufficient attention to developments in international
media, particularly the relation to the interface between the global
and the local. If there is something distinctive about a pedagogy for
globalization, it lies in acknowledging ways in which national media
belong to an international media system yet retain their own national distinctiveness, and that the experience of consuming and studying global media can be a site for critical development, ideological
resistance, and liberation.

REFERENCES

Abu-Said, M. (1993). The methodology of the Islamic behavioural sciences. *The American Journal of Islamic Social Science, 10*(3), 10-
18.

Albrow, M. (1990). Introduction. In M. Albrow & E. King (Eds.), *Colonisation, knowledge and society* (pp. 3-13). London: Cape.

Appadurai, A. (1990). Disjuncture and difference in the global cultural economy. In M. Featherstone (Ed.), *Global culture* (pp. 295-310). London: Sage.

Baudrillard, J. (1985, Winter). Child in the bubble. *Impulse*, pp. 12-13.

Collins, R. (1990). *Satellite television in Western Europe.* London: John Libbey.

Cruise O'Brien, R. (1974). Domination and dependence in mass communications: Implications for the use of broadcasting in developing countries. *Institute of Development Studies Bulletin, 6*(4), 85-99.

Dissanayake, W. (1988). *Communication theory: The Asian perspective.* Singapore: AMIC.

Ferguson, M. (1992). The mythology about globalisation. *European Journal of Communication, 7*, 69-93.

Foucault, M. (1980). *Power/knowledge. Selected interviews and other writings.* Brighton, UK: Harvester.

Giddens, A. (1984). *The constitution of society: Outline of the theory of structuration.* Berkeley: University of California Press.

Giroux, H. (1993). Paulo Freire and the politics of postcolonialism. In P. McLaren & P. Leonard (Eds.), *Paulo Freire: A critical encounter* (pp. 177-188). London: Routledge.

Golding, P. (1974, Summer). Media role in national development: Critique of a theoretical orthodoxy. *Journal of Communication, 24*(3), 39-53.

Golding, P., & Elliott, P. (1979). *Making the news.* London: Longman.

Hall, S. (1991). Old and new identities, old and new ethnicities. In A. King (Ed.), *Culture, globalization and the world system* (pp. 41-68). London: Macmillan.

Hall, S. (1992) . The question of cultural identity. In S. Hall, D. Held, & T. McGrew (Eds.), *Modernity and its future* (pp. 273-325). Cambridge: Cambridge Polity Press.

Hartmann, P., Patil, B., & Dighe, A. (1989). *The mass media and village life: An Indian study.* New Delhi: Sage.

Hebdige, D. (1982). Towards a cartography of taste, 1935-1962. In B. Waite, T. Bennett & G. Martin (Eds.), *Popular culture past and present* (pp.154-211). London: Croom Helm.

Holaday, D. (1992), Globalizing the communication curriculum. *Media Asia, 19*(4), 226-229.

Jameson, F. (1984). Postmodernism, or the cultural logic of late capitalism. *New Left Review, 146*, 53-92.

Katz, E., & Wedell, G. (Eds.). (1978). *Broadcasting in the Third World: Promise and performance.* Cambridge, MA: Harvard University Press.

Lerner D. (1963). Toward a communication theory of modernisation. In L.W. Pye (Ed.), *Communications and political development* (pp. 327-350). Princeton NJ: Princeton University Press.

Massey, D. (1991, June). A global sense of place. *Marxism Today*, 24-29.

Mohammadi, A. (1990). Cultural imperialism and cultural identity. In J. Downey, A. Mohammadi & A. Sreberny-Mohammadi (Eds.), *Questioning the media* (pp. 267-280). London: Sage.

Morley, D. (1991). Where the global meets the local: Notes from the sitting room. *Screen, 32*(1), 1-15.

Negus, K. (1993). Global harmonies and local discords: Transnational policies and practices in the European recording industry. *European Journal of Communication, 8*, 295-316.

Peacock, J.J. (1969). Religion, communications and modernisation: A Weberian critique of some recent views. *Human Organisation, I*, 35-41.

Pool, I. de S. (1963). The mass media and politics in the modernisation process. In L.W. Pye (Ed.), *Communications and political development* (pp. 234-253). Princeton NJ: Princeton University Press.

Robertson, R. (1990). Mapping the global condition: Globalization as the central concept. *Theory, Culture and Society, 7*(2/3), 15-30.

Robins, K. (1991). Tradition and translation: National culture in the global context. In J. Corner & S. Harvey (Eds.), *Enterprise and heritage* (pp. 21-44). London: Routledge.

Rogers, E. (1963). *Diffusion of innovations*. New York: The Free Press.

Sahin, H., & Aksoy, A. (1993). Global media and cultural identity in Turkey. *Journal of Communication, 43*(2), 31-40.

Schiller, H. (1969). *Mass communication and American empire*. Norwood, NJ: Ablex.

Schlesinger, P. (1991). *Media, state and nation: Political violence and collective identities*. London: Sage.

Schramm, W. (1964). *Mass media and national development*. Stanford, CA: Stanford University Press.

Shor, I. (1993). Education is politics: Paulo Freire's critical pedagogy. In P. McLaren & P. Leonard (Eds.), *Paulo Freire: A critical encounter* (pp. 25-35). London: Routledge.

Silverstone, R., Hirsch, E., & Morley, D. (1991). Listening to a long conversation: An ethnographic approach to the study of information and communication technologies in the home. *Cultural Studies, 5*(2), 204-227.

Tunstall, J. (1977). *The media are American*. London: Constable.

Tunstall, J., & Palmer, M. (1991). *Media moguls*. London: Routledge.

Wells, A. (1974). *Mass communication: A world view*. Palo Alto, CA: National Press Books.

Chapter ▪ 12

Breaking Step: South African Oppositional Film and Media Education in Transition

Jeanne Prinsloo

Oppositional communication practices set out to break step, to disrupt what is prevalent and dominant. The account of oppositional filmmaking in South Africa that is presented here is a partial narrative, a selected and selective representation of representations. Like other histories, the account is chronological and refers to what precedes and surrounds it as a cultural practice. Like other histories, the meanings are necessarily relational, contextual, and unstable. This chapter recounts the historical events in order to consider the implications and limitations of the Freirean legacy within development of this specific form of communication and then to advocate the employment of postmodern understandings, not as a panacea, but as a way to move on from an impasse, to continue breaking step. It proposes that these insights should not simply influence production practices, but makes an argument for Media Education that will develop critical thinkers.

    The rise of the dominant forms of cultural expression, whether fiction or nonfiction, has neither been an automatic teleological development, not has it run an uncontested course. Cinematic and film practices that oppose mainstream practices have developed concurrently with the meteoric rise of dominant Hollywood cinema. Soviet cinema of the 1920s, German Expressionism, and

185

Italian Neo-Realism are early oppositional film movements. Considerable debate has addressed oppositional cinema since Mulvey's (1975) attack on dominant cinematic forms as monolithically reproducing dominant (patriarchal) ideology. Feminist film theory and practice has dominated these debates in the Euro-American arena. In South Africa, particular terms that have emerged from recent debates and that have acquired currency include Cinema of Africa, Africa Cinema, Third Cinema, Cinema of Resistance, Black film, and, somewhat more diffidently, feminist film.

The common thrust of these approaches is their attempt to critically confront the discourses of the center that have disregarded all history that does not relate the unfolding of White Euro-American history as uniform, chronological, and teleological. The discourses of the center have articulated the inferiority of all other cultures and histories. They construct both the histories and the cultures as that of "other." These discourses articulate and achieve inscription in the following ways. First, the discourses have been legitimized by an Enlightenment appeal to rationality, progress, and humanism. Second, they have inscribed (and been inscribed by) the subject: Although modernist discourses vary, they arise from a Eurocentric position, defined within totalizing and universalistic theories, that create a transcendental White, male, Eurocentric subject that occupies the center of power and the realm of action. Third, they achieve a representation of those "others" marginalized by these metanarratives as the object of its gaze, both literally and metaphorically. The "other" cannot be a historical agent except by incorporation into the modernist notion of progress. Modernism, then, can only be accompanied by epistemic and material violence to those it produces as peripheral. Beyond the largely rejected explanation of biological superiority, the modernist discourses have not developed cultural criticism capable of redefining the boundaries between itself and its subordinate groups defined in terms of race, sex, class, and colonialism. This does not imply simply or exclusively an indifference by those in the center, but suggests that the humanist emancipatory promise of pluralism and multiculturalism remains unable to reach any kind of fruition. It remains ensnared with the Western models of authority that privileges the White male at the center of history and views history as the unproblematic unfolding of science, reason and technology:

> Though the theoretical sweep is broad and oversimplified here, the basic issue is that modernist discourse in its various forms rarely engages how white authority is inscribed and implicated in the creation and production of a society in which the voices of the centre appear either invisible or unimplicated in the historical and social construction of racism as an integral part of their own collective identity. (Giroux, 1992, p. 116)

Theorists on the left had recourse to Marxism as an oppositional position from which to understand society. However, by extension then, a validation of "history" as a modernist metanarrative
implicates Marxism as well. In the aptly titled *White Mythologies*,
Robert Young (1990) considers Western narratives of history. He
describes Marxism's universalizing narrative of the unfolding of a
rational system of world history as simply a reversed form of the history of European imperialism. He reminds the reader that Hegel
declared that "Africa has no history," and that, although critical of
British imperialism, Marx essentially approved of the British colonization of India because it led India within the narrative of Western
history, thereby producing the conditions for future class struggle
there. A Marxist history thus appears as the other side of the same
coin of that imperial narrative that required the subjugation of
Europe's "others" as the condition of its own authority. The process
is described by Cixous and Clemente (1986) as "the reduction of a
'person' to a 'nobody' to the position of 'other'—the inexorable plot of
racism" (p. 71)

In Africa the development of film is implicated in the plot of
European colonialism.[1] Louis Lumiere is credited with the invention of
the cinema in 1895 and evidently showings of the Lumiere cinemato-
graph took place in the back rooms of cafes in Alexandra and Cairo in
1896 (Thoraval, 1975). The market for films developed around the
tastes of the colonial powers is mirrored in their attempt to protect
Africans from commercial films and conventional film styles: "The
African is, in general, not mature for cinema. Cinematographic conventions disrupt him; psychological nuances escape him; rapid suc-
cessions of image submerge him" (quotation of Belgian authorities in
Belgian Congo cited in Diawara, 1984, p. 29).

It is only after countries achieved independence that there
arose the opportunity to develop an African film industry. Although
the modernist enterprise frequently situates emergent cinema, it also
becomes possible to operate beyond and against the defines of imperial discourse, albeit against the backdrop of competition with and
evaluation by industrial countries:

> Film-making demands close contacts with Europe for aspiring
> filmmakers virtually everywhere outside Egypt. . . . Feature
> films are not made by people coming directly from remote
> rural villages, since the successful realization of a film
> involves both mastery of a Western-originated technology and
> understanding (if not imitation) of Western systems of audio-
> visual narrative. (Malkmus & Armes, 1991, p. 42)

---

[1] The Berlin conference of European powers in the partition of Africa, the so-
called "Scramble of Africa," took place in 1884–5, and the last great outward
surge of European imperialism lasted until the outbreak of the 1914 war.

The politics of identity are thus implicated within the development of film. It is on the lines of gender and race, in which the marks of exclusion are displayed, Cainlike, on the skin, that the conflict of identity is intensified. Undoubtedly the subjects of these narratives need to shift, the discourses to change. The struggles become articulated in and by dissenting and oppositional discourses and social movements. The politics of representation thus pervade these battles. Yet there is a tension between identity and the politics of representation, a tension between what is posed as a cultural struggle and democracy. The practices and texts that readdress difference and identity are acts of resistance and transformation. Yet it is to the latter that attention needs to be given. Identity politics plays a crucial role in challenging those discourses that have positioned them, yet it needs to move to transformation, to a notion of citizenry and democracy.

Identity politics runs the risk of simply reversing the power relations, of demanding the opposite but the same. For it is through binarism and belief in essentialism that the modernist discourse limits and controls. It is the argument of this chapter that to move beyond this there is the need to call on certain understandings of postmodern critique so as to challenge the metanarratives. This chapter presents an overview of oppositional filmmaking in South Africa through the 1970s and 1980s and analyzes the shifts in cultural debate. This leads to an argument for media education as a tool of critical citizenry.

The development of South African filmmaking shows some similarities with that of other African countries. Moreover, the question of identity politics takes on added relevance perhaps because of the differences in historical experience: the White minority government maintained racist power for decades longer than in most other countries and became, in a certain sense, a postcolonial regime representing a domestic, rather than a foreign elite.

Historically, as in other places in Africa, film viewing as a leisure activity was largely confined to the privileged sectors of society. Commercial venues restricted their audiences along overtly racial lines as well as in economic and class terms. Viewers were offered particular and restricted representations and constructions of the "world" as most films were imported from the United States and England, thereby offering classic Hollywood texts and the associated ideological constructions. Moreover, the film industry in South Africa has historically been controlled stringently by the state largely through the deployment of subsidies (Tomaselli, 1989).[2] Feature films made within South Africa have generally been produced by those filmmakers whose films have been considered apolitical or that

---

[2]Rather than launching a national film industry as was the intention, the subsidy system established in 1956 restricted the development of a genuine cinema. The state subsidy system was considered to protect the incompetent as well as to reaffirm the ideology of the Nationalist Party or at least not counter it.

have supported the Nationalist government's position. Documentary films, considered educational and informative, more directly reflected the ideological framework of the ruling party and promoted their interests. Political opposition to the state was also regulated by Draconian laws of control and censorship for which the penalties exacted were high.

Nevertheless, during the 1970s and 1980s, numerous oppositional groupings in South Africa cohered around the notion of the "struggle" that was waged on many fronts, but it was possible to identify a homogenous adversary manifest in apartheid. Groupings opposed to the government began to produce films, particularly documentaries. Oppositional film acquired greater impact and relevance, and identity politics were put into sharp focus. This interest in filmmaking coincided with other forms of cultural action and struggle.

It responded to a desire to present discourses other than those inscribed by the absolute and inflexible position of the South African mainstream film and broadcast industries. There was a sense of righteous indignation that demanded the exposure of the conditions prevalent in South Africa. In another way, in a Freirean sense, there was a commitment and understanding among cultural workers that the experiences of oppression could be represented so as to enable those oppressed to reflect on such experiences as a necessary prelude to action. These responses are evident in two types of documentaries that can crudely be separated in time and audience: Those of the late 1970s were produced for overseas consumption and contrast with the later productions that attempted the fraught enterprise of engaging with local audience and distribution.

During the 1970s the representations of the South African conditions inscribed within the productions would simply not have been acceptable to the South African state and would have been summarily censored or banned. The documentary producers who were working in South Africa were subject to constant surveilance. For example, in 1974, Sven Persson's film "Land Apart" was filmed under continuous scrutiny by the state. Among other things, permission to film in many Black areas was denied, the production fell foul of the Publications Control Board, and the producers battled to have it passed for screening in reedited versions. Also, in 1976, filmmaker Gibsen Kente was jailed while trying to make a film in the Eastern Cape (Tomaselli, 1989). It is therefore not surprising that documentaries were made surreptitiously and screened elsewhere. Cinematic culture was stunted both as a result of censorship and political repression and the consequent self-censorship.

At this stage in northern countries, especially the United Kingdom, there appeared to be a degree of interest in South African documentaries, and these countries broadcast more of these productions than South Africans did. The productions adopted those codes that have characterized broadcast documentaries and are typically considered as BBC conventions. The voice of documentary was presented in the direct-address style with its distinctive formal and ideological qualities. An authoritative off-screen narration presents a single, uncontested position that implicitly claims authorial omniscience and results in didactic reductionism. Known as the Voice of God, predictably the naturalized and invisible voice emanates from a White man sporting a middle-class accent, usually British (and preferably Oxbridge). A shift in broadcast codes, drawing on journalistic practices, incorporated direct address with the narrator on screen presenting an argument to the audience. This was achieved by incorporating the "evidence" of witnesses in the form of interviews. These interviewee-witnesses have the ideological impact of imparting an authentic and representative tone to the argument or position presented. The encoding appears to reconstruct objective and authentic experiences, and posits an unquestioned empiricism: "Very few seem prepared to admit through the very tissue and texture of their work that all filmmaking is a form of discourse fabricating its effects, impressions, and point of view" (Nichols, 1985, p. 261).

"The White Tribe of Africa" provides a typical example of the British television documentaries under discussion. It attempts to offer an explanation of apartheid by considering the Afrikaner both as a beleaguered group and an enigmatic historic occurrence. The simplistic positioning of White people, in this case Afrikaners, in opposition to Black victims typifies this type of exposition. On the one side, interviewees are Afrikaner White men in positions of authority, who become representative of white people. Notably absent are White English-speaking corporate businessmen (or women), whose ideological position of liberalism ironically could well coincide with that of the producers. Other "witnesses" to bear testimony, authenticated by the photographic image, are Black people over a range of classes and occupations (for more detailed analyses, see Tomaselli, Williams, Steenveld, & Tomaselli, 1986). The positioning creates the Afrikaner as the "other." That these productions were also considered instrumental to the extent to which they played a role in influencing investors attitudes to South Africa implies that they were oppositional in the United Kingdom context, even if ambiguously:

> Seen in their historical context, however, these films played a significant role in informing international audiences about apartheid and the way British companies were supporting it, and, in this sense, they have influenced the development of the anti-apartheid movement and the pressure brought to bear on the state and capital in subsequent years. (*FAWO News*, 1989, p. 4)

Although these films are critical of conditions in South Africa, they present discourses that do not interrogate or make visible their paradigm or the ideological perspectives from which they operate. They enable viewers to assume the position as witness to "a window on the world," a transparency, relating to South African history, economy, and so on. They present stereotypes of Black South Africans and Afrikaners that carry particular norms of evaluation and judgment. This can engender the assumption among viewers that they have a privileged understanding of another country peripheral to their own center. This attitude has been sharply criticized as "little more than a product of the liberal moral values—the Western Norm—of a guilt-ridden British public on the consequences of their earlier coloniza-tion of Africa" (Tomaselli et al., 1986, p. 4). What is evident is that by castigating racial capitalism, it effectively ignores the inherent racism within capitalism, thereby fudging the implications for their own economic and social structure.

Many of these films were made by South Africans who con-sulted with the African National Congress (ANC) to varying degrees. Funding was received from overseas agencies and organizations such as UNESCO (as was the case with Peter Davis's "White Laager.")

Historically, 1976 has been understood as a turning point within the history of South Africa. The Soweto school resistance, the ensuing surge of mass opposition to the state which included rent boycotts and mass stayaways, the formation of a mass-based democ-ratic movement, all indicate a growing dissatisfaction and mobiliza-tion. The cultural struggle was premised on Freirean understandings of conscientization as a process. Not surprisingly, media organiza-tions were conceived as agents within the politics of representation. Their vital role was understood to include education, organization, and mobilizing people within the struggle. This role was particularly crucial because of the heterogeneity of those involved in the struggle.

The Nationalist Party was increasingly unnerved by a slip-page of power and conscious of the need for a reformed alliance in order to continue to control. The establishment of a tricameral par-liament proposed representation at a parliamentary level for two racially defined groups ("Coloreds" and Indians) previously excluded. Opposition to the tricameral parliament was mobilized under the banner of the United Democratic Front (UDF) in 1984, which was perceived as a surrogate of the African National Congress (ANC). In the following year (1985) the major labor federation, COSATU, was founded with an overtly political agenda. The restriction of the UDF in 1988 left COSATU in the leading role of what became known as the Mass Democratic Movement (MDM). The MDM incorporated the community organizations, which formed the base of the UDF, and church, educational, and labor organizations. They were united in their opposition to the existing power structures of apartheid and their goal of moving to a democratic society and maintained the UDF's categorical espousal of non-racism.

In 1976, television was introduced in South Africa, which was to have significant implications for film/video production. This tardy arrival coincided with the demise of Albert Hertzog's influence. He was Minister of Posts and Communications until 1968 and remained in the cabinet until 1970, when he was dismissed. He had exerted great influence on his right-wing supporters in their determined battle against television. His opposition to television was premised on the politics of identity.[3] He feared the demise of Afrikaans culture and language in the face of the ideological impact of the importation of English programs from the United States and UK. (In 1970, he went on to lead a right-wing split to form the Herstigte Nasionale Party.)

Initially, television producers were needed in the new broadcast industry and trained mostly in communication departments, which had mushroomed in the conservative Afrikaans universities and technikons. They adopted the Voice of God conventions of broadcast television. Unsurprisingly, God appeared in support of the Nationalist Party. South African history was represented as the teleological narrative of colonialism as seen through the gaze of an Afrikaner. Indigenous people were not the subjects of such discourses, and women were positioned in peripheral roles. The practice thus replicated but exagerated those of the international mainstream.

In reaction, oppositional film aroused interest within the departments of the liberal English-speaking universities. By the 1980s, film theorists began a critical and analytic examination of film and television. They were concerned with notions of culture, hegemony, and change and drew on the Freirean discourse of "knowing subjects" as the ground of authenticity and hence authority. Many students and academics were engaged in community organization. They premised their approach of filmmaking on participatory learning/teaching methods gleaned from Freirean notions of enabling people to attain their voices. Many of the filmmakers also made documentary films with the explicit intention of creating documentaries that consciously imaged those communities which historically were seldom the subject of documentaries.

A number of video collectives were established, some of which have continued to exist and change with circumstances in South Africa. Oppositional film thus introduced subjects and narratives that had been disarticulated by the hegemonic order. Steenveld (1992) documents the development of oppositional documentary film in what she understands as its role to "reclaim" history. She summarizes the topics of the films as ranging from the general political situation to more specific concerns of the forced removals of people both in urban and rural areas, labor struggles, community forms of struggle around specific issues such as literacy or health, the role played by women, the church, and the destruction of indigenous people.

The particular aesthetics that emerged can be attributed in part to educational theory and the notion of participatory practices. To show the oppression of apartheid it became crucial to encode the resistance to this oppression. The immediate effect of this was a change in the "actors" within these discourses. Binary positions

---

[3]The Afrikaner struggle for the recognition of Afrikaans as an official language is well documented. The Nationalist Party fought the 1948 elections largely on these grounds and to institute Afrikaans as a language of instruction.

relate in opposition. In Proppian terms,[4] it appears that the flipside of the apartheid story showed the former villains/victims as active protagonists, the former heroes as the villains. The implicit nature of the quest of these changed stories simultaneously alters from the God-sanctioned quest of keeping control of the thankless minions to that of the struggle for democracy against the villain oppressor.

Whereas the interviewees/authorities within SABC productions continued to be the conventional ones, oppositional productions directed the camera lens at people who had experienced oppression, those who have taken part in resistance to the oppression that they were attempting to expose. Consequently, people engaged in menial work such as domestic workers, unemployed men and women, trade union representatives or shop stewards, squatters, and cultural workers began to be selected as appropriate and authentic witnesses. Although there is a binarism operating here, these productions achieved a broader discourse by introducing many groups of people who had until then been structured as an absence.

"FOSATU: Building Worker Unity" (1981) deals with organized labor. Lack of experience and untheorized gung-ho approaches mark this stage of production. One of the producers, Lawrence Dworkin, acknowledges that "we were all totally naive as to what went into making films for the type of constituency, that type of audience, and under what conditions we would be working" (quoted in Unwin & Balton, 1992, p. 291). Funding for this and similar productions was limited, and production depended on an activist determination. Attempts were made to move from conventional formats. Certain producers adopted a Direct Cinema approach in "Mayfair" (1984) and "Chronicles of South Africa" (1987). Some productions record the increase in grassroot organizations that offer examples of struggle. People who were conceived of as victims in the liberal overseas documentaries are now portrayed as active agents. ("Re Tla Bona" [1985] shows a Learn-and-Teach literacy project in a rural area. "The Ribbon" [1986] is one of the few productions that deals with gender.[5])

It becomes important to consider the nature and degree of change of this film movement and to attempt to problematize it, to consider its limits. If we ask who narrates these histories we confront an old problem: Who is speaking? Most production was centered in the

---

[4]Propp's (1958) *Morphology of the Folktale* offers a structural model of narrative analysis according to units he describes as narrative functions. He also defines seven possible character functions within narrative. Media theorists have appropriated and widely applied his model of analysis to popular culture. In examining the character functions in the productions described earlier, it is tempting to apply the application of the Proppian model further. Do the filmmakers on account of their class position become construed as the helper, and more cynically does the funding from abroad not become the magical agent? For discussion of application of Propp's narrative theory see Lapsley and Westlake (1988).

[5]The paucity of films that deal with gender coherently is evident in the summary report of Annecke and Tomaselli (1990).

greater Johannesburg area, a metropolitan area. The production coop-
eratives consisted, for the most part, of White filmmakers who had the
advantage of a university education. Influenced by participatory practices and electing to work outside more lucrative commercial and professional corporations, they attempted to fulfill the needs of clients
drawn largely from progressive or community organizations, largely in a
service capacity. Most undertook to train other producers who had not
had the opportunity of training. The Media Attachment Programme[6]
was one example of this type of initiative that tried to restructure the
relationship between producer and client/subjects. Its intention was to
create a space for skill transfer and politicization.

In an attempt to understand what are considered the
authenticating tropes of this film movement, one confronts certain
paradoxes or contradictions. These documentaries were validated by
the particular political position to which the producer or production
unit adhered. The need for balance of coverage was considered secondary in a climate of relentless propaganda and censorship from
the state.[7]

The heroes/subjects served as an authenticating trope, which
pertains to the selection of the heroes and interviewees. Mamphela
Ramphela is interviewed in "Ithuseng." As a Black woman doctor (rare
enough as a start), she is a figure of historical significance in terms of
her renowned support of Steve Biko, and she also speaks with confidence and assurance. The knowledge, which is offered during the video,
that she had also been banned to the area suggests that she is to be
trusted. The envisaged audience does not rely on historical analysis,
but on a shared political opposition to apartheid and common expectations that they bring to the viewing of this type or genre of production.
The new canon of heroes is also sung: Mandela, Tambo, Harry Gwala,
Neil Aggett, and David Webster are among those that come to mind
easily. It is worth noting that this appears again to be articulating the
heroic narratives of men. The change in backdrops, speakers, locations,
and scenery become the authenticating icons of the new genre.
Indigenous music also begins to become an iconic refrain signaling this
form. South African music is thus validated.

Whatever I describe relates to tendencies within this period
that was marked by differences. Structures began to change in
response to debates. The "Fruits of Defiance" (1990), which really
marks the end of the period I am discussing, shows the defiance campaign in Mannenberg. This production relies on interviews and cinema verite devices. Avoiding the didactic use of a narrator/interviewer
it showed interviews of a range of people; it intercuts these with
footage of the campaign and police action. It constructed multiple
voices—Black people, women, the subaltern, as if finally, the subaltern might speak. Other experimentation incorporated reflexive prac-

---

[6]The Media Attachment Programme in the Media Resource Centre, University
of Natal, Durban, was established in 1985.

[7]This anti-intellectualism in the early 1980s is discussed in Tomaselli &
Prinsloo (1992).

tices to confront the impact of realist codes and their accompanying naturalization of representation without calling attention to the selection and construction that accompanies any media text. "I am Cliffie Abrahams" (1984) provides one of the rare examples. This approach has had significantly less impact on documentary aesthetics, beyond the occasional presence of the crew and equipment in some productions.[8]

Notions of dialogue and reflection leading to praxis were well taken. By the late 1980s, organizations recorded events for archival purposes frequently, and youth groups recorded cultural days. For the politicized, it marked a stage of greater self-assurance. One of the paradoxes pertains to the frequent strand within these productions of a reclamation of history, in which subaltern issues are "voiced" by middle-class White producers. The issue of authenticity becomes muddied. Yet the filmmakers were political activists in many cases with a concern for the subjects and the audience. To what extent any articulation or representation is authentic and to what extent one can speak for others across any borders is a contentious issue. That any one woman can speak on behalf of other women, that a woman's voice is automatically more representative of other women or of a particular man is not axiomatic. Nor can you have a simplistic binary opposition of oppressor and oppressed:

> The moment the insider steps out from the inside, she is no longer a mere insider (and vice versa). She necessarily looks in from the outside while also looking out from the inside. Like the outsider she steps back and records what never occurred to her—the insider as being worth or in need of recording. But unlike the outsider, she also resorts to non-explicative, non-totalizing strategies that suspend meaning and resist closure. . . . For there can hardly be such a thing as an essential inside that can be homogeneously represented by all insiders; an authentic insider in here, an absolute reality out there, or an uncorrupted representative who cannot be questioned by another uncorrupted representative. (Minh-Ha, 1989, p. 145)

Spivak (1988) debates whether the subaltern can speak. There can be no authentic voice. Our attempts to know or to give voice to the other is literally to forge that knowledge or voice and the subject represented by it (Deacon, 1993).

Perhaps it is more useful to consider the limits of the discourses rather than the question of legitimacy. We need to attempt to expose relationships of social power and its discourses. To defer to

---

[8]Reflexivity is a modernist and postmodernist practice. As a modernist strategy it tends to closure and offers no emancipatory potential. Within postmodernism, although it has been accused of being narcissistic, it advocates a self-consciousness about the act of representation.

simplistic notions of "other" is to accept essential differences that deny contradiction.

Opposition to the political system formed a common ground for these camera guerrillas. Their documentaries played an important role as an antidote to mainstream productions. In addition they offered personal pleasure for people to see and "misrecognize" themselves on the screen in a Lacanian sense, to narcissistically and exhibitionistically enter into the visual pleasures on offer. This is part of the Freirean stage of recognition. Lovell (1983) considers the import of such pleasures as being of a social nature:

> Pleasures of common experiences identified and celebrated in art, and through this celebration, given recognition and validation; pleasures of solidarity to which this sharing might give rise; pleasures in shared and socially defined aspirations and hopes; in a sense of identity and community. (p. 95)

What these pleasures do not evoke is a critical sense of any kind. Mass mobilization is a political intervention that calls for following, and not necessarily reflection. Euphoria reigned temporarily within the early 1990s with the unbanning of political parties. Those within the country who had been concerned about change celebrated the release of the political prisoners. Many South Africans who had been living abroad as enforced or voluntary exiles returned. Difference and rivalry emerged among those who had been struggling on the same front ideologically. The struggle changed its nature in that it was no longer a straightforward reaction against apartheid, but was now engaged within the open political arena. Not only had the parties to negotiation to redefine their identities, but diverse interest groups struggled for recognition and power both within articulated political formations and in a broader society. It is in the demand for recognition that the politics of identity acquires an intense ambivalence, for recognition is always recognition by the other as well as recognition of the self.

In this context, the rallying cries can appear blatantly opportunistic. A very large body of disaffected Black "youth" who had missed the opportunity for education and career training both as a result of the internal civil war and the unequal provision of education on offer, seek inclusion within the symbolics of Western consumerism irrespective of the country's economic potential. In effect, because the future is a predicate of the political economy of modernism, the apparently exorbitant claim of youth equates to the difference between having a "future" or having "no future." Yet there remains an inherent ambivalence between the rejection of the symbolics of racism and an aspiration to the economic benefits of globally structured racism.

Such ambivalence was repeated in a different register when students at the University of the Witwatersrand demanded a "pass one pass all" examination policy. A claim is thus made for the value of certification premised on exclusion, simultaneously demanding its nonexclusivity—a move that would render certificates worthless.

There is little accord. More gravely, there is little tolerance or harmony. Daily violence occurs across the country. Positions are frequently articulated in discourses of polarizing binarisms and exclusion. The identity politics that are emerging inscribe a new racism around an altered construction of patriotism of inclusion/exclusion. Even though identity politics has been central to challenging the discourses of apartheid's power relations, providing opportunities to articulate excluded voices and experiences, it now runs the risk of moving to a new notion of difference that replaces the one master narrative with others, contesting bitterly for ascendancy. It has not moved to a broader political and democratic struggle whose goal would be the elimination of structural and cultural inequalities. I refer to one of the political leaders as an example. On a current affairs TV program entitled "Agenda," broadcast by South African Broadcast Corporation (SABC) on September 14, 1993, Chief Mangosuthu Buthelezi, leader of the IFP, was unable to satisfactorily answer questions put to him by a panel of three journalists. In response he reverted to accusations of racism suggesting that the White interviewer was treating him as a kaffir.[9] Similarly, on Radio Zulu the following day, in an interview with a Zulu-speaking radio journalist who probed his decisions, he resorted to dismissing him as being a traitor to the Zulu nation, again marking the boundaries of exclusion. The positive contribution that identity politics has delivered must be identified; so must the limitations.

The problem is that it gives rise to a logic that chokes off radicalism and ends up supporting domination (Giroux, 1993).

Film organization has not completely escaped the greater political rifts. Forums and networks of oppositional filmmakers are implicated in the wider political environment. Although networks operated in the 1970s, the state repression of the time forced filmmakers to be secretive or at least cautious about their work. Political forums occurred outside the country in the early years. In July 1982, the Culture and Resistance Festival took place in Gaberones, Botswana, where "Film and video workers from inside and outside South Africa featured prominently at this event and pledged to align themselves with the people of South Africa for the liberation of the country by contributing their special skills in a conscious and organized way in their communities and regions" (Feinberg, quoted in Blignant, 1992, p. 299).

In 1987, anti-apartheid filmmakers came together in Johannesburg to establish an institute to secure funding for production and to organize film and video workers aligned with the UDF. In a politically charged atmosphere, manifest differences marred progress. These differences related to several issues including who had not been consulted and who was taking leadership. A steering

---

[9]*Kaffir* is a South African term used for a Black person. It has extremely derogatory connotations—historically implying a nonbeliever.

committee was elected in order to overcome these problems. In 1988, the Culture in Another South Africa (CASA) conference was held in Amsterdam, which led to the formation of regional groupings in South Africa. It played an important role until transformation to a democratic country. The Film and Allied Workers Organization (FAWO) was established in Johnnesburg in the same year, with affiliates in FAWO Western Cape and Natal Organization of Video and Allied Workers (NOVAW) in Durban being formed in 1989.

FAWO engaged actively with the state around issues of distribution, control, and independent broadcasting. It addressed the politics of representation, distribution, and training of film workers. Its considerable achievements were premised on a progressive but nonaligned position. It established a Community Video School to develop filmmakers among Black South Africans. Serious effort created important links with other progressive media groupings, and it engaged with the state to change existing broadcasting conditions.[10]

Since the political jockeying that existed with organizations and was evident in 1987 new groupings and units arose,[11] and other groups have changed their orientation.[12]

The Independent Broadcast Association was established in order to ensure a more representative public broadcasting system. The previously monolithic SABC has acceded to the need for more democratic procedures. In an extraordinary way, the selection of the existing board of the SABC was selected by a panel of jurors following publicly broadcast selection interviews of people proposed by the wider population through organizational channels. A change of faces and interests on such a board is refreshing, but it does not assure us that it will be exposed to a wider more challenging set of agendas and representations. To retain a space for questioning, for critical debate, more is needed than a shift in ideological positions. The development of critical citizenry becomes an urgent challenge. Censorship, repressive laws and conservative education has ensured an extraordinary degree of passivity at one level of society—one that denied debate or a spirit of enquiry.

In the greater political arena, rivalry for power dominates the agenda. Yet civil society has been inclined to anticipate that the new political leaders will ensure their democratic rights. In contrast there were the negotiations at the World Trade Centre, where amidst the parading and strutting, all party political stakeholders have concerned

---

[10]In August 1991, the Jabulani! Free the Airwaves conference took place in Doorn, Holland. This marked the beginning of joint consultation on a wide front of media groupings (commercial and oppositional) to confront monolithic state broadcasting.

[11]These include the Black Film and Television Foundation (BFTV) and National Film and Television Trust of Southern Africa NAFTSA, both ANC aligned.

[12]The industry-oriented grouping, South African Film and Television Association (SAFTA), previously conservative, has now adopted a more progressive position.

themselves with establishing the parameters of power between the political parties rather than giving serious concern with setting the ground rules for a changed democratic society. Commenting on this, journalist Philip van Niekerk (1993) voiced his concern that civil society has not performed well in transition and suggested that

> A major hope is that a cacophony of voices in civil society could graft a new sense of accountability on to political culture. . . . Large sections of the press are still star struck by politicians. The press as a whole has failed to raise freedom of information. . . . The greatest fear that South Africans should face at this new beginning is that we will merely be recycling a new set of politicians into old positions. (p. 14)

The heterogeneous society van Niekerk envisaged as possible needs to find ways of accepting difference and sharing resources.

In a movement away from polarizing binarisms, there is the need to encourage a sense of discourse as being always incomplete, as closure and meaning always deferred. It stresses signification and representation. We also should call on Foucault's understandings of the relationship between knowledge and power, of how discourses operate to entrench power. Postmodernism argues against the doxa; it stresses the need to "dedoxify"[13] the discourses. Like the Buddhist caveat against any arrogant assumption of full knowledge, "If you meet a Buddha on the road, kill him," we need to remain critical and vigilant. However, what is being advocated is a particular form of postmodern critique, a critical or oppositional (is this paradoxical?) postmodernism described by McLaren (1993) as resistance postmodernism, which has been posed in opposition to "ludic" postmodernism.

Resistance postmodernism speaks against the position that disqualifies postmodernism from political involvement because of its narcissistic and ironic appropriations of existing representations and narratives. It argues the necessity of challenging the ideologies by and in which subject positions are inscribed, in relation to an articulated and organized politics. Hutcheon (1989) also envisages the possibility of such strategies. Drawing on postmodernist feminism, which has distinct and unambiguous political agendas, she advocates a form of postmodernism that speaks of resistance. She insists that postmodernism is complicitous and critical of domination:

> Yet it must be admitted from the start that this is a strange kind of critique, one bound up, too, with its own complicity, with power of domination, one that acknowledges that it cannot escape implication in that which it, nevertheless, still wants to analyse and maybe even undermine. (p. 4)

13Hutcheon (1989) adopts Barthes's notion of "doxa" as public opinion, the naturalized consensus, and suggests that postmodernism works to "dedoxify" cultural representations.

Although ambiguous or compromised, the critique does enable a political engagement. Such strategies install the conventions; the critique then challenges and subverts, exploits yet disrupts.

As an educator concerned with the politics of representation and political education in its widest sense, what appears to be of crucial importance is the creation of an understanding of knowledge construction and the discourses of knowledge and power. Media education offers a clear way to confront these areas. A holistic approach to media education that is informed by resistance forms of postmodernism would assist to develop the critically autonomous thinkers that South Africa and any country aspiring to democratic practices rely on. In South Africa educational debates and policy documents have only recently begun to acknowledge media education. To overlook the politics of representation would be a serious neglect. The spaces that have opened up in the curriculum) and the opportunities that exist for situating media education need to be examined.

The relevance of media education has been acknowledged by UNESCO (1982):

> The school and the family share the responsibility of preparing the young person for living in a world of powerful images, words and sounds. Children and adults need to be literate in all three of these symbolic systems, and this will require some reassessment of educational priorities.

Such a reassessment might well result in an integrated approach to the teaching of language and communication.

As the term suggests, "media education" specifically aims to educate about the media. Inherently, because what we describe as popular culture is contained in media texts, whether these are films, picture romances, pop music, computer games, or ads on billboards, media education implicates popular culture. Although it aims at a critical literacy and competence, it advocates a close scrutiny of that which constitutes it as a field of study. This contrasts with other fields of study. Most subject disciplines, especially at school, are constructed around Eurocentric metanarratives that contain and are contained by accepted bodies of knowledge and that do not problematize their own history and legitimacy. It can be argued that science selects and constructs those scientific events it considers of value in a culturally specific manner. Scientific discourse selects its main heroes and valorizes particular narratives. History as a discipline relates the metanarrative of conquest and imperialism. These disciplines construct a body of knowledge accompanied by a common-sensical understanding of what constitutes the field that remains largely unchallenged. History is not referred to as historiography, science does not critique what is considered science. In contrast, media education (as the word education suggests) attempts to educate about the media, to construct a critical approach to information offered by the media, and to contextualize those agencies that produce media. The role attached to media education is to develop and nurture the critical abilities of learners, and to nurture autonomous thinkers who approach information not as transparent, but as constructions that are selective and partial. It is vital for today's learners to approach information in relation to the mass media and those texts considered authoritative precisely because all information is mediated. All information is produced within a signifying system, be it spoken, written or audio-visual. Hence, all knowledge reaches us as representations and mediations whether they be fictive or factual. Consider the description of media education offered by Bob Ferguson (1991) in his opening address as keynote speaker at the conference held in Durban in September 1990 entitled "Developing Media Education in the 1990s":

> [Media Education] is, I suggest, an engagement, over a long period, with all forms of representations. It is concerned with how messages are put together, by whom and in whose interests. . . . It is also concerned with how to construct media messages which are similar to those now available, and how to construct messages that are different; and how to acquire production skills. . . . It is a subject that should be on the agenda for all teachers and students and one which does not lend itself to brief encounters. . . . For, above all, Media Education is an endless enquiry into the way we make sense of the world and the way others make sense of the world for us. Above all it must be genuinely open and critical. (pp. 19-20)

From this definition it becomes clear that this conception of media education situates itself as an aspect of critical education. As with any other field of study, this is considered a choice emanating from particular philosophical positions and understandings of society. This has certainly not always been the case with media education. The position Ferguson described as media education emanates from rigorous debates and shifts in social theory over several decades largely in the United Kingdom and reflects the rejection and revision of certain other positions.

Media education has its origin in the high culturalism of Leavis on the one hand and the critical theory of the Frankfurt School on the other. Both were concerned with inoculating learners against the invidious power of the media. Both assumed an enlightenment view of knowledge, but whereas Leavis focuses on the text and the author in terms of both moral and aesthetic concerns, the critical approach attended to the structural relations of the text. This coupled with notions of Althusserian Marxism lead to a concentration on the need to demystify and to expose the ideological workings of the media. They considered the economic scenario, the contest of media industry, and capitalism.

This shift in approach crucially incorporated new areas of consideration of the media. The concern with language moved from the expression of an individual author to concepts derived from semiotics, in which signification focused attention on representations and mediation of meaning, how codes and conventions work and are used, and how cultural "myths" operate. It introduced structural understandings of narrative and the ideological implications of the structure. In addition, structuralist understandings of audience identificatory positions lead to considerations of Lacan's theories of the formation of the subject in relation to reception.

This produced a closer analysis of what appeared "commonsensical" so as to alert the reader to processes of selection and construction of popular cultural messages. It proposes an investigation of how and why these messages are constructed and in whose interests they operate. Through this shift the concepts of audience, language, representations, technology, and categories and became constitutive of the field of study of media education in the United Kingdom by the early 1980s.

What education and the media shared for the Media Educationists was the purpose of maintaining the status quo by means of ideological production. Drawing on certain insights of liberation pedagogy of Freire, Masterman (1985), a prominent figure in advocating media education in the United Kingdom, espouses an approach to the field of study that is both experiential and demystificatory. Concepts such as the notion of hegemony heralded the notion of culture as a site of struggle and popular culture became the terrain on which such a struggle could take place. This contrasts with the pessimism of the heritage of the Frankfurt school. It also introduced a particular tension into media theory that continues to manifest itself. Inherent in these conflicts are questions relating to a type of enlightenment model around demystification, founded on the notion that superior logic could shift subjective understandings, be they racist or sexist, ageist, homophobic, or sizest.

By drawing on experiential approaches and the ideas of Freire, this work is premised on the model of dialogue, reflection, and action. Implicated in this understanding is "an act of knowing" that would empower the learners. The learning process implicates a decoding of what has appeared as common sense. They become border intellectuals, moving from one position to another. The act of knowing implies the development of strong antagonisms. Antagonisms in turn create borders. There is the danger inherent in this of demystifying one position and replacing it with a binarily opposed position. There is an ambivalence inherent in this kind of border crosser, which perhaps characterizes many of the struggles around the politics of identity, of an enlightenment position.

This situation within media education was further influenced by debates that are underpinned and influenced by postmodernist thought. The enlightenment model was refuted as proposing a return to "true" consciousness and failing to address the complex nature of socialization and subject formation. Beliefs, prejudices, and attitudes of any kind are rooted in material conditions. This has led to ongoing debate between those who assert the ideological power of the media, as described by Postman (1986), and those who argue the dispersal of power through multifarious contradictory readings, as suggested by certain reception theorists who emphasize that meaning is negotiated and celebrate popular culture as a site of resistance.

These poststructural understandings both shook the assumptions of media educators and also offer renewed and exciting potential. The feared "death of the subject" that Althusserian Marxism heralded and the relativism suggested by contradictory reading positions is disarming only if one is attempting to impose a master narrative, a totalizing and rational logic. Those teachers who "failed" to "teach" learners about the stereotypes and undo their prejudices are able to reconsider their aims.[14] Postmodernism offers a path for educators to engage in the insights offered both by understandings of the ideological power of discourses within society and the concept of multiple readings. Such an enterprise moves beyond being only deconstructive in considering the workings of the metadiscourses, but no longer anticipates a single answer.

The potential for postmodernist understandings in South Africa with a particular heritage of an educational system based on gross inequalities needs some elaboration. What postmodernists were responding to was the totalizing metanarrative of modernity. The discourses of modernity entrench a single Eurocentric rationality, the belief in the power of logic, progress, and technological development as part of the inevitable route to "civilization." For Lyotard (1984), such grand narratives assume their legitimacy and deny their social and historical construction as they oppose and take up position against difference and particularity. Postmodern texts and, in particular, certain feminist investigations challenged and critiqued the construction of the constant "other" relegated to the role of victim of enemy and displaced somewhere at the margins of history and society. Henry Giroux (1992) takes up the notion of the margins and the "other" when he outlines what he terms "border pedagogy." It provides fertile ground for teachers concerned with difference, for teachers who have to address learners who have been constructed as peripherally, or for those who have accepted such constructions, whether they are situated centrally or peripherally.

Giroux suggests that the rigid boundaries imposed by modernist culture exclude and privilege according to categories of race, class, gender and ethnicity. It creates a frame that centers European culture. For him, postmodernism questions the way such culture is inscribed. It offers a way of rereading history, of reconsidering what is high culture and what is low or popular culture. A crucial characteristic of border pedagogy is the rejection of binary oppositions as postmodernism refutes the possibility of a single truth. Eurocentric history cannot summarily be dismissed and replaced by a single

---

[14]Williamson (1981) discusses teaching against subject positions.

oppositional history. Rather, border pedagogy demands that we examine all representations in our culture; it requires an acknowledgment of the borders, and that we understand difference as social and historical constructions positioned within hierarchies of domination and opposition.

In this way crucial questions are raised for what I consider to be vital aspects for critical education in South Africa today. Critical education calls for our focused attention on the cultural representations that circulate. It requires that we attend to popular culture and to all media texts, whether they be considered high or low. It calls for their consideration in terms of the discourses they are presenting for us to ask the questions around who is represented, how are they represented, who is omitted, who has made the message, and in whose interest this discourse is working. These questions reflect the key notions of media education mentioned earlier. However, border pedagogy goes further. It aspires to the creation of learners who are able to cross borders and locate knowledge historically, socially, and critically. Beyond this they need to understand that codes have limits and that codes are partial and historically specific, and it is at the limits that they become productive: students need to construct their own narratives and histories while recognizing the narratives that locate them, that constitute their subjectivity:

> Within this discourse, students should engage knowledge as border crossers, as people moving in and out of borders constructed around co-ordinates of difference and power. . . . Border pedagogy becomes decentered as it remains. The terrain of learning becomes inextricably linked to the shifting parameters of place, identity, history and power. . . . This is not an abandonment of critique as much as it is an extension of its possibilities. (Giroux, 1992, pp. 29-30)

This chapter is assuming an agreement that education should be democratic, open, and tireless in its spirit of enquiry. Such democratic aspirations contrast with present circumstances. Reacting to the pervasive violence, repeated calls are being made by leaders, the clergy, and ordinary people for an atmosphere of tolerance. What future education has to contend with in South Africa are inherited constructions around the "other," an intolerance around race and gender to mention but two aspects. It needs to deal with the powerful discourses that have entrenched power in this country and to create the kind of critical thinkers who are not simply reactionary, angry, or defensive, but can aspire to democratic principles. We need the border crossers that Giroux described. Media education seems to be crucially implicated.

These histories of media education relate to thinkers and writers based in Europe; this chapter locates them there. In deciding their relevance to South African educational situations, it is necessary to recall that South African academic traditions have their roots in British academia. Leavisite approaches to language and literature have persisted, and we find these exclusionary notions and approaches prevalent in much of what is considered literary studies both at school and in tertiary education.

The full text of imperialism remains as inscribed within the dominant institutions of South African society. It remains inscribed within institutions of education, in which Leavisite approaches to language and literature persist, and in media that carry the unremitting narrative of modernism. General audiences call for Rambo and Kung-fu movies when progressive organizations organize film festivals in townships. This chapter calls for media education that will develop understandings of constructions of knowledge and their implications. Critical "readers" can both "read" and "write" the differing narratives; the two are inseparably enmeshed. Thus, as the film theory of the 1980s was moved by Freirean notions, filmmaking in the 20th century needs to absorb some of the lessons of postmodern thought.

Postmodern strategies go beyond demystifying and deconstruction to an understanding of discourses and social interrelations. Hutcheon (1989) suggests that postmodernist film strategies include "irony, playfulness, historical reference, the use of vernacular materials, the continuity of cultures, an interest in process over product, breakdown of boundaries between art forms and life, and new relations between artist and audience" (p. 9).

These strategies attempt to challenge the seamless quality of life. The notion of history as an uninterrupted narrative can be contested by plural, unrepressed, discontinuous, and interrupted histories. Storytelling becomes both an historical and political act with a postmodernist emphasis on particularizing and contextualizing. These proposed strategies transgress the rigid borders between fiction and fact and advocate a self-consciousness about the act of representation and parody that is ironic yet critical.

Changing production practices that draw from such postmodernist understandings are evident in certain South African projects. One example lies in the change of focus of the Community Video School, which responds to changing theoretical threads and has moved from "reclaiming" history in documentaries to telling new stories (there are many stories to be told). Stories that do not replace one master narrative with others retain their status as political acts and these short films reflect this. Another strategy has been to offer different perspectives of the same event. In a series of programs screened on South African television, entitled "Ordinary People," in 1996, each program presented an event patterned by the representational conventions of the series.[15] A camera team followed each of

---

[15]They included the invasion of the World Trade Centre by a right-wing group, the auction of a bankrupt farm belonging to an Afrikaner, the monitoring of a political rally, a soccer match between Orlando Pirates football team and a prison team, and a fascinating scrutiny of Ponte City, a vast apartment center in central Johannesburg.

two or three "ordinary people" who were participants in the event. These "actors" were clearly selected for their difference in subject position. The edited footage then moved frequently between the chosen subjects, thereby developing ironies and comparisons in these interrupted and plural stories. These is no Voice of God, no binary opposition that posits a teleological consolation. But the narrative produced by the cameras—by the representational conventions—partakes of the vulnerability of the actors.

The strategies of resistance postmodernism take on the ethical considerations of Freire, particularly the commitment to equity and justice, but such commitments are no longer founded within a totalizing discourse. Hutcheon (1988) rejects the notion of modernism as a world in need of mending and postmodernism as a world beyond repair. This indicates that there is no closure to history, no millenarian end of history. Postmodernism points to the possibility of political action that acknowledges that it is caught within what is always already said, that is caught within the economy of representation. But it works at the borders of what is said to challenge the will to closure and the forms of inclusion and exclusion that accompany such a will.

REFERENCES

Annecke, W., & Tomaselli, R. (1990). In A. Kuhn with S. Randstone (Eds.), *The women's companion to international firm.* Virago.

Cixous, H., & Clement, C. (1986). *The newly born woman* (B. Wing, Trans.). Manchester, UK: Manchester University Press.

Deacon, R. (1993, December). *Discourses of discipline in South Africa: Rethinking critical pedagogies in postmodernity.* Paper presented at Communication and Development in a Postmodern. Era: Reevaluating the Freirean Legacy conference, Penang.

Diawara, M. (1984). *African cinema.* Bloomington: Indiana University Press.

FAWO News, Take 4 (1989). *1*(4), p. 4.

Ferguson, B. (1991). What is media education for? In J. Prinsloo & C. Criticos (Eds.), *Media matters in South Africa Durban* (pp. 19-24). South Africa: MRC.

Giroux, H. (1992). *Border crossings: Cultural workers and the politics of education.* New York: Routledge.

Giroux, H. (1993). Living dangerously: Identity politics and the new cultural racism: Towards a critical pedagogy of representation. *Cultural Studies, 7*(1).

Hutcheon, L. (1988). *The poetics of modernism.* New York: Routledge.

Hutcheon, L. (1989). *The politics of modernism.* New York: Routledge.

Lapsley, R., & Westlake, M. (1988). *Film theory: An introduction.* Manchester, UK: Manchester University Press.

Lovell, T. (1983). *Pictures of reality: Aesthetics, politics and pleasure.* London: British Film Institute.

Lyotard, J.-F. (1984). *The postmodern condition.* Minneapolis: University of Minnesota Press.

Malkmus, L., & Armes, R. (1991). *Arab & African film making.* London: Zed Books.

Masterman, L. (1985). *Teaching the media.* London: Comedia.

McLaren, P. (1993). Multiculturalism and the postmodern critique: Towards a pedagogy of resistance and transformation. *Cultural Studies, 7*(1), 118-416.

Minh-Ha, T. (1989). Outside in, inside out. In J. Pines & P. Willemen (Eds.), *Questions of third cinema* (pp. 133-149). London: BFI.

Mulvey, L. (1975). Visual pleasure and narrative cinema. *Screen, 16*(3), 6-18.

Nichols, B. (1985). The voice of documentrary. In B. Nichols (Ed.), *Movies and methods* (Vol. 2, pp. 258-273). Los Angeles: University of California Press.

Postman, N. (1986). *Amusing ourselves to death.* London: Heinemann.

Propp, V. (Trans.). (1958). *Morphology of the folktale.* Austin: University of Texas.

Spivak, G. (1988). Can the subaltern speak? In C. Nelson & L. Grossberg (Eds.), *Marxism and the interpretation of cultures* (pp. 277-311). New York: Macmillan.

Steenveld, L. (1992). Reclaiming history. In M. Blignaut & J. Botha (Eds.), *Movies moguls and mavericks* (pp. 301-328). Johannesburg, South Africa: Showdata.

Thoraval, Y. (1975). *Regards sur le cinema Egyptien* [A view of Egyptian cinema]. Beirut: Dar-el-Mashreq.

Tomaselli, K. (1989). *The cinema of apartheid.* New York: Routledge.

Tomaselli, K., & Prinsloo, J. (1992). Third cinema in South Africa. In M. Blignaut & J. Botha (Eds.), *Movie moguls and mavericks* (pp. 329-373). Johannesburg, South Africa: Showdata.

Tomaselli, K., Williams, A., Steenveld, L., & Tomaselli, R. (1986). *Myth, race and power.* Bellville, South Africa: Anthropos.

UNESCO. (1982, January). *Declaration on media education.* Grunwald, Federal Republic of Germany.

Unwin, C., & Balton, C. (1992). Resistance cinema. In M. Blignaut & J. Botha (Eds.), *Movie moguls and mavericks* (pp. 277-300). Johannesburg, South Africa: Showdata.

van Niekerk, P. (1993, September). Like father, like son? *Weekly Mail & Guardian.*

Young, R. (1990). *White mythologies: Writing history and the west.* New York: Routledge.

FILMOGRAPHY

Abrahams, C., Hayman, G., Pinnock, D., & Tomaselli, K. (Directors). (1984). *I am Cliffie Abraham* [Film]. (Production company: Rhodes University Department of Journalism, Grahamstown)

Bensusan, T., Schwegmann, W., Tilley, B., & Weinberg, P. (Directors). (1984). *Mayfair* [Film]. (Production company: Ad Hoc Video Group, Johannesburg)

Coleman, D., & Dworkin, L. (Directors). (1981). *FOSATU: Building Worker Unity* [Film]. (Distribution: Mayibuye Centtre, Johannesburg)

Direct Cinema (Production). (1987). *Chronicles of South Africa.* (Distribution: Film Resource Unit, Johannesburg)

Gavshon, H. (Executive Producer). (1983). *Ordinary People.* Johannesburg: SABC.

Person, S. (Director). (1974). *Land Apart* [Film].

Proctor, E. (Director). (1985). *Re Tla Bona* [Film]. (Production company: Frontline Video, Johannesburg.

Schmitz, O., & Tilley, B. (Directors). (1989). *Fruits of Defiance* [Film]. (Production Company: VNS. S. Africa)

Wilson, L. (Director). (1987). *Ithuseng: Out of Despair* [Film].

Chapter ▪ 13

From Pedagogy to Praxis: Freire, Media Education, and Participatory Communication

Zaharom Nain

INTRODUCTION

This chapter is about alternatives; that is, alternatives not only as regards communication policies and structures, but on a wider scale viable alternatives as regards the process of development and the crucial role communication plays in this process. In this sense, therefore, what is discussed in these pages are cultural strategies that are necessary if an egalitarian world is what we wish for future generations. These discussions come at a time when, as Hamelink (1995) puts it, "The new world order poses a serious threat to the project of an egalitarian democracy since it exacerbates existing inequalities and results in a deep erosion of people's liberty to achieve self-empowerment" (p. 31).

The modest aim of this chapter is to try to locate the relevance of Paulo Freire in two areas of communication studies: namely, media education and participatory communication for development. In so doing, the main issue this chapter attempts to grapple with is whether the Freirean project of liberation and the strategies he proposes are applied to these two areas and to what extent these two areas in communication studies could become inextricably linked, particularly in the context of the so-called developing world, given current social, political, and economic realities?

THE DOMINANT PARADIGM

In recent years, the debate regarding development—particularly that of the developing world—appears to have come around full circle, with the "dominant paradigm" of development apparently reasserting its dominance in many parts of the world, having survived the many theoretical and methodological critiques hurled at it. Like a persistent, recurring nightmare, the paradigm continues to be espoused in the policy statements and development strategies of many governments, particularly in the developing world and international aid agencies.

Although it has been stated (see Shah, 1996) that Everett Rogers was the first to use the term "dominant paradigm" in relation to communication and development, it is nonetheless widely agreed that the paradigm was originally conceived in the late 1950s and provided the theoretical framework for much media research and policy making in the 1960s and 1970s.[1]

The basic assertion was that more media were a good thing because they speeded the modernization process. For Golding and Harris (1997), this was the phase of "happy optimism," in which the media were assumed to be "magic multipliers, bringing development advice instantly, effectively and extensively to the information-hungry multitudes" (p. 4).

---

[1]The belief of this orthodoxy was that the poor and supposedly backward Third World nations *should* develop and "modernize" and, inevitably, would do so according to the patterns and structures designed by the industrialized nations, particularly the United States. As one critic succinctly put it, "Development becomes a question of how *'we'* (the bearers of modernity) can make *'them'* more like *'us'* (Foster-Carter, 1974, p. 81; emphasis in original).

The problem of underdevelopment, according to this school of thought, can be traced back to the individual. Underdevelopment, quite simply, is due to the outmoded, counterproductive attitudes of the peoples of the Third World. Hence, modernization can primarily be achieved through individual, psychological change. Lerner (1958), for example, utilizing a simplistic traditional-modern dichotomy in his study of the Middle East, stressed the need for the emergence of "mobile" persons in the region. According to him, to do so the individual in "traditional" society needed to have and subsequently cultivate the ability to empathize. In his words:

> This is an indispensable skill for people moving out of traditional settings . . . high empathic capacity is the predominant personal style only in modern society, which is distinctively industrial, urban, literate and participant. Traditional society is nonparticipant—it deploys people by kinship into communities isolated from each other and from a centre. (p. 50)

As Shah (1996) puts it, "In the most general terms, the dominant paradigm promised happiness and security that was supposedly enjoyed in abundance in the West" (p. 147). Indeed, the dominant belief, pioneered by Schramm and Lerner, was that:

> Increasing urbanisation would raise. . . literacy levels, which would lead to increased use of information media which would in turn increase per capita income and an interest in democratic citizenship, thereby binding the new societies together and increasing economic prosperity. (Smith, 1980, p. 61)

To be sure, the Western-style modernization proposed by this paradigm did come to many Third World countries: Their gross national product rose, accompanied by improvements in health care, education, transportation, and mass communication. The emphasis certainly was on a top-down flow of information, very often paying little attention to the needs of people at the grassroots level, the marginalized, and the disenfranchised. Invariably, imposed modernization of this nature had its price. As Shah (1996) notes:

> The price was growing structural inequality, that is, the process of disparities emerging over time in the spatial distribution of resources . . . while workers and peasants experienced a decline in earning power and wealth, there was an increasing concentration of power in the hands of rural and urban elites whose prosperity became increasingly tied to and dependent on the West. (pp. 148-149)

Schramm (1964), clearly supportive of Lerner's argument that psychological factors are central to the process of development, similarly argued that for social change to take place:

> First the populace must become aware of a need which is not satisfied by present custom and behaviour. Second, they must invent or borrow behaviour that comes closer to meeting the need. A nation that wants to accelerate this process, as all developing nations do today, will try to make it's people more widely and quickly aware of needs and of the opportunities for meeting them, will facilitate the decision process, and will help the people put the new practices smoothly and swiftly into effect. (p. 115)

Both saw the mass media as playing a pivotal role in this process of behavioral change. Calling them the "mobility multiplier" (Lerner, 1958, p. 52) and seeing them as performing "watchmen" functions and creating "a climate for development" (Schramm, 1964, pp. 131-132), both scholars argued for an all-round expansion of the mass media systems in developing countries. This, they believed, would trigger economic growth.

This aside, Shah (1996), borrowing from the ideas of Giddens, argues convincingly that this form of modernization has also had personal implications. For him:

> The separation of space from time, leading to disembedding and reflexivity . . . created a situation in which temporal and spatial realities were experienced as discontinuous phenomena. . . . The consequences of these discontinuities is that biographical narratives—people's knowledge about and sense of power within the world—are undermined and self-identities are threatened because a sense of self is dependent on a sense of continuity across time and space. The resulting feeling is one of existential anxiety characterised by insecurity about externally impinging events, a preoccupation with risks to personal existence because of rapid changes in social and physical environment and a feeling of emptiness because of doubts about the integrity of self-identity. (p. 149)

It is relatively easy to recognize and understand the theoretical and political naivete of the Schramm-Lerner view. For instance, it fails to consider the notion of power and the nature of power relations within and between societies; it neglects the international dimension and international relations, or, in the words of Elliott and Golding (1974), it "systematically skirts around the existence of an international social system, initially of colonialism, subsequently of economic imperialism, to which these separate states are tied" (p. 234). It even views development in an ahistorical manner, assuming developing countries to have emerged from static isolation and simply needing stimuli such as the mass media to bring them out of the Dark Ages and into the 20th century.

However, because of its adherence to—and reinforcement of—the status quo, for a long time this paradigm has endured, despite the systematic and comprehensive academic critiques that have been leveled against it (see, e.g., Elliott & Golding, 1974, 1977; Hedebro, 1982) and the equally convincing critiques that have been leveled against the philosophical underpinnings of modernization theory (see Bernstein, 1979; Frank, 1969; O'Brien, 1979).

Indeed, to take just three published case studies—India, Thailand and Taiwan—as examples, it would appear that the dominant paradigm, albeit reformulated, clearly is still dominant as regards media's role in the development of these countries.

In his study of information technology (IT) in India, Thomas (1991) has argued convincingly that the

> reasons for the large-scale use of IT in India are couched in the language and ideology of modernisation. The lack of information has once again been resurrected as the main reason for underdevelopment. Well-worn phrases like the "takeoff"

stage of growth, and the "trickle-down" theory have once again come into fashion. It is widely stated that IT will catapult India into the 21st century. (p. 35)

Siriyuvasak (1991), in looking at the role of the state in Thailand's media, has argued in turn that "the State, the TNCs and the media industries are employing the public communication systems for their own interests. There is little space provided for information to develop the communicative competence and actions of the public" (p. 30). For her:

> The goal of the present Thai State to establish an industrialised economy, by emphasising economic growth over and above economic distribution and social development, demonstrates the antagonism between a capitalist system and egalitarian social order introduced by the 1932 Revolution (led by Kana Rasadorn) around the concept of citizenship. (p. 28)

As for Taiwan, Fang (1991), in his study of the growth of IT, has argued that "in general Taiwan is a model of dependent development, but nowhere is it more pronounced than in the IT sector. It epitomizes clearly the ways the State works actively to bridge domestic capital and the transnational corporations" (pp. 44-45). He goes on to argue that while it

> can hardly be denied that, building on historical legacies, Taiwan has achieved substantial economic growth during the post-war decades . . . [nonetheless] . . . such growth is not equal to articulated development and is by no means a product of market mechanisms. Rather the State has provided every possible means, including a docile and educated labour force, to help Taiwan's national capital grab a niche in an IT market tightly oligopolised by certain transnational corporations. Recent situations in Taiwan seem to prove that, rather than being an "exception," Taiwan's economic story sticks to "the rule" of dependency. (pp. 44-45)

The ideas of the dominant paradigm are even more explicitly articulated by Cesar M. Mercado, Planner/Programme and Monitoring and Evaluation Specialist of the UNDP/OPS Asia and Pacific Programme for Development Training and Communication Planning in the Philippines. For Mercado (1991):

> A development communicator writes a radio broadcast or a news story with the clear intent of changing the knowledge, attitude, skill and/or behaviour of listeners or readers towards a certain person, group, institution or technology.

Development communication wants to achieve more than knowledge, it further attempts to achieve understanding, attitude, skill and practice. Communication is effective when it accomplishes its intended objectives; such as change in knowledge, attitude, skill and/or behaviour.

The causes of poverty are basically man-made. It is brought about by illiteracy and rapid population growth: overuse of natural resources, and degradation of the environment. (pp. 17-21)

Of course, the political, economic, and cultural contexts have changed in many countries since the heyday of the dominant paradigm. In turn, the global contemporary media/culture spectrum is indeed more complex than that proposed by, primarily, the media imperialism/dependency perspective that emerged to challenge the ideas of the dominant paradigm.[2] As far as development thinking is concerned, Escobar (1995) has argued that "a critique of development as discourse has begun to coalesce in recent years . . . [aiming] . . . to examine the foundations of an order of knowledge about the Third World, the ways in which the Third World is constituted in and through representation" (p. 214).[3]

---

[2]Martin-Barbero (1993), for example, has argued that instead of simply resulting in the homogenization of cultures, the transnational media have actually caused the dislocation of cultures. In their commentary on the contributions of major Latin American cultural theorists, Schlesinger and Morris (1997) argue that, for Martin-Barbero, the old modernizing phase in which the media, especially radio, were utilized "for the political project of forming a 'national sentiment'" had now been replaced by a situation in which

> the process has now gone into reverse: the media devalue the national, memories have become deterritoralised, images have become denationalised, the youth are appealed to through music and video. . . . The consequence . . . is that from a global point of view, the national is seen as provincial and weighed down by statism, whereas from a local point of view the nation is perceived as centralising. These combined pressures mean that there are no ways of defining the boundaries of a common national culture, policed by the sovereignty of the state. (p. 10)

[3]Escobar (1995) argues that the number of scholars involved in this rethinking is increasing:

> Rather than searching for development alternatives, they speak about "alternatives to development", that is, a rejection of the entire paradigm. They see this reformulation as a historical possibility already underway in innovative grassroots movements and experiments. . . . New spaces are opening up in the vacuum left by the colonizing mechanisms of development, either through innovation or the survival and resistance of popular practices. . . . What is at stake is the transformation of the political, economic and institutional regime of truth production that has defined the era of development. (pp. 215-216)

While taking all this into consideration, it is also true—and needs to be stressed nevertheless, as indicated in the examples mentioned earlier—that elements of the dominant paradigm of development still exist with "governments designing ambitious development plans, institutions carrying out development programs in cities and countryside alike, experts studying development problems . . . foreign experts everywhere and multinational corporations brought into the country in the name of development" (p. 214).

THE NEW WORLD ORDER AND THE DOMINANT PARADIGM

The collapse of communism and the emergence of what are now often termed the "post-Cold War era" and a "new world order" have certainly contributed to a reemergence of faith in the dominant paradigm. This has happened at a time when new—more complex—political, economic, social, and cultural configurations have emerged globally and consolidated themselves, making the project of liberation even more urgent and certainly no less daunting. These new actors and structures include what Sreberny-Mohammadi (1996) terms "supranational forces" (intergovernmental organizations such as the IMF, the ITU, and INTERPOL), "transnational forces" (including a variety of public interest nongovernmental organizations, transnational corporations, trade unions, and religious bodies such as the Organisation of Islamic States), and "regional structures" such as the European Community, ASEAN, and NAFTA, whose importance in the post-Cold War era appears to have superseded the importance of geopolitical regional groupings (NATO, Warsaw Pact), groupings that were accepted as being important during the Cold War.

Recent history also indicates the reemergence of identity politics and subnational forces. Tribal conflict in Rwanda, competing ethnicities in the Balkans, and religious antagonisms in India and Lebanon are but just a few examples of how identity politics now threaten to fragmentize and separate communities in—and between—many countries.

Hence, what we currently have with the "new world order" appears to be a situation in which control is in the hands of "the world's largest business corporations, the most powerful industrial states and their political and intellectual elites, often with the generous support of the media moguls of the late twentieth century" (Hamelink, 1995, p. 31). It is an order that pins its faith on deregulation, a "free" global market that, it is asserted, represents the best interests of the people. As Hamelink (1995) puts it, "A key belief is the gospel of privatisation. It declares that the world's resources are basically private property, that public affairs should be regulated by private parties on free markets, and that the state should retreat from most—if not all—domains that affect people' s daily lives" (p. 33).

Also, eerily almost echoing the sentiments of the original proponents of the dominant paradigm, another key belief is that "people cannot be trusted to make sound and sensible decisions about their own lives. . . . Their choice of a system of governance is best left to those in control and their allies in engineering consent" (p. 33).

ALTERNATIVE STRATEGIES

This is not to suggest, however, that alternatives are no longer forth-coming or valid. On the contrary, given the growing inequalities internationally and within nation-states, it would appear that alter-natives are very much needed. Indeed, during this same period, there evidently has been a resurgence of interest—among academics and activists—in the work of Paulo Freire and its relevance for cul-tural action and alternative development strategies: alternatives that recognize the dehumanizing aspects of current, dominant develop-ment strategies and policies in many countries, particularly those in the developing world; alternatives that, in response, argue for a more humanizing approach, one that puts human beings at the forefront of the development agenda; alternatives that, in turn, have been picked up and utilized by communication scholars and activists evi-dently committed to the emergence of a more egalitarian world order.

Although it has been widely acknowledged (see, e.g., Mackie, 1980; McLaren & Leonard, 1993) that Freire's contribution to critical education has been immense, his influence on the field of communi-cation thus far has been less frequently documented. Before moving to a discussion of Freire's contributions to alternative media educa-tion and participatory communication for development, it would be pertinent to briefly state some of the key elements of Freire's ideas on development.

Two related themes that form the bedrock of Freire's concerns are oppression and liberation. Stated boldly, Friere's analysis of devel-opment is grounded on the premise that current dominant world and domestic structures by and large are inegalitarian and exploitative in nature. For him, genuine development entails social transformation that would lead to the dismantling of these structures and their replacement with more egalitarian ones (Freire, 1978):

> The central problem is this: How can the oppressed, as divided, unauthentic beings, participate in developing the pedagogy of their liberation? Only as they discover themselves to be "hosts" of the oppressor can they contribute to the midwifery of their liberating pedagogy. As long as they live in the duality where *to be* is *to be like*, and *to be like* is *to be like the oppressor*, this con-tribution is impossible. (p. 26; emphasis in original)

Believing in the liberatory potential of oppressed human beings, Freire then outlines how he believes "cultural action for freedom" may take place. For him (Freire, 1985), "cultural action for freedom is characterised by dialogue, and its pre-eminent purpose is to conscientise the people, cultural action for domination is opposed to dialogue and serves to domesticate the people. The former problematizes, the latter sloganizes" (p. 85). His strategies, as they relate to communication and media, are referred to in the following sections. Briefly put then, Freire's project is that of the liberation of the oppressed. His is the language of hope, believing in the potential of the oppressed to overcome their oppression. His is also the language of possibilities, as he outlines the ways—primarily through education and, more broadly, cultural action—in which liberation may be a reality.

ALTERNATIVE MEDIA EDUCATION

For Paulo Freire (1976, 1978), true education begins with the questioning and testing of established knowledge, norms, values, ideas, and practices that define our reality and shape our consciousness to see whether they are necessarily true or otherwise in our own social, historical, and ideological reality. This he calls "conscientization"—in which the people are given the tools to perceive and name their world. These "tools" are, rightly, communication tools—language and literacy, and numerous forms of expression (e.g., newspapers, posters, dramas, films, photography).

Hence, to improvise from Freire, true media education does not lie primarily in the acquisition of language fluency, social skills, or the ability to collect and string together facts. Neither does it lie in our dexterity at twiddling knobs and manipulating hard- and software. Rather, education that conscientizes creates a critical awareness of the structural boundaries set up by the dominant groups and classes to control our lives and the realization that radical transformation of our social reality is possible. For Freire (1976): "Conscientization is a permanent critical approach to reality in order to discover it and discover the myths that deceive and help maintain the oppressing dehumanising structures" (p. 225).

A critical approach to media education does offer us that opportunity to "penetrate" the media, "and know it." This, however, requires a grasp of the fundamental links between the numerous realms—social, cultural, political and economic—in society. It is essential that media students not only learn how to construct media artifacts, but also to "deconstruct" media messages and recognize the underlying institutional and organizational power relations as well.

In this regard, British media educationist, Len Masterman (1985), acknowledging the influence of Freire in his classic text, *Teaching The Media*, stresses "the importance of the processes of dialogue, reflection and action within media education" (p. 28). For Masterman (1985):

Dialogue-reflection-action: the component parts of Freire's formula for a liberating education are all to be understood dialectically. Dialogue is both the basis of reflection and action, and the site to which they return for continuing regeneration. . . . Dialogue . . . involves a genuine sharing of power even if differential power relationships exist outside of the dialogue. . . . Dialogue does not attempt to dissolve contradictions into consensus, but actively seeks contradictions out as the motivating power for change. . . . Finally dialogue is oriented towards action. Using and intervening in the media are important parts of any media education course. (p. 323)

Masterman (1985) rightly acknowledges that "it will obviously be helpful if they [media students] have first-hand experience of the construction process from the inside" (p. 26). However, he equally rightly points out that "practical activity does not, in itself, constitute media education" (p. 26). It can never be assumed then that students involved in practical work automatically acquire critical abilities and can demystify the media. Critical awareness and understanding are elements to be worked at. They are based on a conscious effort to link practical work with analytical activities. It is an effort that must be made by both students and educators.

If media education is to be truly critical and liberating, there must be freedom and opportunity to be critical and skeptical of media messages and artifacts that shape our lives. Students must be equipped with "radical doubt" (Illich, 1969, 1970) in order to be perceptive and critical to the sociopolitical structures that exploit and constrain.

It is apparent that what future—and present—media practitioners need is a form of education that, in Gramsci's words, will develop "the love of free discussion; the desire to search for truth rationally and intelligently" (cited in Blackledge & Hunt, 1985, p. 308). Unfortunately, as long as media education is constrained by the pressures of the marketplace, the freedom and opportunity to be critical of the media and media education will continue to be severely restricted. Indeed, as indicated by French and Richards (1996), "In terms of course content, the communication and media departments of the world have faced a common set of dilemmas. To be specific, pressure is often experienced from students, and some potential employers, for vocationally-oriented training" (p. 16).

However, if those who have had the privilege of being conscientized through some form of alternative education are "unwilling to be constrained by the apparently all-determining forces and structures of the industrial age" (Illich, 1969, p. 18), then perhaps there will still be a ray of hope left for media education. As Illich further suggests, "our freedom and power are determined by our willingness to accept responsibility for the future" (p. 18).

In this regard, it is quite obvious, therefore, that the concept of "public service" is essential to media education. Media education and communication too for that matter must not be allowed to merely serve only the power structures or dominant groups in society.

However, important though this alternative form of media education may be, especially in problematizing the media, its potential must not be overstated. As Freire (Freire & Shor, 1987) himself notes:

> We must know, or at least we must make clear here, we are not falling into an idealistic position where consciousness changes inside of itself through an intellectual game in a seminar. . . . Liberating education can change our understanding of reality. But this is not the same thing as changing reality itself. No. Only political action in society can make social transformation, not critical study in the classroom. The structures of society, like the capitalist mode of production, have to be changed for society to be transformed. . . . At the level of the classroom only, you can achieve much better understanding of [an] . . . issue without changing it as a reality. (p. 175)

Or, as he puts it in another work (Freire, 1985):

> A true revolutionary project . . . to which the utopian dimension is natural, is a process in which the people assume the role of subject in the precarious adventure of transforming and recreating the world. . . . The people, standing at the threshold of their experience as subjects and participants of society, need signs that will help them recognise who is with them and who is against them. (pp. 82-83)

PARTICIPATORY COMMUNICATION FOR DEVELOPMENT

Suffice it to say at this juncture that what Freire proposes is that in order to begin working for social change, intellectuals (or researchers) need to privilege and learn from the experiences of the people at the grassroots (the ordinary people). It is this proposal that has spawned interest in participatory approaches to media development programs over the past two decades. It has come at a time when small, alternative organizations—media and non-media—have been set up by workers' collectives and other people's organizations around the world (see Fals Borda & Rahman, 1991).

Where the dominant paradigm stressed the top-down nature of development program, where governments and other agencies of power were given the legitimacy to design programs for the ordinary people whose "counterproductive" attitudes needed changing, the participatory model turns this belief on its head, arguing—more democratically—that what the people want, their fears, their ideas, should be privileged.

One of the foremost advocates of this approach, Jan Servaes (1989, see also his chapter in this volume), rightly problematizes Freire's arguments about culture and cultural action by advancing his "multiplicity in one world" model. Servaes's argument (see Huesca, 1996) is that "cultures are not monolithic and unified, but they contain multiple interpretations and meanings of many notions, such as poverty and oppression" (p. 26). Operating under this presupposition, Servaes elevates the role of communication in exploring, cataloguing, and mediating the multiplicity of meanings within a single culture.

It is evident then that the task of the participatory researcher is to understand what development means for the people, how they strategize and resist oppressive structure (see Fals-Borda & Rahman, 1991; Scott, 1985). The emphasis is on case studies, believing that oppressive structures operate differently in different contexts, and that equally counterhegemonic strategies vary according to differing circumstances. The aim, through Freire's notion of "dialogue," is a "critical reading" of the situation, leading to an unmasking of the myths that contribute to the oppression of the peoples concerned. Or, as Fals-Borda (1991) puts it:

> The final aims of this combination of liberating knowledge and political power within a continuous process of life and work are: (1) to enable the oppressed groups and classes to acquire sufficient creative and transforming leverage as expressed in specific projects, acts and struggles; and (2) to produce and develop sociopolitical thought processes with which popular bases can identify. (pp. 3-4)

NEGOTIATING MINEFIELDS

It is, of course, all too easy—and potentially disastrous—to romanticize these alternatives, to overstate their viability, especially at a time when the tide of global events appears to go against their successful long-term development. Indeed, as far as media education is concerned, in the fast developing countries of Asia, where it has been added to the curricula of many universities, the development of any alternative to the market-based, vocational-training model of media education is becoming increasingly harder, although not necessarily impossible. To take Malaysia as an example, where media or communication education has been part of the curriculum in many universities for about two decades, the current emphasis on the corporatization of the country's universities has resulted in the curricula having to be modified in order to suit even further the requirements of the Malaysian media industry (Zaharom, Mustafa, & Kirton, 1996).

As for participatory communication, it remains problematic as to how long small, largely voluntary, media organizations will endure, given the tight controls imposed by many regimes and, not surprisingly, the current pressures imposed by the commercial media. It would seem that, to resurrect the problems raised by Landry and his associates (1985) in their analysis of the failure of the alternative media in Britain, participatory communicators would need to take cognisance of, among other things, market pressures and the need for organizational skills. As they put it (Landry et al., 1985):

> We believe that it is vital to develop a strategy for the "independent"... sector, one which will enable it to secure its own economic infrastructure. This is the necessary underpinning to a Gramscian political strategy—whereby the subordinate culture can develop the economic base it needs to sustain itself on the long road to hegemony. (p. 97)

Indeed, the same sentiments are echoed by the Chairperson of the Community Media Network, Sean O. Siochru (1996) in his discussion on alternative media:

> The fragile and often sporadic nature of democratic media is demonstrated by the many initiatives that emerge with great hopes, only to disappear through lack of a permanent sustainable base and averse circumstances beyond their control. It would be a mistake to underestimate the scale of the task ahead for democratic media if it is to become a significant force in people's lives, from local to global levels. Building beyond isolated, often spontaneous and self-sacrificing, media projects towards an enduring and mutually sustaining democratic media sector is going to demand a qualitatively new level of organisation. (p. 3)

But alternatives, despite the hurdles, are certainly necessary, and indeed possible, as indicated by many of the other contributors to this volume. Change, following from Freire, must emerge from continuous struggle within particular sites. As Hamelink (1995) rightly puts it, "World political reality is not very encouraging for those who adopt this egalitarian perspective. But then, unless one is beyond caring about our common future, there is no other sensible perspective available" (p. 35).

REFERENCES

Bernstein, H. (1979). Sociology of underdevelopment versus sociology of development? In D. Lehmann (Ed.), *Development theory: Four critical case studies.* London: Frank Cass.

Blackledge, D.A., & Hunt, B. (1985). *Sociological interpretations of education.* London: Croom Helm.

Elliot, P., & Golding, P. (1974). Mass communication and social change: The imagery of development and the development of imagery. In E. De Kadt & G. Williams (Eds.), *Sociology and development.* London: Tavistock.

Elliot, P., & Golding, P. (1977). *Making the news.* London: Longman.

Escobar, A. (1995). Imagining a post-development era. In J. Crush (Ed.), *Power of development.* New York: Routledge.

Fals-Borda, O. (1991). Some basic ingredients. In O. Fals-Borda & M. A. Rahman (Eds.), *Action and knowledge: Breaking the monopoly with participatory action-research.* New York: Apex Press.

Fals-Borda, O., & Rahman, M. A. (Eds.). (1991). *Action and knowledge: Breaking the monopoly with participatory action-research.* New York: Apex Press.

Fang, C.S. (1991). The state and information technology in Taiwan. *Media Development, XXXVII*(3), 43-45.

Foster-Carter, A. (1974). Neo-Marxist approaches to development and underdevelopment. In E. De Kadt & G. Williams (Eds.), *Sociology and development.* London: Tavistock.

Frank, A.G. (1969). *Latin America: Underdevelopment or revolution?* New York: Monthly Review Press.

Freire, P. (1976). A few notions about the word "conscientisation." In R. Dale et al. (Eds.), *Schooling and capitalism.* London: Oxford University Press.

Freire, P. (1978). *Pedagogy of the oppressed.* Middlesex, UK: Penguin.

Freire, P. (1985). *The politics of education: Culture, power and liberation.* London: MacMillan.

Freire, P., & Shor, I. (1987). *A pedagogy for liberation: Dialogues on transforming education.* London: Macmillan.

French, D., & Richards, M. (Eds.). (1996). *Contemporary television: Eastern perspectives.* New Delhi: Sage.

Golding, P., & Harris, P. (Eds.). (1997). *Beyond cultural imperialism: Globalisation, communication and the new international order.* London: Sage.

Hamelink, C. (1995). The democratic ideal and its enemies. In P. Lee (Ed.), *The democratization of communication.* Cardiff: University of Wales/WACC.

Hedebro, G. (1982). *Communication and social change in developing nations: A critical view.* Ames: Iowa State University Press.

Huesca, R. (1996). New directions for participatory communication for development. *Media Development, XLIII*(2), 26-30.

Illich, I. (1969). *Celebration of awareness.* London: Pelican.

Illich, I. (1970). *Deschooling society.* London: Calder and Boyers.

Landry, C. et al. (1985). *What a way to run a railroad: An analysis of radical failure.* London: Comedia.

Lerner, D. (1958). *The passing of traditional society.* New York: Free Press.

Mackie, R. (Ed.). (1980). *Literacy and revolution: The pedagogy of Paulo Freire.* London: Pluto Press.

Martin-Barbero, J. (1993). Latin America: Cultures in the communication media. *Journal of Communication, 34*(2), 18-30.

Masterman, L. (1985). *Teaching the media.* London: Comedia.

McLaren, P., & Leonard, P. (Eds.). (1993). *Paulo Freire: A critical encounter.* London: Routledge.

Mercado, C.M. (1991). Development communication management. *Journal of Development Communication, 2*(2), 13-25.

O'Brien, R.C. (1979). *The political economy of underdevelopment: Dependence in Senagal.* Beverly Hills, CA: Sage.

Schlesinger, P., & Morris, N. (1997). Cultural boundaries: Identity and communication in Latin America. *Media Development, XLIV*(3), 5-17.

Schramm, W. (1964). *Mass media and national development.* Stanford, CA: Stanford University Press.

Scott, J.S. (1985). *Weapons of the weak: Everyday forms of peasant resistance.* New Haven, CT: Yale University Press.

Servaes, J. (1989). *One world, multiple cultures: A new paradigm on communication and development.* Leuven, Belgium: Acco.

Shah, H. (1996). Modernization, marginalization and emancipation: Toward a normative model of journalism and national development. *Communication Theory, 6*(2), 143-166.

Siriyuvasek, U. (1991). Communication, privatization and the state in Southeast Asia. *Media Development, XXXVII*(3), 28-30.

Siochru, S. O. (1996). Strategies and opportunities for democratic media. *Media Development, XLIII*(3), 3-7.

Smith, A. (1980). *The geopolitics of information.* London: Oxford University Press.

Sreberny-Mohammadi, A. (1996, June). *Whither national sovereignty: Cultural identities in a global context.* Paper presented at the 25th Anniversary Conference of AMIC, "Asian Communication: The Next 25 Years," Singapore.

Thomas, P.N. (1991). The state and information technology in India: Observations on emerging trends. *Media Development, XXXVII*(3), 31-38.

Zaharom, N., Mustafa K., & Kirton, C. (1996). Communications, curricula and conformity: Of national needs and market forces. *Educator and Education, 14,* 115-135.

Chapter ▪ 14

Latin American Political, Cultural, and Educational Changes at the End of the Millennium

Adriana Puiggros
(translated by Ann Shakespeare)

Latin America's contemporary education systems are in crisis at the most crucial time in their history since their introduction in the second half of the 19th century. The crisis is affecting education throughout the countries of Latin America and among the Latin American population of the United States (Torres & Puiggros, 1997). Its cause lies not only in the public expenditure cuts, which led to the recent collapse of the education systems; there are also political and cultural factors that need to be examined and that, along with the spending cuts, lead us to hypothesize that we are facing a crisis in the education system that I will call "organic" (see McLaren, 1995), with certain reservations. The most important elements of this situation include:

- The decline of modern Western education systems caused by changes in the legal and political lives of the nation-states and in national political culture. These changes have been brought about by the scientific and technological revolution, combined with the loss of consensus regarding statehood and the advance of neoconservatism.

- The accumulation of unresolved problems that have existed in Latin America since the introduction of education systems: Illiteracy, truancy, repetition, and unequal education structures have affected different countries in different ways.
- The interruption by military dictatorships of educational reforms that were introduced by democratic governments at the end of the 1960s and the beginning of the 1990s.
- Neoconservative policies applied as "adjustments" to Latin America's state economies since the end of the 1980s. Among the most influential have been the dramatic reduction in the financing of public education by the state and subsequent deterioration (Argentina), the lack of resources for schools (Venezuela), or simply the abandonment of schools on the part of the state (Peru).

These factors, along with migration and changes of population, have damaged the various forms of cultural expression in Latin America that had become established by the end of the 19th century, remaining relatively stable until the 1980s. At present, some regions can be defined as embracing a political and cultural mixture transcending the boundaries of the nation-state and offering alternatives to the modern education system. These regions include:

- the Chicano Anglo-Hispanic population of northern Mexico and the United States
- those parts of Mexico and Central America that are characterized by violent migration, ancient unresolved sociocultural and political antagonism
- the Andean region with its culture of drug trafficking and fundamentalist guerrilla activity
- the "Mercosur" region, where new political and cultural links are taking shape, although less strongly than in other regions
- the political and cultural factors surrounding childhood and youth, involving "street children," hired assassins, children who have suffered from civil war, and children and young people who have been expelled from school or denied schooling and who are illiterate. Modern education systems are deeply flawed, but new ideas and very different perspectives are beginning to emerge.

The combination of factors that led to the current crisis affected education systems in different ways. The effects can be grouped together in the following way.

First, in the more advanced education systems that had managed to meet almost all demands at all levels, such as in Argentina and Uruguay, the current crisis led to deep cultural divisions that plunged the middle classes into poverty and salaried workers into misery. The ideals of education and cultural integration held by the liberal Latin American educators of the 19th century (Ramos, 1910; Safford, 1989) have been pushed out of sight, and new systems are emerging, very separate from each other. Education, previously considered to be a role, duty or service of the state, becomes a marketable consumer good. Characterized by inequality and persistent political and cultural antagonism, it is weighed down by unresolved problems. Educators face neoliberal reform with trades unions, including more flexible working conditions and the reduction of public education.

The situation in Chile is an example of the process that is affecting this group. Chile's modern education system was dismantled on a wide scale by Pinochet's government between 1979 and 1981. The state formally laid down its responsibility for education, reserving authority only for providing basic teaching. All secondary and higher levels of education were privatized, either by charging fees or by total handover to private businesses. The methodology and state subsidy were passed on to private enterprise, and the agricultural, commercial, and industrial schools were handed over to commercial associations. Thus, the unity of national education policy was broken, and in its place came flexible curricula that reflected the fragmentation of the new system.

Applying the logic of market forces to education, the authorities dismantled the existing model of state education. Titles such as "managers," "employees," and "clients" replaced those of directors, teachers, and pupils. The handing over of the majority of educational institutions to town councils effectively placed them under the direct control of political authorities representing the Ministry of Home Affairs. As a result of the restrictions and the oppression imposed on the educational system by the military authorities since 1973, combined with the reduction in public spending, growth in registrations fell from 6.54% between 1970 and 1973 to -0.03% between 1973 and 1981, and spending on education fell from $601.9 million in 1972 to $497.4 in 1980 (Nunez, 1996). The government of President Alwin inherited a seriously damaged system that left more than one third of Chileans marginalized. At present, President Frei is trying to reverse the excesses of decentralization and privatization, but is discovering that it will not be easy to restore the benefits of the public education system.

Second, we find countries whose education system only reached a half of the population of which the majority is indigenous. Differences in culture and language led to deep clashes. We refer especially to the Andean countries and to Guatemala. This group is affected by diminishing education budgets, squeezing the education system and teachers' salaries, and by the closing down of cultural integration programs. The gap between the elite and the poor widens considerably, while at the same time there is an increasing tendency to undermine the identity of grassroots culture through the use of mass media. The indigenous populations of the Andes and Central America are now unable to prevent cultural genocide by maintaining their own tradition and language. The growth of commercially driven education makes them vulnerable to the messages of the mass media while at the same time excluding them from the educational opportunities of the dominant elite. Nongovernment organizations involved in grassroots education fulfill an important role in areas the state fails to reach, but it is not enough to meet the needs that exist.

For about 10 years, new doors have opened to enable the Quechua, Aymara and Guarani populations and other indigenous groups to find a way out of poverty. One new opportunity has been that of placing traditional agricultural systems, based in large part on the cultivation of the coca plant, at the service of the drug trade. This is corrupting the ancient culture and leads to the destruction of communities. Another possibility open to indigenous groups has been to ally themselves with the regressive influences of fundamentalist left-wing groups. Both cases combine the worst of contemporary culture with the lifeless remains of ancient traditions, resulting in dangerous consequences for education.

Third, in Brazil, the relative political autonomy of the states (or provinces) had allowed different educational strategies to develop in the midst of the crisis, some of which are important experiments for the future. For example, there is the experiences of Darcy Ribeiro in Rio de Janeiro, of Paulo Freire in Sao Paulo, and others. But since Fernando Henrique Cardoso became president, neoliberal reform of the state is well underway, including the changes in public education. The withdrawal of the state from its responsibility for education affected the integrity of the system in a more severe way than in other countries because historically the integration was late in coming and was a difficult process. The number of small children entering education increased by millions, and the universities suffered from lack of funds.

Fourth, education in Mexico has survived better than in other countries with more rigid, less diversified systems. It has shown a clear tendency to follow the Chilean model, although forces opposed to it are stronger than elsewhere in Latin America. By 1987, Mexican education had lost a third of the budget that had been available in 1982; a primary school teacher lost half the value of his or her salary, and a university professor lost 45%. The Mexican education system is complex. One factor that led to major changes in the system was the need to address problems in the 1970s and 1980s following the violent repression of the student movement. So when the crisis of the 1990s developed, the Mexican state was prepared to continue exercising control over education, adapting policy according to neoliberal thinking. However, difficulties and divisions began to arise. The most significant change arose on the northern border, where North American and Chicano influence spreads as rapidly into Mexico as Mexican and Latin American culture spreads into the United States. The new political and cultural issues that are emerging there have been described by the feminist Chicano author Gloria Anzaldua in her book entitled *Borderlands, the Frontier, the New Mestiza*. She explores a complex situation, characterized by profound divisions and differences that are not served by a homogeneous, unbending education policy. There is firm resistance both to education that reflects the "American way of life" as well as to that which is offered by the Mexican state.

Fifth, education in Costa Rica demonstrates positive changes that were introduced as part of social democratic reformist policies in the 1980s and that were made possible by the interest of the United States in keeping Costa Rica out of Central America's hostilities. Illiteracy in the country was reduced with the result that the percentage of population over 10 years old who were illiterate in 1973 (10.2%) dropped to 6.9% in 1984. The system was diversified and decentralized among state-run educational institutions throughout the country, and new educational initiatives were introduced among grassroots sectors and marginalized areas. In addition, recent years have seen a process of economic and educational change become established in Costa Rica. Measures to reduce costs at all levels have affected public education, but the authorities have maintained negotiations with the teaching unions that have resulted in agreements that protect teachers' salaries as well as the national integrity of the education system.

Finally, education in Cuba has been affected by the collapse of socialist states as well as by the negative consequences of the breakdown in affiliation with grassroots education movements elsewhere in Latin America. In addition, Cuba's educational system is suffering from the consequences of economic ties between politics and education under socialism, despite the wide-ranging process of modernization and democratization that is taking place. However, in spite of this situation, on top of the poverty caused by North America's blockade, Cuba retains a good deal of its capacity to provide education to its population and to guarantee a high standard of quality.

DIFFERENT INTERPRETATIONS

The situations described previously are viewed from a different perspective by politicians, intellectuals, and teachers. The prevailing viewpoints in Latin America are discussed in the following sections.

Entrenched Defense of Neoliberal Reform

International consultants, especially conservatives or technocrats who espouse the thinking of the World Bank and of Latin America's neoliberal governments, believe that it is essential that governments withdraw as much as possible from their role as provider of education and that they place restrictions on public investment in this area. They justify their position by citing the inefficiency of short-term investment and the enormous outlay needed to educate the masses, without the assurance of immediate and substantial returns on the capital invested. They believe that the centralized, public system of education is old and rigid, and that the state should fulfill a secondary role, leaving market forces to regulate the provision of education and limiting its intervention to welfare programs. Investment should be restricted to a minimum, and commercial criteria should be followed to allocate the budget between the most profitable education sectors. It will involve developing a flexible way of enrolling students and applying commercial standards.

In order to make investment efficient, the old educational institutions of the past will be closed, and those programs currently designed for sectors of society that have no place in the workforce of the neoliberal economic model will be disbanded. For this reason, there is a lack of interest in grassroots education programs, adult education centers are closing, and education for minority groups is waning.

"Adjustment" with Reduction

Some political and technical sectors reject the idea that the neoliberal education model may have caused structural problems within the education system, which they consider to be defunct. They acknowledge the serious problems facing education, but according to them the "adjustment," or changes, in education are as indispensable as the economic changes designed to modernize the country. They criticize the restrictions on investment in education, but they consider that the social consequences of the adjustment are not inherent in the neoliberal model; rather, they are the unwanted and inevitable results of an "adjustment" with a human face. Corruption and poor administration are to be blamed more than the model itself. They support strong, market-driven intervention in education without defining the problem of distribution and encourage competition to improve quality, coinciding with the views of conservative neoliberalism. They see the state as having a balancing role, giving it responsibility for ensuring equality in the distribution of education. With the exception of social assistance and education programs there are no strategies of this kind, combining neo-Keynesian social policy with a neoliberal economic policy. It is claimed that the same government that introduces market economy into education, with destructive results, repairs the damage caused by this very model. Technical solutions are given priority over political solutions based on the participation of teachers and others involved in education. More favorable loans from the World Bank for education and the restriction imposed by the state depend on the development of technical policy.

Democratic Position

Various interpretations, tendencies, and strategies exist, all of which recognize the seriousness of the situation but believe that it is necessary to recover a substantial part of the existing system in order to bring about a transformation. Teachers strongly support this position because the existence of their profession and their source of work depend on the subsidizing of public education. In addition, teachers and professors are directly affected by the poverty of their students (Hargreaves, 1966). Grassroots educators, previously opposed to public education, should now defend it. The sectors they serve are now broader than marginalized communities and minorities. The grassroots educator needs to join together with the school teacher and with a variety of subjects, old and new, in order to defend public opportunities for education. Many secondary teachers are now grassroots educators. Grassroots educators face the task of motivating communities as well as taking part in the struggle for public education. From the theoretical point of view, the controversy over grassroots education in the 1970s and 1980s has been displaced by another issue. There is a need to discuss the relationship between the education that the state should provide and the rights and responsibilities that should be addressed in the community.

A LITTLE HISTORY

Latin America's traditional school curricula were designed by liberal-oligarchic politicians, influenced by the positivism of the 19th century. The founders believed that it would be possible to wipe out all vestiges of the ancient indigenous and mestizo cultures by means of public education. For this task, the centralization of curricula was fundamental, but different countries chose different ways of approaching it. An example is the comparison between the approaches of Argentina and Mexico.

In Mexico, dealing with indigenous and grassroots resistance to the imposition of modern culture required a system of education that was capable of addressing the complexities of the situation. At the beginning of the 1920s, the ruling class that emerged after the Mexican Revolution (1910–1917) believed that the way to achieve hegemony was to mix races and cultures. Jose Vasconcelos, the country's first Secretary of Public Education, considered that a superior race, which he called "cosmic race," would develop as the new society grew. Although the school system was the most important, the education system was designed as a series of different strategies, both formal and informal, urban and rural, and that included literacy campaigns, and so on. The school curricula contained elements of different grassroots cultures, which were all, however, made to fit into the national plan. In Mexico, the dominant pedagogical thinking of that time clearly demonstrates profound differences between the attitude and behavior of the Mexican state and the attitude of the grassroots groups, reflected in myriad activities and a remarkable ability to adapt themselves to different political, social, and cultural situations. It remains to be seen what effect the neoliberal policies will have in Mexico and Latin America as they place importance on both the most ancient and the most modern of existing unresolved social differences.

In Argentina, the indigenous population was slaughtered during the 19th century. The mestizos were ignored by the dominant class who identified with everything European. Later, at the turn of the 19th century, immigrants arrived from Europe, and the governing class, despite its identification with European values, rejected the political culture, language, and religion of the immigrants, except Catholicism. The Latin American education system was modeled to reflect the aspirations of a particular sector of the population: male chauvinist, White, Catholic, racist, hostile to indigenous people, mestizos, and Jews. The system also tended to foster the intellect at the expense of productivity and pragmatism. Educational activities were focused at one level: the school. Once at school, each child and adult was obliged to leave behind his or her cultural context. School life was based on a myth that defined how society should be organized. This myth claimed that national unity is only possible if all differences are suppressed and rendered homogeneous. In Argentina, school custom abolished any kind of expression that deviated from the established norm. The education system developed a facade of homogeneity, but serious differences were hidden beneath the surface. The rigidity of the system made it impossible to address the variety of regional, political, and cultural needs, and it could not stand up to the current crisis.

Since 1930, several countries in Latin America had launched vigorous programs to combat illiteracy and had made schooling available to the whole population. The literacy campaigns of the government of Lazaro Cardenas in Mexico and of Getulio Vargas in Brazil and the education programs offered to grassroots sectors by Peronists in Argentina were highly significant and went a long way toward meeting the educational needs of the populations of the region's three major countries.

Since the end of the World War II, international organizations invested large sums in literacy programs, training for the workforce, and women's education. With highs and lows, school enrollment increased and truancy and illiteracy dropped in almost all countries. According to published research (Puiggros, 1977), secondary and higher education has developed most in recent decades. In 1950, over 15% of the population in only three countries had received secondary schooling, and in most countries the figure was under 7%. With regard to higher education, in 1950, only one country had enrolled 10% of its population between 19 and 22 years, another enrolled 8%, and the majority enrolled below 4%. However, in 1990, the enrollment percentage in Latin America surpassed 27%.

Taking examples from different countries, in Argentina the rate of primary schooling rose between 1869 and 1991 as follows (Pereyra et al., 1996):

1869	20,0
1896	31,0
1914	48,0
1947	73,5
1960	85,6
1970	87,7
1980	93,4
1991	95,3 (estimated; see Gramsci, 1982; Weber, 1982)

The percentage of secondary school (see Ramos, 1910; Safford, 1989) attendance between 1980 and 1991 rose from 33.4% to 53.5%, and higher education rose from 5.1% in 1980 to 10.6% in 1991 (Braslavsky, 1995).

The Brazilian education system showed growth throughout the 1980s (Schwartzman, Durham, & Goldemberg, 1995):

Year	Pre-school	Primary	Secondary	Higher
1981	115,58	99,44	100,04	100,65
1984	185,84	109,70	104,68	101,60
1989	264,42	122,31	122,06	110,24

From the perspective of neoliberal debate, it is important to emphasize that the system is not an uncontrollable monster, piling up errors and inefficiency. A look at three important elements will illustrate this: illiteracy, repetition of classes, and streaming (desgranamiento).

Illiteracy in Latin America continued to fall in 1990. According to UNESCO estimates, the adult literacy rate in Latin America and the Caribbean in 1980 was 79.5%, and in 1990 it was 84.9%, with an estimated rate of 88.5% in the year 2000 (Nunez, 1996).

Illiteracy (Percentage of the population 15 years and older; Schifelbein, 1997):

Country	1970	1980	1985	1990
Argentina	7.4	6.1	5.2	4.7
Bolivia	36.8	27.5	22.5	
Brazil	33.8	25.5	21.5	18.9
Colombia	19.2	12.2	15.3	13.3
Ecuador	25.8	16.5	17.0	14.2
Guatemala	54.0	44.2	48.1	44.9
Mexico	25.8	16.0	15.3	12.4
Paraguay	19.9	12.3	11.7	9.9
Dominican Republic	33.0	31.4	19.6	16.7
Uruguay	6.1	5.0	4.3	3.8
Venezuela	23.5	15.3	14.3	11.9

The repeating of classes tended to drop in most Latin American countries, but in some countries it increased. There are no comparative studies analyzing the causes of this variation. The following chart, showing rates of repeated primary classes, is based on information provided by UNESCO (Pereyra et al., 1996):

Repeated Classes in First Grade

	1973	1984
Colombia	50.5	45.6
Chile	32.6	18.3
Paraguay	37.2	29.5
Uruguay	20.3	21.5
Brazil	54.4	54.3
Peru	41.2	46.8
Venezuela	20.8	25.6

At the end of the 1960s and beginning of the 1970s, democratic reforms were introduced that affected education at preschool, secondary, and higher levels, and adults. Parallel with the growth of formal education an important nonformal education movement developed that was deeply influenced by the work of Paulo Freire. Many nongovernment organizations (NGOs), both lay and religious, initiated a variety of programs, including education for adults and indigenous groups, literacy schemes, and training for migrant and marginalized communities. Toward the end of the 1970s almost all countries were in a position to provide basic education for their population. However, military dictatorships and authoritarian governments restricted or prevented its development, persecuted the grassroots educators, and hindered the work of the NGOs. The climate of repression caused additional damage to systems already affected by difficulties and divisions.

At the end of the 1980s, schools were in need of wide-ranging reforms. The situation was different in each country. Some had not even begun to modify the system they had had for over a century. Others had introduced reforms that adapted the system to new technologies and cultural changes. In general, Latin America suffered from a combination of old, new, and future problems, with few prospects for solutions, given the paucity of democratic thinking. The objections to formal education, which had been voiced by democratic educators several years previously, had hampered methodological and technological progress. Planning, educational technology, and other new developments were not sufficiently explored. The numerous initiatives in alternative education that took place between the early 1960s and mid-1980s fell away as international organizations and private institutions were restricted in their investment in research and grassroots education. Politicians, technocrats, and intellectuals moved away from the grassroots movements in favor of hegemony, and alternative, democratic educational programs were almost abandoned.

At the start of the 1990s, schools, colleges, and universities were faced with strong demands for a new approach to education.

While neoliberal education policy extended its influence, the democratic movement criticized the problems caused by "adjustment." Taking a more radical position than the left of the 1970s, the neoliberal leaders declared that the public education system had failed as a model: They threw the baby out with the bath water, using existing problems to justify selling off a major part of Latin American public education.

At present, many Latin Americans are not learning to read nor write. Sixteen cities of more than 20 million inhabitants will contain most of the population of the Third World by the year 2000. Poverty will be combined with information systems and with cultural and social control that today seem like science fiction. Illiterates will be defenseless.

Illiteracy threatens a large percentage of young people and adults throughout the subcontinent. These are people who cannot read a newspaper, political and commercial propaganda, street signs, public service announcements, nor instructions for electronic appliances. There are others who have completed primary and perhaps secondary or higher education, but who are also technically illiterate because of the weaknesses in the education system and economic difficulties.

Millions of children and young people live on the margins of society or on the streets and organize their own micro-society. They are used as hired assassins by Colombian drug dealers; in Mexico they are known as *bandas* or *panchitos*, falling outside the law; in Rio de Janeiro they sleep under bridges and in train stations. More than 35% of the economically active population in Argentina is unemployed or underemployed. Their children are more likely to attend primary school than before because there they receive food and protection from the community. For this reason, truancy has diminished, but cases of repeated classes and failure in basic learning increased dramatically, pointing to future illiteracy. Arrangements for learning are determined by the law of hunger and the law of the street. In many schools on the outskirts of Buenos Aires pupils are rubbish collectors, and they feed themselves with leftovers they pick up. They were disastrous at learning, but when their teachers introduced the theme of rubbish as a topic, they were streets ahead of their fellow pupils.

Latin America's population has been pushed to the backwater of history, plundered not just economically but also culturally. The destruction of the public education system, including universities, will prevent future development. For decades hence, Latin America will lack a critical mass of educated men and women who will build a productive and relatively autonomous society and culture because the majority of citizens will not be able to play a productive part in their society.

THE SITUATION FACING GRASSROOTS EDUCATION

The fact that the optimistic predictions and proposals of the progressive sectors and the left in Latin America have failed is due not only to the defeat suffered by socialism and leftist policies, but also to internal obstacles in the grassroots education movement. Major contradictions remained unresolved, such as those between awareness-raising and indoctrination, between respect for cultural differences and authoritarian education, and between education for the oppressed minorities and education for the majority. Most grassroots educators were critical of the public education system. They ranged from those who adopted a position of "reproductivism," which dismissed all public teaching initiatives in favor of grassroots education and reduced activity to the imposition of the dominant ideology, to those who believed that grassroots education should be offered by the public system. However, they view the crisis facing Latin America's schooling systems in a different way. The school, previously criticized as being an "old and fat sacred cow" (as Ivan Illich referred to it in his talk in La Paz, Bolivia, in 1970) is regarded as indispensable in guaranteeing education for millions of children who were left vulnerable with regard to their right to education. The educational role of the state has been reevaluated, acknowledging that the demand for greater democratization of educational bodies, of curricula, and of the management of educational institutions depends on the extent to which governments are prepared to take responsibility for guaranteeing adequate education for their citizens.

A major step taken by neoliberal governments has been to transfer centrally governed educational programs and establishments to the provinces and town councils, with the aim of handing them over to private management. Provincial authorities and town councils in Latin America are notoriously impoverished or else, as in the case of large cities, are weighed down by problems and are unlikely to be able to finance education or to take responsibility for the administration of the programs transferred to them. The result has been the reduction and impoverishment of the public education service. The privatization initiative has failed badly because in the current economic recession no sector, be it social, religious, or economic, is in a position to take charge of the education of millions of children and of the salaries of millions of teachers. The private initiative, with the exception of a few less developed countries, was directed specifically at secondary and higher levels, but no interest was shown in basic education nor in adult education among the poorer sectors (Benjamin, 1986).

According to the previously mentioned situation, formal education was gaining strength in the 1970s but lost its way in the 1990s. In the 1970s criticism leveled by progressive educators against authoritarianism and bureaucratism led to a search for more democratic education systems. In the present day, the focus is more on the need to reclaim the right of Latin Americans to a structured, accessible system of basic education.

Since the period of the conquest, Latin America's education systems have developed within the context of a complex combination of inequalities, which continue today in different forms. Whatever political ideologies prevail in the continent at the start of the 21st century, it is clear that this inequality should be addressed in the development of education systems, in the selection and organization of knowledge, in the curricula, and in the way it is presented. It is likely that there will still be conflict between different ways of distributing and employing knowledge. Education in the 21st century will suffer from clashes between old and new ideologies. There will be conflict between different theories underpinning the understanding, logic, and management of reality in the context of education. The right of different social groups to take an active part in the development and evaluation of teaching and learning will become a high priority.

The path of neoliberalism, which serves to deepen the injustices of society, further alienates the different factions and pushes away the possibility of consensus or at least a way of living with differences. If there is to be a form of education that will lead to democracy, social justice, mental health, and happiness, then there must be options that will embrace the different viewpoints, languages, and political ideologies and that will transcend former antagonism. These options must bring together modern Western thinking with that of the oppressed and marginalized sectors of society. New political and cultural attitudes are needed in the conception and development of curricula, based on more democratic processes. A major objective for the democratic movements is to share power in the management of educational institutions, in community education programs, and in the planning of curricula.

SOME METHODOLOGICAL FORECASTS

There is an insufficient body of theory around grassroots education, given the changes that have come about over the decades. The education needs of the population have changed, as have the institutions. There are new ways of looking at nonformal education, and there was a revolution in the forms of communication. Faced with this scenario, there is a need to reflect on the philosophical and political thinking behind educational strategies. This reflection should consider various issues that are defined as follows (Bernstein, 1990).

The most complete information and best overview of education is in the hands of national governments and international organizations. These have recourse to technical equipment and economic resources in abundance and have influence over public and private institutions, which enable them to carry out quality control, research, and other forms of assessment. They also involve the grassroots sectors by evaluating and classifying them.

The information and interpretations obtained from centers of power should be critically assessed and tested against the daily experience of educators, pupils, and the community. In particular, they should question theories that endorse discriminatory education programs (Gasche, 1986).

There is a need to identify knowledge and know-how that is not simply able to be classified, but that is also capable of bringing about change in the power structures in education, that generates new teaching alternatives, and that fosters creative ways of combining modern technology with grassroots education.

We also need to look inward, within ourselves, and in this sense to reconsider the term "grassroots education," to reflect on its historical meaning and its relationship with formal education, to consider the theories it embraces, to classify and study the experiences it offers, and to bring to light its contradictions. We need to embark on a profound study of the composition of society. There have been changes in the distribution of wealth, social structure, and the organization of work. Not only are there more people who are poor, but also the meaning of poverty has changed over the decades. Many of those who are the focus of grassroots education now often live in large urban communities, rather than remote areas. Those living in poverty are not a homogeneous mass but are varied in their culture, their ways of living and of thinking about the present and the future. In many cases they have different ways of communicating with government and with the education system.

Of the ideas bequeathed to us by Paulo Freire, one that stands out is that the educator and the pupil are not given positions but are historically and politically constituted. Official pedagogy (all official pedagogies always have a positive heart) tends to consolidate these positions, desiring to monopolize society's educational message. But this clashes in an irreconcilable way with historical development, which is a complex tapestry of human desires (Laclau, 1987, 1990). The pupil of today can be the educator of tomorrow if policies are introduced that will encourage democratic alternatives. The community will count on educators to discover paths that lead away from the cross-roads in which neoliberalism has trapped us. They should find a different perspective to the neoliberal "adjustment"—one that rises above the traditional education system which they criticized years ago (McLaren & Lankshear, 1992; Puiggros, 1997).

REFERENCES

Anzaldua, G. (1987). *Borderlands, the frontiers, the new Mestiza*. San Francisco: Spinsters/Aunt Lute.

Benjamin, W. (1986). Desembalo mi biblioteca revista Punto de Vista [Unpacking my library]. *Ano, IX*(26).

Bernstein, B. (1990). *Sobre el discurso pedagogico en la construccion social del discurso pedagogico* [On pedagogic discourse in the social construction of pedagogic discourse]. Bogota: El Griot.

Braslavsky, C. (1995). Tranformaciones en curso en el sistema educativo Argentino [Changes under way in the Argentine education system]. In J. Puryear & J. J. Brunner (Eds.), *Educacion, equidad y competitividad economica en las americas: Un proyecto de dialogo interamericano* [Education, equity and economic competitiveness in the Americas: A plan for interamerican dialogue]. Washington, DC: OEA.

Gasche, R. (1986). *The tain of the mirror, Derrida and the philosophy of reflection.* Cambridge, MA: Harvard University Press.

Gramsci, A. (1975). *Notas sobre Maquiavelo, sobre politica y sobre Estado moderno* [Notes on Machiavelli, on politics and on the modern state]. Mexico City: Juan Pablos.

Hargreaves, A. (1966). *Profesorado, cultura y postmodernided* [Teaching, culture and postmodernity]. Madrid: Morata.

Laclau, E. (1987). *Mouffe Chantal. Hegemonia y estrategia socialista* [Mouffe Chantal. Hegemony and social strategy]. London: Verso.

Laclau, E. (1990). *New reflections on the revolution of our time.* London: Verso.

McLaren, P. (1995). *Multicultural education, critical pedagogy and the politics of difference.* Albany: State University of New York Press.

McLaren, P., & Lankshear, C. (1992). *Conscientization and oppression.* New York: Routledge.

Nunez, I. (1996). La educacion chilena en el periodo 1945-1990 [Education in Chile in the period 1945-1990]. In G. Valadez (Ed.), *Historia de la educacion en Iberoamerica* [History of education in Latin America] (Vol. 1). Mexico City: Siglo XXI.

Pereyra, M. et al. (1996). *Globalizacion y descentralizacion de los sistemas educativos* [Globalization and decentralization of education systems]. Barcelona: Pomares-corredor.

Puiggros, A. (1997). *Imperialismo, neoliberalismo y educacion en America Latina* [Imperialism, neoliberalism and education in Latin America]. Buenos Aires: Paidos.

Ramos, J. P. (1910). *La instruccion primaria en la Republica Argentina* [Primary teaching in the Argentine Republic]. Buenos Aires: Consejo Nacional de Educacion.

Safford, F. (1989). *El debate de lo practico* [The debate about practice]. Bogota: Empresa Editorial Universidad Nacional/El Ancora.

Schifelbein, E. (1997). Financing education for democracy in Latin America. In C. A. Torres & A. Puiggros (Eds.), *Latin American education.* Boulder, CO: Westview Press.

Schwartzman, E., Durham, R., & Goldemberg, J. (1995). A educacao no Brasil em una perspectiva de transformacao [Education in Brazil from the point of view of change]. In J. Puryear & J. J. Brunner (Eds.), *Educacion, equidad y competitividad economica en las americas: Un proyecto de dialogo interamericano.* Washington, DC: OEA.

Torres, C. A., & Puiggros, A. (1997). *Latin American education.* Boulder, CO: Westview Press.

Weber, M. (1982). *Escritos politicos* [Political writings]. Mexico City: Folios Ed.

Chapter ▪ 15

Freirean Futures: Toward a Further Understanding of Participatory Communications

Pradip N. Thomas

PARTICIPATORY COMMUNICATION: THE FREIREAN LEGACY

Paulo Freire's (1982) classic study *Pedagogy of the Oppressed* has been a key referent in social and cultural struggles around the world during the preceding 25 years. During this time Freirean concepts and pedagogical methods have acquired wide currency, even a certain notoriety. *Cultural action, participation,* and *action-reflection* are some Freirean terms that have been adopted, adapted, used, abused, celebrated, or coopted by a variety of actors inclusive of activists, development specialists, pedagogists, and government officials.

If anyone were to write a history of participatory communications, the place of key Freirean terms in that history, inclusive of "participation" and "cultural action" as idea, process, and praxis, will surely need to be acknowledged. Although the praxis of critical pedagogy has been Freire's key concern, it seems extraordinary that writings on Freire (McLaren & Lankshear, 1994; McLaren & Leonard, 1993) have ignored Freire's contribution to the communicational dimensions of pedagogy, inclusive of the theory and practice of participatory communication. The growing library of literature on the subject of participatory communications (Riaño, 1994; Servaes,

Jacobson, & White, 1996; White, Nair, & Ascroft, 1994) and any number of articles in a variety of journals—*Chasqui, Africa Media Review, Group Media Journal, Media Development*—have to some extent redressed this imbalance. Continuing this trend, this volume celebrates Freire's contribution to the transdisciplinary field of development communications by acknowledging the influence of his theory as praxis on academics and activists working in the area of international communication, development communication, pedagogy, and participatory grassroots communications.

A primary objective of this chapter is to examine the Freirean legacy to participatory communications in light of contemporary challenges stemming from new theories of liberation and his own subsequent revaluation of the meaning of social change as liberation. An implicit assumption accompanying this text is the faith that participatory communication, in order to remain of "cutting-edge" relevance, will have to dialogue with and reflect on emerging instances of critical theory, particularly that body of knowledge that throws light on the increasingly complex, variable relationships between consciousness, power, and social change. This chapter is organized into three sections: (a) an introduction to "liberation crisis" in contemporary cultural politics, which will include a brief critique of postcolonial thought that, along with critical postmodernist thought, informs the theoretical stance of the post-1985 Freire; (b) a contrastive reading of Habermas and Freire as a means to illustrate the basis for a "fusion of horizons," which remains a central objective of participatory communications; and (c) an assessment of key Freirean concerns, in particular, the notion of participation for liberation in the context of non-Western ideas, moralities, and modes of sociability that inspire trust and lead to integrated understandings of community.

LIBERATION CRISIS IN CONTEMPORARY CULTURAL POLITICS

The credibility of reigning theoretical orthodoxies in the social sciences, both of the right and left, but most critically the left, has been called into question in light of their inability to account for contemporary motivations of social change. New variants of critical theory have emerged to fill the void. Its proponents include those who do not owe allegiance to any particular theoretical lineage as well as critical insiders from both the left and the right who have radically altered their links to traditional bodies of theory in favor of contextualized, multivariant understandings of social change shaped by contemporary theories—postcolonialism, poststructuralism, and postmodernism. Contemporary readings of social change reflect growing awareness of the inherent limitations of all-encompassing, essentialized categories such as class and for the need to understand and theorize a cultural politics for those who inhabit the "in-between" spaces, who live "difference," and whose identities are formed in the context of predatory cultures, forced and unforced migrations, and fractured along the lines of race, ethnicity, gender, sexuality, class, caste, tribe, and nationality. Readings of participatory communications based on unitary foundations have also come under critical scrutiny in light of perceived complexities at local levels—the increasing salience of individual identities, the spread of the politics of "difference" and its implications for communication strategies founded on the primacy of collective identities (Melucci, 1996). The postcolonial theorist Bhabha (1994) captures the mood for a "new" cultural politics, the need

> to think beyond narratives of originary and initial subjectivities and to focus on those moments or processes that are produced in the articulation of cultural differences. These "in-between" spaces provide the terrain for elaborating strategies of selfhood—singular or communal—that initiate new signs of identity, and innovative sites of collaboration, and contestation, in the act of defining the idea of society itself. (pp. 1-2)

One may add that the objective is not merely to "think" the spaces of difference but also to "act" on this new terrain. While the task of rebuilding radical cultural theory has begun to be enunciated by a diverse group of theoreticians, both old and new, including the likes of Escobar (1995), Melucci (1996), Canclini (1995), Spivak (1988), Bhabha (1994), among others, there remains a nagging doubt, a sense of unease with the form, content, and objectives of the new vision of social change, particularly the versions that are shaped by postmodernism and postcolonialism. For instance, one could quite easily make the point that despite their protestations against any form of essentialism, postcolonial readings tend to be essentialist. Binary readings and categorical assumptions pepper their texts. Tradition, for instance, is deemed to be sacrosanct and beyond the ken of critique except from within the parameters generated by an internal value system.[1] Such readings, at least in the South Asian context, feed into and corroborate ultraconservative discourses. Similarly, even though their readings of colonial history and representations have in general been immensely insightful, the same can-

---

[1]The social critic Sarah Joseph (1991) has called our attention to the need for multidimensional, translocally valid criteria in the evaluation of tradition:

> An approach to tradition which relies solely on internally generated standards of rationality can be questioned on a number of grounds such as how we could (sic) recognise violations of internal standards, how we could understand the causal factors which give rise to these standards of rationality, and the possible conflicts and contradictions between different parts of social life. (pp. 60-61)

not be said of their readings of Christian Mission, for instance, which tend to be unoriginal in the sense that they have not sufficiently considered self-critiques made by critical insiders both during the colonial and postcolonial eras.[2] The tremendous variety of readings from a liberation theology perspective is a case in point. But the most damaging critique relates to their inability to go beyond the theorizing of difference, in other words, their inability to reconstruct the basis for liberatory discourses after the deconstructions. Although difference has to be acknowledged and theorized and hybridity and in-betweenness taken seriously, a politics for liberation must necessarily have multisectoral objectives based on an acknowledgment of commonalities. What is missing in these exercises is a vision of cultural politics built on the recognition of continuities rather than discontinuities.[3]

The project of reconstruction is of particular relevance to those involved in grassroots work and social movements in the South, who have witnessed the fracture of collective consensus, the decentering of the project of capturing power at a national level, and the dismemberment of unified approaches to development in light of identity politics at local and national levels based on both "real" and "imagined" struggles that are on occasion framed by global identity politics. Participatory communication projects in South Asia have, for instance, been affected by the politics of resurgent religious revivalism and ethnic chauvinism, but they have also been affected by exogenous trends—sustainable development, environmentalism, and so on. Although a few notable initiatives have attempted to deal with this trend, for the most part the bypassing of collective strategies and their replacement by particular, narrowly circumscribed strategies of participatory communication has accelerated the sectoralization of cultural action.

---

[2]See, for instance, a predictable reading of the Mission in the otherwise excellent treatise by Gauri Vishwanathan (1989).

[3]One of the continuing legacies of modern Western scholarship, inclusive of its critical variants, is a tendency to the overgeneralizing and univerzalizing of economic, cultural, and political trends that are often abstracted from finite, parochial experiences. Steven Robins (1996) recalls an incident that took place at the Congress on Globalisation and Culture, Duke University, November 1994, when the Egyptian scholar and writer Nawaal Sadaawi, after listening to the various presentations on the demise of the nation-state and the decline of nationalism, voiced her indignation at the "trend-setters" who generalize aspects of the fall, without providing any scope for certainities, for progressive understandings of what she termed the "reconstruction of nationalism." See also van der Gaag (1996), who deals with contemporary trends in the break-up of the nation-state. It celebrates a romanticized Pan-Africanism without stating the case for a need for a new "nations-state" with defined boundaries, that is founded simultaneously on a respect for the identities of its "nations" within and on an inter-"nation"ally agreed to Right to Nations.

THE UNIVERSAL AND THE PARTICULAR—FREIREAN PERSPECTIVES

It is significant that Freire, inspite of his schooling in a Western scholastic tradition, attempts to read the world from distinctly critical, at times anti-Enlightenment perspectives. For instance, he takes a non-dualistic, even an *advaiten*[4] stance with respect to knowing the world. His philosophy stresses continuities rather than discontinuities between subject and object, consciousness and the world, reflection and action, the oppressor and the oppressed. Although Freire has always maintained the right of the oppressed to be free, this act is subject to the larger objective of humanizing the world through the resolution of the contradiction between the oppressor and the oppressed. This resolution is born out of a spirit of love and humility. In his *Pedagogy of the Oppressed*, Freire (1982) acknowledges the need to bridge the chasm between the oppressor and the oppressed through the humanising action of the oppressed: "As the oppressed, fighting to be human, take away the oppressor's power to dominate and suppress, they restore to the oppressors the humanity they had lost in the exercise of oppression" (p. 32).

This privileging of continuities remains a Freirean concern. In his most recent publication *Pedagogy of Hope* (1994) he recalls that "there are historical moments at which the survival of the social whole imposes on the classes a need to understand one another" (p. 93). This position echoes Gandhian notions of liberation that suggest that the liberation of the Brahmin is tied to the liberation of the Dalit, and vice versa. Whereas Henry Giroux (1993) has called our attention to the problematic nature of Freire's theory of trusteeship, the evaluation of a common order out of the present chaos cannot but be based on a joint project, however remote it seems at the moment. Otherwise, we would need to rest content with a dissaggregated, lopsided vision of liberation. If we are to hold onto a vision of liberation that is common to all, then we must, with Freire and in the spirit of inclusive discourses, ground our perceptions in the notion of conti-

---

[4]Sankara, the 8th-century Indian philosopher, is credited with having formulated the philosophy of *advaita* or nondualism, which advocates a stress on continuities, the sole reality of Brahman (the supreme spirit), and the unreality (Maya) of all else.

The language of continuities is most eloquently expressed in poems by the 11th Indian, Virasaivite poet, Basavanna, from the book *Speaking of Siva* (1973).

Here is one example:

The sacrifical lamb brought for the festival
ate up the green leaf brought for the decorations.
Not knowing a thing about the kill,
it wants only to fill its belly.
But tell me:
did the killers survive?
O Lord of the meeting rivers!

nuities based on a conviction of wholeness often expressed by "other" philosophical traditions and their "incommensurate," non-Cartesian readings of reality. The social critic Ashis Nandy (1978) draws our attention to another interpretation of liberation:

> Often drawing inspiration from the monisitic traditions of their religions, the civilizations of the Third World have carefully protected the faith that the concept of evil can never be clearly defined, that there is always a continuity between the aggressor and his victim, and that liberation from an oppression is not merely the freedom from an oppressive agency outside, but also ultimately a liberation from a part of one's own self. (p. 171)

Such a reading provides the basis for a more complete understanding of the project of liberation. It is one that Freire acknowledges in his writings, and it is to his credit that Freire, while acknowledging the multidimensionality of human identity, grounds his analysis in a vision of the universal in the particular and the particular in the universal.

HABERMAS AND FREIRE: REDEEMING UNIVERSALS

Freire's (1994) most recent book available in English is called *The Pedagogy of Hope: A Reliving of the Pedagogy of the Oppressed*. In it Freire affirms his faith in critical pedagogy as an exercise in the fulfillment of hope, an exercise that is carried forward by what McLaren and da Silva (1993) call a "Utopian dreaming" through which the past, with its layers of privileged interpretations of right and wrong, is opened to the possibility of inclusive futures engendered by the dreams of the oppressed.

The project of participatory communication is built on the assumption that individuals and communities share the right to speak their word, to name reality, and to act on it. It is a means to both apprehend and critique the logic of dominant power flows and its resultant inequalities and to create a shared conviction in another orientation to development. It is founded on the knowledge that mutuality and trust are central to communication as action. Although Freire and Habermas have dwelt at length on the dialogic basis of communication, they seem to part ways on the project of "understanding the other," which is crucial to the formation of a universal ethic of communication that forms the very basis for inclusive strategies of participatory communication. In spite of the many correspondences between Habermas and Freire, for instance, their belief in the progressive strands of Enlightenment thought, particularly notions of freedom and rights, there are key divergences, in particular, Habermas's inability to theorize "difference," to affirm universals in the particulars of non-Western cultures and civilizations, and to validate other public spheres. Freire, however, is open to the reality of difference, the variegated colors of oppression, and to the possibility for provisional Utopias. Freire, unlike Habermas, does make an attempt to answer (albeit in a fragmentary and incomplete manner) the troubling question: If it is no longer possible to conceive of an all-encompassing, liberal, extensive understanding of human liberation from the top-down, is it at all possible to evolve an understanding of liberation from the bottom-up as the universal is expressed in and through the particular?

A by now familiar postmodernist critique against modernist theories is its inability to account for the myriad differences between subjects, the fractured identities, and representative needs of people who desire frameworks for a cultural politics based on nontotalizing, limited forms of collective action. In turn, the uncritical celebration of difference has been questioned for its tendency to make a medley of conflict. More importantly for the purposes of this argument is the critique often brought against the modernity project—the inherent limitations of its ontological, epistemological premises, its reading of origins, history, and development that are deemed to be based on particular and restricted understandings of progress, reason, and rationality. The most consistent, counter-response to the critique of modernity has been made by Habermas (1981). Habermas, taking a critical modernist stance, defends the emancipative potential of modernity based on the legitimation of multiple, differentiated rationalities grounded in a common pool of universal proto-norms. He implicitly defends the rationality of the moral-political in modernity—its espousal of the values of truth, freedom, and justice—and upholds this trinitarian value system in his defense of modernity and as a counter to his critics who take what he terms "premodern" and "counterenlightenment" perspectives (Steuerman, 1988). However, Habermas's critics argue that in order to evolve universal protonorms there is a prior need to dialogue with the postcolonial subject, whose consciousness is often shaped by a life lived in the in-between spaces of different epistemic traditions and who recognizes different emancipatory goals animated by a host of "incommensurate" particulars. In other words, there is little gained by arriving at a reading of universal protonorms that is grounded in what is patently a Western epistemic.

In the authoritative text of the *Theory of Communicative Action* (Habermas, 1981) there is a section entitled "Some Characteristics of the Mythical and the Modern Ways of Understanding the World," in which Habermas develops his understanding of the modern "conduct of life." This is constructed by contrasting the development of "savage thought" with modern thought. Through an interrogation of the foundations of the mythical worldview Habermas proceeds to come to an understanding of the rationalized "lifeworld."[5] His argument is built on a critical reading of

---

[5]In Habermas's (1981) words:

> What irritates us members of a modern life world is that in a mythically interpreted world, we cannot, or cannot with sufficient preci-

anthropologists Evans-Pritchard, Levi-Strauss, and Maurice Godelier, among others; the cognitive psychologist Jean Piaget; and the sociologist Max Weber. The mythical worldview is, as Habermas points out, characterized by "the levelling of different domains of reality" (p. 47), between "language and the world," "internal connections of meaning and external connections of objects" (p. 49), and its "closedness" (p. 52). This stands in sharp contrast to the modern worldview based on categorization, differentiation, and the "decentration of world understanding and the rationalisation of the life world that are necessary conditions for an emancipated society" (p. 74).

Inspite of what seem to be profound, irreconcilable differences in the two worldviews, Habermas echoing Gadamer, in Part II of his argument, does recognize the need for a "fusion of horizons" and intercultural dialogue as a means to come to a universal, fuller understanding of a theory of rationality. However, as one of his critics, Johann Arnason (1991) notes, it is precisely Habermas's "built-in conceptual obstacles" that hamstring his efforts to fuse horizons. As Arnason points out:

> If the specific characteristic of mythical and traditional worldviews are reduced to symptoms of an inability to grasp the differences between object domains (particularly those of the natural, the social and the subjective world) as well as between ways of relating to them, there is no scope for an authentic fusion of horizons. (p. 182)

In the making of universals, it is mandatory that there be an openness when it comes to constructing First Principles. In order to do this one needs to abandon the tendency to monocentricity in the envisioning of universals and replace it with intersubjectively valid understandings.

In this regard, Freire too has by no means been consistent. Until the mid-1980s, his understanding of liberation was open to critique precisely for its inability to deal with the reality of "difference," for leaning to a "phallocentric reading of liberation" (hooks, 1993, p. 148). Yet, inspite of this blindspot, hooks celebrates Freire's openness and willingness to dialogue with more inclusive understandings of liberation.

The future of inclusive approaches to participatory communication is by no means a certainty. Its survival is dependent on its openness to universal protonorms—the commonalities that undergird the mutualities of community. However, these protonorms need to be arrived at on the basis of a dialogue with the living cultures and traditions in our world. The Freirean legacy points us in this direction.

---

sion, make certain differentiations that are fundamental to our understanding of the world. From Durkheim to Levi-Strauss, anthropologists have repeatedly pointed out the peculiar *confusion between nature and culture.* (p. 48; emphasis in original)

AFFIRMING THE OTHER IN AND THROUGH PARTICIPATORY COMMUNICATION

Central to Freirean discourse is the stated intention of wanting to affirm the other through dialogue and participatory processes of interaction. In practice, however, as contemporary reality seems to suggest, affirmation can often result in a schizophrenic, sectoral approach to radical politics. The sloganeering of participation has had deep, negative effects on the practice of both critical pedagogy and participatory communications. In the South Asian context, which I am most familiar with, this has led to the downgrading of the creative potential of "participation" as an inclusive strategy of affirmation. In a context that is fractured, some would say endemically across ethnic, religious, and caste lines, participatory communication has not resulted in the creation of a multiethnic/religious public sphere at local levels. The remaking of a national consciousness along ethnic and religious lines has affected the viability of existing strategies of participatory development precisely because the politicization of identity has heightened tendencies to the "othering" of peoples. What should an enabling pedagogy deal with in such contexts? How can solidarities be maintained in situations characterized by shifting populations, weak support structures, and the closure of public space? And what should be the basis for participatory communication in already enfeebled, fragile contexts plagued by ethnic, religious, nationalist conflicts? It would seem that what is needed today is to engage with the vision of participation expressed in the *Pedagogy of the Oppressed* (1982) and extended in the *Pedagogy of Hope* (1994).

Even though the postmodernist Freire has recognized the reality of diversity and difference, he has failed to theorize the basis for an inclusive Utopia. In the following he (1993) affirms difference from an experiential standpoint:

> I have always challenged the essentialism reflected in claims of a unitary experience of class and gender, inasmuch as it is assumed that suffering is a seamless web always cut from the same cloth. Oppression must always be understood in its multiple and contradictory instances, just as liberation must be grounded in the particularity of suffering and struggle in concrete, historical experiences, without resorting to transcendental guarantees. (p. x)

Although the acknowledgment and celebration of difference in and through self-limiting forms of radicalism expressed through single-identity politics need to be affirmed, it could be argued that contemporary, postmodernist faith in sector-specific approaches to liberation and to a systems approach to dealing with the question of

human suffering do not contribute to the making of a truly universal, multiethnic public sphere.[6] It would seem that this celebration
of "otherness" is wholly self-referential, with little or no bearings on
the project of inclusive futures. Even though the chaos engendered
by difference may be the means to the making of a new order, we
need explicitly to theorize the universal in the particular as the
means to forging common solidarities across the reality of multiple
differences.

This then remains a key problematic. How does one evolve
innovative approaches to participatory communication that are quite
fundamentally based on conversations with emerging rationalizations? And more importantly, while respecting the need and the
space for difference, how can one continue to envision, dream, and
work to inclusive utopias, translocal projects of liberation? This
seems to be a critical concern—an unfinished agenda of the contemporary, internationalist Paulo Freire.

PARTICIPATION IN CONTEXT

The relationship of power to social change is of fundamental importance to the discourse of participatory communication. All too often
the term *participation* is used in a glib, off-hand manner and is
rarely, if ever, rooted in an understanding of the prevailing dynamics
of change. These dynamics of change rooted in relational situations
vary from situation to situation and are not often amenable to easy
analysis. One-dimensional understandings of power flows in contemporary readings of participatory communication mask the many
ways in which an introduced policy of change becomes textured in
its encounter with the social fabric and the many ways in which the
dominant intent is filtered through a prism of power and knowledge
at local levels. In some contexts the basis for participation is drawn
and defined locally and bounded by intracommunity ideals.

In situations in which a community is comfortable with a particular understanding of participation, that model of interaction must
be respected irrespective of the availability of models that might universally be considered to be more just and equal. Although "reason of tradition" cannot be used as a sufficient excuse to remain beyond the pale
of evaluatory critique, nevertheless, there is a need to recognize the fact
that in situations characterized by heightened, accelerated processes of
marginality, the cohesiveness and continuity of the social fabric and its

---

[6]The enterprise of development too has not been spared the postmodern
turn. Long and Villarreal (1993), writing in a volume on new directions in
development theory, call for a return to "objectivity" and urge their readers to
refrain "from the tendency to empathise ideologically with the hapless victim"
and to "instead, explore the extent to which specific actors perceive themselves capable of manouevering within given contexts or networks and develop strategies for doing so" (p. 158).

attendant structures may need to be considered a primary objective, over and above the pursuit of other equalities. Vital to the survival of already enfeebled communities is their ability to have faith in their own meanings, a view that is echoed in the writings of the social critic Owen Kelly (1984): "When meaning is constructed within a community by means of the steady accumulation of acquired knowledge, then the concerns of that community, however localised or idiosyncratic they might be, will form the core of the process of constructing meaning, as well as providing its motive force" (p. 78).

To belabor the point, if participation is to lead to empowering discourses and lasting change, then communication strategies need to be built on the basis of conversations with local value systems. Mina Ramirez (1990), in an analysis of people power in the Philippines, refers to an ethos of participation built on an edifice of traditional Tagalog values—the relationship between *loob* (inner self), *labas* (exterior reality), *ganda* (the ethic of goodness), and *lakas* (strength)—key words crucial to the organization of popular education. Clifford Geertz (1993), in attempting to explain the meaning of the Malay term *adat* (custom), calls attention to the extrajuridicial meaning of the term, a sense of "propriety" that is born out of a fusion between inner and outer realms of life, leading to a vision of a just order of things. In fact, the more successful examples of mass cultural politics in India, inclusive of the Chipko and Narmada valley movements,[7] have been grounded in root values and animated by the languages of continuity, spirituality, and the self (Nandy, 1987). True participation that leads to the creation of freedom in "another development" is attained when a balance is achieved between inner freedom and outer freedom leading to the recovery of root qualities and values—of sensitivity, tolerance, love, compassion, conviviality, and simplicity (see Rahnema, 1992). As long as variety and pluralism continue to define human diversity, there are bound to be other moralities animating local civil society, and ways of relating that affirm collective solidarities in a moral community. These traditions have a lot to offer in the making of global solidarities.

Participatory communications strategies need to anchor their practices in context. That context is incredibly varied. It consists of ever-changing developments in the field; variable forms of consciousness; political, social, and economic exigencies; and challenging interpretations of that reality. In the context of multiethnic, multireligious societies, dialogue across cultures will need to form the basis for the practice of participatory communication as a "pedagogy of hope."

---

[7]Both the Chipko and Narmada valley movements highlighted the strength of popular solidarity and local values in the face of the destructive march of modernization. Both are environment movements—Chipko, an antideforestation movement, paved the way for the environmental movement in India. The Narmada valley movement was an anti-dam lobby consisting of poor peasants, indigenous peoples, and activists. Women played a major role in both movements.

CONCLUSIONS

There is much that Freire has given. He will be remembered as an open intellectual, but more importantly his contributions to the humanization of our world will surely place him in the company of the 20th century's great champions of freedom. In the spirit of Freire there is the need to explore new spaces for possibility, new places for the birthings of liberation, in the "publics" old and new, in the recognized and unrecognized centers of human creativity, in all the places where people think and dream and work toward inclusive futures. In conclusion, the words of Carlos Alberto Torres (1993) provide a fitting tribute: "there are good reasons why, in pedagogy today, we can stay with Freire or against Freire, but not without Freire" (p. 140).

REFERENCES

Arnason, J.P. (1991). Modernity as project and field of tension. In A. Honneth & H. Joas (Eds.), *Communicative action*. Cambridge, UK: Polity Press.

Basavanna. (1973). *Speaking of Siva* (A. K. Ramanujan, Trans.). Delhi: Penguin Books.

Bhabha, H. (1994). *The location of culture*. New York: Routledge.

Canclini, N.G. (1995). *Hybrid cultures: Strategies for entering and leaving modernity*. Minneapolis: University of Minnesota Press.

Escobar, A. (1995). *Encountering development: The making and unmaking of the Third World*. Princeton, NJ: Princeton University Press.

Freire, P. (1982). *Pedagogy of the oppressed*. Harmondsworth, UK: Penguin Books.

Freire, P. (1993). Foreword. In P. McLaren & P. Leonard (Eds.), *Paulo Freire: A critical encounter* (pp. ix-xii). New York: Routledge.

Freire, P. (1994). *Pedagogy of hope: Reliving pedagogy of the oppressed*. New York: Continuum.

Geertz, C. (1993). *Local knowledge: Further essays in interpretive anthropology*. London: Fontana Press.

Giroux, H.A. (1993). Paulo Freire and the politics of post-colonialism. In *Paulo Freire: A critical encounter* (pp. 177-188). New York: Routledge.

Habermas, J. (1981). *The theory of communicative action: Vol. 1 Reason and the rationalisation of society*. London: Heinemann.

hooks, b. (1993). bell hooks speaking about Paulo Freire—The man, his work. In P. McLaren & P. Leonard (Eds.), *Paulo Freire: A critical encounter* (pp. 146-154). New York: Routledge.

Joseph, S. (1991). Culture and political analysis. *Social Scientist, 19*, 10-11.

Kelly, O. (1984). *Community, art and the state: Storming the citadels*. London: Comedia Publishing Group.

Long, N., & Villarreal, M. (1993). Exploring development interfaces: From the transfer of knowledge to the transfer of meaning. In F. J. Schuurmann (Ed.), *Beyond the impasse: New directions in development theory*. London: ZED Books & Johannesburg, South Africa: Witwatersrand University Press.

Melucci, A. (1996). *Challenging codes: Collective action in the information age*. Cambridge, UK: Cambridge University Press.

McLaren, P., & da Silva, T.T. (1993). Decentering pedagogy: Critical literacy, resistance and the politics of memory. In P. McLaren & P. Leonard (Eds.), *Paulo Freire: A critical encounter* (pp. 47-89). New York: Routledge.

McLaren, P., & Lankshear, P. (Eds.). (1994). *Politics of liberation: Paths from Freire*. London: Routledge.

McLaren, P., & Leonard, P. (Eds.). (1993). *Paulo Freire: A critical encounter*. New York: Routledge.

Nandy, A. (1978). Oppression and human liberation: Towards a Third World utopia. *Alternatives, 4*(2), 165-180.

Nandy, A. (1987). Winners and victims. *Development: Seeds of Change, 1*, 7-12.

Rahnema, M. (1992). Participation. In W. Sachs (Ed.), *The development dictionary*. London: ZED Books.

Ramirez, M. (1990). *Communication from the ground up*. Manila, Philippines: Asian Social Institute.

Riaño, P. (Ed.). (1994). *Women in grassroots communication: Furthering social change*. Thousand Oaks, CA: Sage.

Robins, S. (1996, Winter). Fried chicken democracies and the new South Africa. *Cultural Survival Quarterly*, pp. 4-6.

Servaes, J., Jacobson, T. L., & White S.A. (Eds.). (1996). *Participatory communication for social change*. Thousand Oaks, CA: Sage.

Spivak, G. C. (1988). *In other worlds: Essays in cultural politics*. New York: Metheun.

Steuerman, E. (1988). Habermas vs. Lyotard: Modernity vs. post modernity? *New Formations, 7*, 51-66.

Torres, C.A. (1993). From the *Pedagogy of the Oppressed* to a *Luta Continua*: The political pedagogy of Paulo Freire. In P. McLaren & P. Leonard (Eds.), *Paulo Freire: A critical encounter* (pp. 119-145). New York: Routledge.

van der Gaag, N. (March, 1996). Bullets and borders. *The New Internationalist*, No. 277.

Vishwanathan, G. (1989). *Masks of conquest: Literary study and British rule in India*. New York: Columbia University Press.

White, S. A., Nair. K. S., & Ascroft, J. (Eds.). (1994). *Participatory communication: Working for change and development*. Thousand Oaks, CA: Sage.

Postscript ∎

Some Words from Freire:
An Unfinished Journey

I would like to listen attentively to what women and men from other countries, other cultures, have to say about their dreams or against the very act of dreaming, about utopias or their disavowal. It is not just that I would like to, but that I need to find out how people see modernity, without which it is impossible to talk about postmodernity. What distinguishing marks make us say that someone is a modern or purely postmodern thinker about education? I would like actively to take part in the discussions about whether postmodernity is a historical province in itself, a kind of *sui generis* moment in history, or if it inaugurates a new history, almost without continuity, with what was and what will be, without ideology, without utopias, without wishful thinking, without social classes, without struggle. It would be a "rounded time," "plump," "smooth," without "edges," in which men and women experiencing it would end up discovering that their fundamental characteristic was neutrality. Without social classes, without struggle, without thought of quarrel, without the need for choice, therefore for rupture, without the yoke of ideologies that clash, an empire of neutrality would arise. It would be the disavowal of history itself.

Alternatively, does postmodernity, like modernity, like traditionality, on which weighs its substantial combination of connotations, imply a necessary continuity that characterizes history itself, considered as human experience, whose way of existing flows from one province of time into another? In this sense, each province is characterized by the preponderance not the exclusivity of its connotations. For me, postmodernity today, like modernity yesterday and

255

traditional antiquity the day before yesterday, while conditioning the women and men in them and enveloping them, does not and did not destroy in them what we call their nature, which not being a priori of history is constituted in it and only in it.

One might be able to say, using this argument, that the strength of the history in whose experience human nature was constituted or is constituted or reconstituted is enough to redo it completely in such a way that one day men and women might not recognize themselves in general terms as anything like their predecessors.

It seems unquestionable, however, that certain expressions, or certain ways of being as components of human nature, manifest themselves in time and space in a different way. The different way they reveal themselves does not, however, contradict them.

Throughout history, for example, the need to have certainties about the world has been imposed on men and women, certainties held back by doubts.

This need so imposed itself on human beings that its absence was an obstacle to how humans lived together.

One characteristic of modernity, resulting from the scientificity that developed into scientificism, was the mystification of certainty. Scientific thought dogmatically established a too-certain certainty on certainty itself, as religiosity had previously made its certainty dogmatic.

Rigorous methods for approaching and capturing the object turned certainty into a myth, previous to a different quality, in the absence of methodical rigor. It was this methodical rigor or its mythification, and also the mythification of the greatest accuracy of findings, in modernity, that negated the importance of feelings, desires, emotions, of passion in the ways and practices of knowing.

However, I see that as well as there having been progressivists and reactionaries in antiquity and modernity, they are also present in postmodernity. There is a reactionary as well as a progressivist way of being postmodern. Postmodernity is not exempt from conflicts as a consequence of choices, ruptures, and decisions.

For me, the progressivistically postmodern practice of education—in which I have always placed myself ever since I shyly emerged in the 1950s—is founded on democratic respect for the student as one of the subjects of the process: It is what is there in the act of teaching—coming to know an inquisitive and creative moment in which educators recognize and recreate knowledge previously known and students are open to or produce the as-yet unknown. It is what uncovers truths instead of hiding them. It is what promotes the beauty of purity as a virtue and fights against puritanism as the negation of virtue.

It is what, in all humility, learns from differences and rejects arrogance.

With warm greetings,
Paulo Freire.

Author Index

A

Abu-Said, M., 180, *182*
Aburge, C., 165, *168*
Aksoy, A., 177, *184*
Albrow, M., 174, *183*
Alexander, N., 141, *148*, 156, 160, *168*
Althusser, L., 138, *148*
Alvarez, S., 21, *31*
Amin, S., 127, *129*
Anderson, B., 21, *31*
Annecke, W., 193n, *206*
Anzaldua, G., 228, *238*
Appadurai, A., 48, 50, *61*, 177, *183*
Argyris, C., 103, *106*
Armes, R., 187, *207*
Armstrong, W., 97, 98, *106*
Arnason, J.P., 248, *252*
Arnst, R., 5, *12*
Ascroft, J., 242, *253*
Attali, J., 110, *129*

B

Balton, C., 193, *207*
Basavanna, 245n, *252*
Baudrillard, J., 174, *183*
Bauman, Z., 142, 143, 144, *148*
Beck, U., 21, *31*
Beltran, L.R., 24, *31*
Benjamin, W., 236, *238*
Berlin, J., 115, *129*
Bernstein, B., 237, *238*
Bernstein, H., 212, *222*
Besas, P., 59, *61*
Bhabha, H.K., 120, 121, *129*, 243, *252*
Blackledge, D.A., 218, *222*

Bourdieu, P., 140, 142, 143, *148*
Bozzoli, B., 135, *148*
Braslavsky, C., 233, *238*
Brauchi, M., 61, *62*
Brown, A., 68, 70, 75, *79*

C

Cabezas, A., 24, *31*
Camilo, M., 27, *31*
CANA Business, 78, *79*
Canclini, N.G., 243, *252*
Cassey, R., 105, *106*
Castles, S., 51, *52*
Chesterman, J., 66, *79*
Ciespal, 24, *31*
Cixous, H., 187, *206*
Clement, C., 187, *206*
Cloete, N., 140, *149*
Cohen, S., 116, 117, 118, *129*
Collins, R., 50, 52, 53, *62*, 176, *183*
Contreras, E., 24, *31*
Cope, B., 51, *62*
Criticos, C., 135, 141, 142, *148*, 151n, 157, *168*
Cruise O'Brien, R., 172, *183*

D

da Silva, T.T., 246, *253*
Deacon, R., 135, 137, 140, 143, 144, *148*, 195, *206*
Delcourt, X., 50, 53, 54, *62*
Derrida, J., 137, 138, 142, 146, *148*
Desai, G., 120, *129*
Development Resources Centre, 159, *168*

257

Dewey, J., 103, *106*
Diamond, J., 38, *43*
Diawara, M., 187, *206*
Dighe, A., 172, 173, *183*
Dissanayake, W., 180, *183*
Dreyfus, H., 144, 146, *148*
Durham, R., 233, *239*

E

Elliot, P., 172, *183*, 212, *222*
Ellsworth, E., 141, *148*
Escobar, A., 21, *31*, 214, 214*n*, *222*,
    243, *252*
Eurich, C., 23, *31*
Eyerman, R., 21, *31*

F

Fals-Borda, O., 100, 101, *106*, 219,
    220, *222*
Fang, C.S., 213, *222*
Farmers Assistance Board, 23, *31*
Featherstone, M., 54, *62*
Fell, L., 60, *62*
Ferguson, B., 201, *206*
Ferguson, M., 36, *43*, 174, 175, *183*
Fisher, M., 21, *32*
Fiske, J., 51, *62*
Foster-Carter, A., 210*n*, *222*
Foucault, M., 138, 139, 140, 142,
    143, 144, 145, *148*, *149*, 180,*183*
Fox, E., 55, *62*
Frank, A.G., 212, *222*
Freire, P., ix, x, xi, xii, *xiii*, 4, 5, *12*,
    13, 18, *31*, 34, 35, *43*, 102, 104,
    106, 109, *129*, 141, *148*, 155,
    168, 216, 217, 219, *222*, 241,
    245, 246, *252*
French, D., 218, *222*
Fuentes, M., 21, *32*

G

Garnham, N., 53, 57, *62*
Gasche, R., 238, *239*
Gee, J., 115, *129*
Geertz, C., 14, *31*, 251, *252*
Giddens, A., 20, 21, *32*, 180, *183*
Gilmour, D., 157, *168*
Giroux, H., 115, *129*, 160, 161, *168*,
    179, *183*, 186, 197, 203, 204,
    206, 245, *252*
Goldemberg, J., 233, *239*
Golden, T., 57, *62*
Golding, P., 35, 39, *43*, 172, 175,
    183, 210, 212, *222*
Goll, S., 61, *62*

Gramsci, A., 233, *239*
Gran, G., 23, *32*
Grundy, S., 103, *106*, 154, *168*
Gunder, F., 21, *32*

H

Habermas, J., 102, *106*, 154, *169*,
    247, 247*n*, *252*
Hall, B., 100, *106*
Hall, S., 176, *183*
Hamelink, C., 209, 215, 221, *222*
Hargreaves, A., 231, *239*
Harris, P., 39, *43*, 210, *222*
Hartmann, P., 172, 173, *183*
Hebdige, D., 176, *183*
Hedebro, G., 212, *222*
Hegel, G., 138, *149*
Heidegger, M., 139, *149*
Heller, P., 38, *43*
Hirsch, E.D., Jr., 111, *129*, 176,
    178, *184*
Hitchcock, P., 121, *129*
Holaday, D., 179, *183*
hooks, b., 122, 123, *129*, 248, *252*
Hoskins, C., 51, *62*
Huesca, R., 5, *12*, 220, *222*
Huizer, G., 23, *32*
Hunt, B., 218, *222*
Hutcheon, L., 199, 199*n*, 205, *206*

I

Illich, I., 142, *149*, 218, *222*

J

Jacobson, T.L., 241, *253*
Jameson, F., 49, *62*
Jamison, A., 21, *31*
Joseph, S., 243*n*, *252*

K

Kalantzis, M., 51, *62*
Kassam, Y., 23, *32*
Katz, E., 172, *183*
Kelly, O., 251, *252*
Kincheloe, J., 114, *129*
Kirton, C., 221, *223*
Kronenburg, J., 23, *32*
Kruss, G., 133, *149*

L

Laclau, E., 139, *149*, 238, *239*
Landry, C., 221, *223*
Lankshear, C., 115, *130*, 238, *239*
Lankshear, P., 241, *253*
Lapsley, R., 193*n*, *200*
Lefebvre, H., 109, *129*

Leonard, P., 34, *43,* 115, *130,* 216, 223, 241, *253*
Lerner, D., 175, *183,* 210n, 211n, *223*
Lewin, K., 104, *106*
Lipman, A., 66, *79*
Llorente, P.G., 24, *31*
Long, N., 250n, *253*
Lovell, T., 196, *206*
Lyotard, J.-F., 203, *207*

M

MacBride, S., 18, *32*
Mackenzie, F., 135, *149*
Mackie, R., 216, *223*
Mahoney, M., 138, *149*
Malkmus, L., 187, *207*
Mannheim, K., 68n, *79*
Marcus, G., 21, *32*
Marques de Melo, J., 59, *62*
Martin-Barbero, J., 51, *62,* 112, 116, *130,* 214n, *223*
Marx, K., 146, *149*
Mashamba, G., 134, *149*
Massey, D., 175, *184*
Masterman, L., 5, *12,* 202, *207,* 217, 218, *223*
Mata, M.C., 27, *32*
Mattelart, A., 50, 53, 54, *62*
Mattelart, M., 50, 53, 54, *62*
McAnany, E., 51, 56, *62*
McCarter, M., 59, *62*
McLaren, P., 34, *43,* 112, 114, 115, 116, *129, 130,* 199, *207,* 216, 223, 225, 238, *239, 241,* 246, *253*
McQuail, D., 19, *32*
Melucci, A., 243, *253*
Mercado, C.M., 213, *223*
Merod, J., 120, *130*
Minh-Ha, T., 195, *207*
Mirus, R., 51, *62*
Miyoshi, M., 110, *130*
Mkatshwa, S., 134, *149*
Moffett, M., 59, *63*
Mohammadi, A., 176, *184*
Morley, D., 50, 52, *63,* 176, 178, *184*
Morris, N., 214n, *223*
Morrissey, M., 51, *62*
Mouffe, C., 139, *149*
Mowlana, H., 18, *32*
Muller, J., 140, *149*
Mulvey, L., 186, *207*
Mustafa, K., 23, *32,* 221, *223*

N

Nain, Z., 221, *223*
Nair, K.S., 242, *253*
Nandy, A., 246, 251, *253*
Nasson, B., 135, *149*
National Eduation Policy Investigation, 136, *149*
Negt, O., 22, *32*
Negus, K., 176, *184*
Nichols, B., 190, *207*
Nunez, I., 227, *239*

O

O'Brien, R.C., 212, *223*
OECD, 38, *43*
Oliver, K., 146, *150*
Olssen, M., 110, *130*

P

Palmer, P.J., 153, *169,* 172, *184*
Parker, B., 137, 142, 143, 144, *148, 150*
Parry, B., 111, *130*
Passerson, J.-C., 140, 142, 143, *148*
Patil, B., 172, 173, *183*
Peacock, J.J., 176, *184*
Pereyra, M., 232, 234, *239*
Philippine Partnership, 22, *32*
Pool, I de S., 175, *184*
Postman, N., 203, *207*
Prinsloo, J., 194n, *207*
Project Inspire, 164, *169*
Propp, V., 193n, *207*
Puiggros, A., 225, 232, 238, *239*
Putnam, R., 103, *106*

Q

Quinlan, T., 135, 141, 142, *148*

R

Rabinow, P., 144, 146, *148*
Rahman, M.A., 100, 101, *106,* 219, 220, *222*
Rahnema, M., 251, *253*
Ramirez, M., 251, *253*
Ramos, J.P., 227, 233, *239*
Riaño, P., 241, *253*
Richards, M., 218, *222*
Roberts, J., 59, *63*
Robertson, R., 49, *63,* 174, *184*
Robins, K., 50, 52, *63,* 176, *184*
Robins, S., 244n, *253*
Rogers, E.M., 16, *32,* 61, *63,* 175, *184*
Ros, J., 24, *31*
Rosario, A., 24, *31*

Ross, A., 112, *130*
Ross, K., 111, 125, 126, *130*

S

Safford, F., 227, 233, *239*
Sahin, H., 177, *184*
Salmon, C., 143, *150*
Sanders, B., 142, *149*
Saunders, C., 133, *150*
Schement, J., 61, *63*
Schifelbein, E., 233, *239*
Schiller, H., 172, *184*
Schlesinger, P., 50, 52, 53, *63*, 176, 177, *184*, 214n, *223*
Schramm, W., 175, *184*, 211n, *223*
Schwartzman, E., 233, *239*
Scott, J.S., 220, *223*
Scott, J.W., 121, *130*
Seguier, M., 23, *32*
Servaes, J., 5, *12*, 15, *32*, 220, *223*, 241, *253*
Shah, H., 211, 212, *223*
Shaull, R., 71, *79*
Shor, I., 141, *148*, 180, *184*, 219, 222
Shor, L., 157, *169*
Silverstone, R., 176, 178, *184*
Sinclair, J., 52, 55, 56, 58, 59, 60, *63*
Singh, M., 159, *169*
Siochru, S.O., 221, *223*
Siriyuvasek, U., 213, *223*
Smart, B., 144, 145, *150*
Smith, A.D., 36, *43*, 53, *63*, 211, *223*
Smith, D., 103, *106*
South Commission, The, 38, *43*
Spivak, G.C., 135, 142, *150*, 195, *207*, 243, *253*
Sreberny-Mohammadi, A., 215, *223*
Stanton, T., 154, *169*
Steenveld, L., 190, 191, 192, *207*
Steuerman, E., 247, *253*
Strategy Research Corporation, 55, *63*
Straubhaar, J., 55, *63*

T

Tapson, D., 135, *150*
Taylor, D., 135, *150*

Taylor, N., 142, *150*
Thomas, P.N., 212, *223*
Thoraval, Y., 187, *207*
Tobias, K.J., 23, *32*
Tomaselli, K., 188, 189, 190, 191, 194n, *207*
Tomaselli, R., 190, 191, 193n, *207*
Torres, C.A., 252, *253*
Touraine, A., 141, *150*
Townsend, P., 37, 41, *43*
Trejo Delarbre, R., 57, *63*
Tunstall, J., 53, *63*, 172, 173, *184*

U

Ulmer, G., 146, *150*
UNESCO, 39, *43*, 200, *207*
Unwin, C., 193, *207*

V

van der Gaag, N., 244n, *253*
van Niekerk, P., 199, *207*
Villarreal, M., 250n, *253*
Vishwanathan, G., 244n, *253*

W

Warburg, S.C., 58, *63*
Weber, M., 233, *239*
Wedell, G., 172, *183*
Wells, A., 172, *184*
West, C., 122, 123, *129*
Westlake, M., 193n, *206*
White, R., 17, *32*
White, S.A., 241, 242, *253*
Williams, A., 190, 191, *207*
Wilson, L., 18, *32*
Witcher, K., 61, 62
World Almanac, 54, *63*

X

Xavier Institute, 18, *32*

Y

Yngvesson, B., 138, *149*
Young, R., 187, *207*

Z

Zaharom, N., 221, *223*
Zizek, S., 138, *150*

Subject Index

A

Academy
  critical pedagogy vs. the, 114-115
  nocturnal, 119-128
Action in depth
  confronting cultures of
  domination through, 5
Action research, 104
Action Research for
  Development Communications,
  97-106
  context of, 98-99
  developing communication plan
  for, 100
Activity
  Freirean emphasis on, 35
"Adjustment"
  with reduction, 230
Adult education, 94
Adult literacy
  See Literacy
Affected Organizations Act, 159
Africa Cinema, 186
Agri-business, 51
Aguinaldo, General Emilio, 83
ALER
  See Latin American Association
  of Radio Education (ALER)
Alpha Lyracom, 59
Alternative communications
  developed in popular education, 9
  theory and practice of, 2
Alternative Media Education, 217-219
Althusserian Marxism, 201, 203
American Publishing Group, 59

Anglophone Caribbean, 70
Anselmo, Rene, 56, 58-59
Anticapitalist social theory, 9
Apartheid society, 153
Appadurai, Arjun, 48-49, 177
Aquino, Corazon, 93
Argentina
  education system in, 232-233
Aristide, Haitian President Jean-
  Bertrand, 25
Attitude
  paramount for facilitators, 31
Audience studies
  recent "ethnographic" trend in, 49-
  50
Awareness
  key Freirean idea, 1
Azcarraga Milmo, Emilio, 58-59
Azcarraga Vidaurreta, Emilio, Sr., 55-
  56
Aztecland, 118

B

Bam, Fiks, 156
Basic Integrated theater arts work-
  shops (BITAW), 86
Benjamin, Walter, 125
Black film, 186
Black intellectuals, 122-124
Bolivia
  See Radio San Gabriel
Bonifacio, Andres, 83
Book production
  Western dominance of, 39-40
Border environments, 163-164

"Border pedagogy," 10, 161-162, 204
Borderlands, the Frontier, the New Mestiza, 228
Borders
  created by antagonisms, 202
  of difference, 162
  elastic, 160, 162-163
  plastic deformation of, 163
Bourdieu, P., 9
Brazil
  education system in, 228, 233
Brazil's National Literacy Programme
  Paulo Freire's coordination of, 4
Brecht, Bertolt, 92
Broadcast media
  linking telephone to, 73
  worldwide distribution of, 40
Brown, Aggrey, 65-79
Building Basic Christian
  communities, 88
Buthelezi, Chier Mangosuthu, 197

C

Canadian International Development
  Agency, 97
Capitalism, 13, 36
  global, 127
  See also Anticapitalist social theory
Caribbean
  case studies from, 73-78
Caribbean Broadcasting Union
  (CBU), 75-77
Caribbean News Agency (CANA), 77-78
Caribvision, 8, 76
Center for Studies in Development
  and Social Change, 113
Center-periphery model
  inherent limitations in, 49, 61
Che Guevara, 48
Chile
  education system in, 227
Chilean Agrarian Reform
  Corporation, 113
Cinema of Africa, 186
Cinema of Resistance, 186
Citizenry
  critical, 198
  liberated, 72
CNN
  ubiquity of, 36, 60
Cohen, Sande, 116-119
Collective research, 101
Collins, Richard, 52-54

Colonialism
  barbaric practices of, 13
  plot of, 187
  social system of, 212
Commodity prices
  falls in, 38
Communications
  as dialogue, 105
  "horizontal," 27
  as knowledge reconstruction,
    101-102
  making multiple meanings, 5
  models of, 15
  relationship to development, 1-106
  as transfer of information, 16
  See also Alternative communica-
    tions; Instant communication;
    Participatory communication
Communications gradient, 39-41
Communications industry
  Western dominance of, 47
Communications media
  See Media
Communications paradox
  of inequality, 33-43
Communications policies, 18-19
Communications resources
  inequalities in, 40-42
Communicative pedagogy
  of globalization, 179-182
Communities
  interdependency of, 15
  and shared meanings, 106
Community based approach, 28-29
Community Media Network, 221
Community participation, 29
Community Video School, 198, 205
"Conscientization" method, 4-5, 9,
  22, 105, 115
Consciousness
  infocom technologies shaping, 69
  social, 106
Contemporary People's Movement,
  84-89
Costa Rica
  education system in, 229
Creative subjects
  learners asserting themselves as, 4
Critical citizenry
  development of, 198
Critical pedagogy
  rethinking in postmodernity, 131-
    150
  vs. the academy, 114-115

Critical recovery
  of history, 101
Criticos, Costas, 9-10, 151-169
Cuba
  education system in, 229
Cultural action
  Freire's concern with, 4
  and the limits to solidarity and
    participation, 4, 151-169
Cultural Action for Freedom, 113
Cultural critiques, 20
Cultural identity, 7, 15
Cultural imperialism
  Dallas perfect symbol of, 50
  debate over, 46-49
  decentering of, 45-63
  limited perspective of, 61
  threat to national cultures, 52
Cultural influence
  international flows of, 50
Cultural invasions, 71
Cultural Marxism
  tradition of, 53
Cultural multidimensionality, 15
Cultural politics
  liberation crisis in contemporary,
    242-244
Culture
  as resistance through mediation,
    49-50
  See also Global culture
Culture and Resistance Festival, 197
Culture in Another South Africa
  (CASA), 198
"Culture of silence," 72
  breaking, 77
Cultures of domination
  confronting through action in
    depth, 5
  Freire's condemnation of, 2
Cultures of struggle
  Freire learning from, 2

D

Dallas (soap epic)
  "perfect hate symbol," 50
Davis, Peter, 191
DBS
  See Direct Broadcast satellites
    (DBS)
de Man, Paul, 125
Deacon, Roger, 9, 131-150
Death of history, 119
Defiance campaign, 194

Democracy
  imperatives toward, 110, 230-231
  meanings of, 13
  struggle for, 13
"Democratisation movement" (radio
  popular) phase, 26
Dependent societies
  challenging the Eurocentrists, 14
  opposed to metropolitan societies,
    4
Derrida, J., 9, 137, 142, 146-147
"Desiring machines," 9, 119
Development
  anchored on faith in people, 18
  cautions regarding, 29-31
  emerging definitions of, 15
  modernity paradigm of, 164
  participatory, 2
  participatory communication for,
    10, 219-220
  post-war defining of, 14
  in practice, 164-165
  reflected versions of, 2
Development communications
  models underpinning, 7
  waning interest in, 6
Dewey, John, 104
Dialogue
  across cultures, 12
  communications as, 105
  education based on, 4
  and the globalization of culture,
    71-73
  key Freirean idea, 1
Difference
  politics of, 119-28
"Diffusion/mechanistic" communication model, 15-17
  main characteristics of, 17
Digital television standards
  battle over, 66
Direct Broadcast satellites (DBS), 70
Direct Cinema approach, 193
Disappearances
  involuntary, 89
Discipline
  discourses of, 131-150
  and the intellectuals, 142-144
Disclosure of Foreign Funding Act,
  159
Discourses
  of discipline, 131-150
  as forms of subjection, 139
  See also Alternative discourses;
    Modernist discourses

Disneyland, 118
Documentary productions, 10
Dominant paradigm, 210-215
  alternative strategies, 216-217
  new world order and, 215-216
Domination
  See Cultures of domination
Dominican Republic
  See Radio Enriquillo

E

ECO, 56
Economy
  See Global cultural economy;
    World economy
Ecuador
  See Radio ERPE
Edu-tainment, 29
Educational institutions
  as a moral agent, 115-119
  in South Africa, 153-155
  See also Popular education;
    Traditional educational processes
Einsiedel, Edna F., 8, 97-106
Emancipation
  right to, 5
Emancipatory participation, 10
Empowerment, 7
Enablement
  language as source of, 4
Enterprise program
  See University of the West Indies
    Distance Teaching Experiment
    (UWIDTE)
Environmental Development Agency,
  165
"Ethnographic" trend
  in audience studies, 49-50
Ethnography of thought, 13
Eurocentric perspective
  challenged by dependistas, 14
  conquering the dynamism of, 110
  metanarratives of, 200
Evaluation
  participatory approach to, 27-28
Evangelista Crisanto, 83
Exclusion
  marks of, 188

F

Facilitators
  attitude paramount for, 31
Fanon, Franz, 34, 111
Farmers Assistance Board, 22-23
Feminist film, 186

Film and Allied Workers
  Organization (FAWO), 198
Film industry
  centers of, 52-53, 185-186
First, Second, and Third Worlds
  demarcation breaking down, 15
Folk culture
  valuing and applying, 101
Foucault, M., 9, 48, 122-123, 145-
  147
Frank, A. G., 48
Frankfurt School, 201
Freire, Paulo, 34-35, 71-72, 89, 104,
  109, 216-217, 219, 228, 238
  impact in South Africa, 155-158
  social pedagogy of, 178-179
  unfinished journey of, 255-256
Freirean legacy, 3-12, 81-95
  future possibilities for, 11-12,
    241-253
  interwoven with art and literary
    movement, 89-94
Freirean pedagogy, 107-253
  and higher education, 109-130
Friedrich Ebert Stiftung (FES), 75-77
Fundamental pedagogics, 132

G

Galian sa Arte at Tula, 87-88
Gangsterland, 118
Gavin, John, 58
Geertz, Clifford, 13-14, 251
GEMS Television, 60
"Geolinguistic" regions, 52
Giroux, Henry, 11, 161, 204, 245
Global alliances, 9
Global capitalism, 127
Global cultural economy, 49
Global culture
  essence of, 35-36
  syndication of, 7
Global homogenization, 126
Global inequalities
  structured, 68-71
Global infocom industry
  structure of, 66-68
Global media
  studying, 10
Global networks, 4
Global syndication
  of culture, 7
Globalization, 2
  categories of, 174-175
  of culture, 65-79
  debates about, 7, 10

defined, 65, 171-178
myth and reality, 35-37
part of agenda about communication and development, 8
pedagogy for, 10
questioning the concept of, 171-
184
Globo-ization
in the Latin world, 45-63
Golding, Peter, 7, 33-43, 175
Grassroots movements
controlling, 135
for education, 231, 236-237
Freire's support for, 3
key Freirean ideas in, 1
Grundy, S., 154-155

H

Habermas, M., 102-103, 117, 154,
246-248
Hegemony
notion of, 202
Hernandez, Amado V., 84
Herzog, Albert, 191
"Heterodoxal Freireans," 9
Higher education
Freirean pedagogy and, 109-130
Historiography
Marxist, 134
History
critical recovery of, 101
death of, 119
language the site of enactment of,
121
History Workshops, 141
hooks, bell, 123-124
"Horizontal" communications, 27
"Hotline," 74
Humanism
new, 14
Humanization of life, 11
Humans
as reflective, 34-35
"Hybrid" genres
international growth of, 53

I

IMF
See International Monetary Fund
(IMF)
Imperialism
See Cultural imperialism
Improvisation for the Theater, 87
Inca-Blinka, 118
Income gaps, 37-39

Incommensurability of translation,
121
Independent Broadcast Association,
198
India
information technology in, 212-
213
Indigenous media, 8
Indigenous peoples, 228
Individuals
bringing to critical reflection, 22
Inequalities
in communications resources, 40-
42
structured global, 68-71
in wealth, 41-42
world of, 37-39
Influence patterns
analysis of, 21
Infocom technologies
information transmitted by, 72
shaping consciousness, 69
See also Global infocom industry
Information
commodifying of, 78
communication as transfer of, 16
Information industry
domination of, 8
Information-rich and -poor, 7
Instant communication, 4
Institute of Cultural Action, 113
Institutions
educational, 115-119
"mixed mode," 75
Intellectuals, 117-118
Black insurgent, 122
discipline and, 142-144
proselytizing power of, 144
reconstituting as "ordinary people,"
141
Intelsat, 60
Intergovernmental organizations,
215
International Commission for the
Study of Communication
Problems, 18
International level
paradox of communications
inequality, 33-43
International Monetary Fund (IMF),
38, 78, 112
Internationalization
of cultural production, 7
Iquitos, Peru
See "La voz de la Selve"

J

Jamaica
  radio call-in programs in, 73-74
Jamaica Broadcasting Corporation
  (JBC), 73-74

K

Kabataang Makabayan, 84
KAISAHAN organization, 88
Kataastaasang Kagalanggalang
  Katipunan ng mga Anak ng
  Bayan (The Katipunan), 83
Kente, Gibsen, 189
Kgositsile, Baleka, 158
Khumbane, Tshepo, 165
KLAS-FM, 74
Knowledge
  resident in participants, 100, 102
Knowledge reconstruction
  communication as, 101-102
Kwedi, Max, 156

L

La Paz, Bolivia
  See Radio San Gabriel
"La voz de la Selve," 24
Laclau, E., 11, 147
Language
  constructing social reality power,
    9
  the site of history's enactment, 121
  source of power and enablement,
    4
Latin America
  political, cultural, and educational
    changes in, 225-239
  regions in, 226
Latin American Association of Radio
  Education (ALER), 25, 27
Learners
  asserting themselves as creative
    subjects, 4
Liberation
  limits to absolutization of, 5
  struggle for, 13
Liberation crisis
  in contemporary cultural politics,
    242-244
Liberation theology
  force of, 89
Liberatory praxis, 9
Literacy
  in Latin America, 233-235
  significance for freedom and par-
    ticipation, 3-4

Lobotomies, 115-116
Local community
  changing from the "bottom-up,"
    15
Local media structures, 8
Lopez, S. P., 83-84

M

Mandela, President Nelson, 72
Manley, Michael, 73
Mao Tse Tung, 89
Marinho, Roberto, 59
Martial law, 85-86
Martin-Barbero, Jesus, 50-51, 214
Marxism, 36, 83, 85-86, 122
  Althusserian, 201, 203
  cultural, 53
  historiography of, 134, 187
Mass Democratic Movement (MDM),
  191
Materialist-idealist distinction, 20
Mattelart, Armand, 46, 53
"McDonaldization" of everywhere, 36
McLaren, Peter, 9, 109-130
Media
  globalizing tendencies of, 42
  "hypodermic needle" effect of, 16-
    17
  paradox of communications
    inequality, 33-43
  See also Popular media
The Media Are American, 53
Media Attachment Programme, 194
Media distribution
  skewed nature of, 7
Media Education, 185-223
  alternative, 217-219
Media imperialism model, 6-7
  questioning, 172-173
Media Resource Centre, 166
Mediation
  resistance through, 49-54
Megaconglomerates
  listed, 67
Memorization
  discouraged by Freire, 4
Mercado, Cesar M., 213-214
Message "receivers," 16
Mestre, Goar, 55
Metanarratives
  of Eurocentric perspective, 200
Methodology
  forecasts of, 237-238
Metropolitan societies
  opposed to dependent societies, 4

Mexico
    education system in, 231-232
"Mixed mode" institutions, 75
Mkatshwa, Father Smangaliso, 157
Mobile recording unit (unidad movil),
    13
Modern consciousness
    multiplicity of, 13
Modernist discourses, 138
    objectification of, 9, 146-147
Modernity
    marks of, 136-139
Modernity paradigm
    of development, 164
Mokaba, Peter, 158
Moniz, Egas, 115-116
MTV Networks, 60
Multidimensionality
    cultural, 15
Multinational corporations, 127
Multiplicity paradigm, 5, 29
    of modern consciousness, 13

N

Nain, Zaharom, 10-11, 209-223
"Naming the world," 5
Nandy, Ashis, 246
Nation state
    break-up of, 36, 174
National cultures
    cultural imperialism a threat to,
        52
    erosion of discrete, 176
National Education Policy
    Investigation (NEPI), 135, 141
National Educational Crisis
    Committee (NECC), 132-134, 140,
        157
Nations
    interdependency of, 15
    paradox of communications
        inequality among, 33-43
Neoliberal reform
    entrenched defense of, 229-230
New Right constituencies
    facing, 111
New World Information and
    Communication Order (NWICO),
        14, 47, 50
New world order
    and the dominant paradigm,
        215-216
News agencies
    international, 47
Nocturnal academy, 119-128

Non-Aligned Movement, 15
Non-Aligned Nations, 15
Nongovernmental organizations,
    215, 228, 234
NWICO
    See New World Information and
        Communication Order (NWICO)

O

OECD countries, 38
Oppositional film making, 10, 185-
    208
"Ordinary people"
    reconstituting intellectuals as,
        141
Orthodoxies
    challenges to in South Africa,
        132-136

P

Palmer, P. J., 153-154
PanAmSat, 56-58
Paradigms
    See Dominant paradigm;
        Modernity paradigm; Multiplicity
        paradigm
Participation
    community, 29
    in context, 250-251
    emancipatory, 10
    key Freirean idea, 1
    not behavioral response, 1
    practicing, 165-167
    right to, 5
Participatory approach
    to evaluation, 27-28
    to research, 28
Participatory communication, 5, 7,
    209-223, 241-242
    affirming the other in and
        through, 249-250
    for development, 10, 219-220
    minefields in, 220-21
Participatory communication
    research, 20-24
    major characteristics of, 23
    perspective of, 21-22
    quantitative and qualitative
        methods, 28
    strategies for, 22-24
Participatory model, 7, 18-20
    main characteristics of, 19-20
"Participatory/organic" communica-
    tion model, 15

Particular
  vs. universal, 245-246
Partido dos Trabalhadores, 113
Patriarchy
  crucible of, 115
Pedagogical praxis, 116
Pedagogy
  of communication, 11
  fundamental, 132
  for globalization, 10, 171-184
  moving to praxis, 209-223
  Paulo Freire and, 107-253
  points of focus of, 180-182
  See also People's pedagogy
*Pedagogy in Process: Letters to
  Guinea-Bissau,* 113
Pedagogy of Hope, 245, 249
Pedagogy of the Oppressed, 4, 71,
  82, 90, 113, 155, 241, 245, 249
People's Education, 132-134, 140,
  157-158
People's movement
  proponents of, 8
People's pedagogy, 81-95
  contemporary challenges and
  imperatives, 94-95
Persson, Sven, 189
Peru
  See "La voz de la Selve"
PETA
  See Philippine Educational
  Theatre Association (PETA)
Philippine Educational Theatre
  Association (PETA), 86, 90-91
Philippine Partnership for the
  Development of Human Resources in
  Rural Areas, 22-23
Philippines
  fisheries sector in, 98-99
  progressive cultural movement in,
  81-95
  Propaganda Movement in, 83
Plastic deformation, 163
Pluralization
  of cultural production, 7
Politics of cynicism and despair, 9
Politics of difference, 119-128
Politics of the concrete, 9
Popular education, 94
Popular media
  Freire's use of, 5
Popular sovereignty, 13
Positivist-functionalist approaches, 20
Postmodernism, 160, 174, 249
  academic, 9

"ludic" vs. resistance, 9
  resistance, 119
  rethinking critical pedagogy in,
  131-150
Power
  language as source of, 4
Praxis, 103-104
  key Freirean idea, 1, 112-113
  moving from pedagogy to, 209-
  223
  pedagogical, 116
  of solidarity, 113
Prinsloo, Jeanne, 10, 185-208
Process
  integrated understanding of, 1
"Project Satellite," 75
"The Public Eye," 73-74
Publications Control Board, 189
Puiggros, Adriana, 11, 225-239

R

"Radio as a communication medium"
  (sistema de communication)
  phase, 26
Radio Enriquillo, 15, 24-29
  objectives of, 26-27
  origins of, 24-26
  participatory communication
  strategies employed, 27-29
  phases of development, 25-26
Radio ERPE, 24
Radio San Gabriel, 24
"Radio schools" (escuelas radio-foni-
  cas) phase, 25-26
Reagan, President Ronald, 58
Reduction
  "adjustment" with, 230
Reflexivity, 195
Reform Training and Research
  Institute, 113
Regions
  "geolinguistic," 52
  interdependency of, 15
  media structures of, 8
Reproductivism, 236
Research
  action, 104
  collective, 101
  participatory approach to, 28
Resistance
  through mediation, 49-54
Resistance postmodernism, 119, 199
Ribeiro, Darcy, 228
Richards, Michael, 3-12, 171-184

Riobamba, Ecuador
  See Radio ERPE
Rizal, Jose, 83
Ross, Andrew, 111-112, 125-126
Rural commitment, 19-20

S

SABC
  See South African Broadcast
    Corporation (SABC)
Samahang Demokratikong
  Kabataan, 84
San Banadov, 118
Schiller, Herb, 46
Scott, Joan, 121
Self-determination, 14
Semiotic codes, 115
Servaes, Jan, 5, 7, 13-32, 220
Shah, H., 211-212
Sign systems, 115
Sihlangu, Kate, 165
Sinclair, John, 45-63
Social consciousness, 106
Social justice
  achieving equality of, 13
Social reality
  as a text, 9
Social trust
  development of, 19
Socialism
  definitions of democracy opposed
    to, 13
Society
  apartheid, 153
  civil, 159
South Africa
  cultural action in, 151-169
  "culture of silence" in, 72
  discourses of discipline in, 131-
    150
  film making in, 187-189
South African Broadcast Corporation
  (SABC), 132, 197-198
South African Students
  Organization, 155
Sovereignty
  See Popular sovereignty
Spelling Entertainment Group, 60
Spivak, G., 9, 146, 195
Spolin, Viola, 87, 90
Strangification, 118
Structured global inequalities, 68-71
Struggle
  for democracy, 13
  for liberation, 13

Subjugated discourses, 139-140
Supranational forces, 215
Supranational ideologies, 35-36
"Syndicalization of experience," 36

T

Taiwan
  information technology in, 213
Tamayo, Dominican Republic
  See Radio Enriquillo
Teaching the Media, 217
Technocratic capitalism, 9
Telecommunications
  worldwide distribution of, 40
Telemontecarlo, 59
Telephone
  linking to broadcast media, 73
Televisa, 7, 54-61
Televisa-ion
  in the Latin world, 45-63
Thailand
  information technology in, 213
Theory of Communicative Action, 247
Third Cinema, 186
Third world
  becoming a meaningless conglom-
    erate, 38
  defined, 111
  See also First, Second, and Third
    Worlds
Third-worldism, 36
Thomas, Pradip N., 11-12, 212, 241-
  253
Time-Warner, 67
Top-down model, 7
Traditional educational processes
  echoing globalization, 10
  Freire's condemnation of, 4
Training design
  essentials of, 91-92
Transcendence
  of class struggle, 127-128
Translation
  incommensurability of, 121
Transnational corporations, 215
Transnational forces, 215
Tropical Television Network (TTN), 76
Trujillo, Dominican President R. L.,
  24
Turner, Ted, 60
TV Globo, 7, 54, 59-61
TVROs, 70

U

UNCTAD, 39
UNESCO, 77
    commitment to NWICO, 6, 47
    media model based on, 7
UNICEF, 38
UNISA, 156
United Nations
    founding of, 14
United States
    decline as a global force, 37
Universal
    vs. particular, 245-246
Universities, 117
    White, 124
University Christian Movement, 155
University of the West Indies (UWI),
    74-75
University of the West Indies
    Distance Teaching Experiment
    (UWIDTE), 75
USAID-funded experiments, 75
Utopia
    philosophy of, 9, 246

V

Valdes, Miguel Aleman, Sr., 55
Vandenbuleke, Humberto, 24-25
Video game systems, 69
Voice of God broadcasts, 192, 206

W

Wealth
    inequalities in, 41-42
White Mythologies, 187
White supremacy
    crucible of, 115
    myth of, 155
Women's liberation movement, 95
World Bank, 78, 112, 135, 229-230
World Council of Churches, 113
World economy
    recent changes in, 36-37
    See also Global cultural economy
World Educational Television
    (WETV), 76-77
World Radio Network, 77
World Trade Centre, 198
"World trends"
    invoking, 47

X

Xenophobia, 122

Y

Young, Robert, 187

Z

Zapatistas, 112
Zarate, Maria Jovita, 8, 81-95